Bethany Erin Hicks

Migration and the Construction of German Identities, 1949–2004

Migrations in History

Edited by
Catherine Brice, Maddalena Marinari,
Anna Mazurkiewicz and Machteld Venken

Volume 2

Bethany Erin Hicks

Migration and the Construction of German Identities, 1949–2004

—

DE GRUYTER
OLDENBOURG

ISBN 978-3-11-221374-2
e-ISBN (PDF) 978-3-11-071622-1
e-ISBN (EPUB) 978-3-11-071626-9
ISSN 2701-1437

Library of Congress Control Number: 2023938630

Bibliographic information published by the Deutsche Nationalbibliothek
The Deutsche Nationalbibliothek lists this publication in the Deutsche Nationalbibliografie;
detailed bibliographic data are available on the internet at http://dnb.dnb.de.

Contents

Introduction

Around 2 a.m. at Checkpoint Charlie . . .

The first border crossing allows ten people through every twenty seconds. The second guard wants an ID, a *taz* business card will also do. The third – grimly – wants to see an exit visa. Once more the *taz* card, this time along with a [western] bank account card . . .

[The West German guard calls] to the waiting crowd: "We don't want you here, go back!" [Once through the border] A West German greets the *taz* reporter and grabs him by the collar. The next one shakes his hand, thinking he is from the East: "Need an apartment? I have work."

Shortly after 2 a.m.: for the first time, one hears the first verse of the German national anthem, the Japanese are filming, and the bear – brown and real – is dancing.[1]

The Berlin scene described above on the early morning of November 10, 1989, by two West German reporters from the Berlin newspaper *Die Tageszeitung (taz)* paints quite a different picture of the "fall of the Berlin Wall" than the one that exists in popular memory. Away from the spectacle of the Brandenburg Gate, the chaotic joy of unification is bound up with bittersweet notes of anxiety, fear, and rejection. That the well-documented cries of *"Wir sind ein Volk!"* (We are one people!) existed alongside such statements as "We don't want you here, go back!" is not what most Germans – or the world – have chosen to remember about the symbolic moment surrounding the end of the division between the Cold War German states.

This fairytale ending to the story of the victory of the West over the East after 40 years of Cold War has become a dominant fixture in the popular memory of the history of the end of the twentieth century. The view of the fall of the Berlin Wall as the final stage in the inevitable and manifest drive toward German unity obscures not only the nuanced and often contradictory consequences of unification but also the complexity of the historical relationships between Cold War nations as well as within the two German states themselves. When examined in historical context, it becomes clear that German unification did not simply restore a so-called "natural order" by incorporating East and West Germans under a common flag. Instead, it has involved overwhelming political, economic, social, and cultural renegotiation and transformation for East and West Germans alike. Digging deeper into this disjuncture reveals tensions that fundamentally call in to question basic assumptions regarding German nationalism, German identity and historical memory, and the history of German regionalism dating back to the

---

1 Elmar Kraushaar and Gabriele Riedle, "Wir wollen rein! An der Grenze tanzt der Bär", *taz*, November 11, 1989.

https://doi.org/10.1515/9783110716221-001

eighteenth century, well before the politically unified entity of "Germany" officially existed.

Just 2 months after the collapse of the German–German border, and well before political unification was a given end to the transition process, the West German weekly national newsmagazine *Der Spiegel* grimly announced the "end of the honeymoon" between East and West.[2] Reporting on an increase in shoplifting the "morning after the Wall opened," West German businesses characterize GDR citizens with the newfound freedom to travel as being "seduced" by the consumer goods in the West. In addition, the article states that West German department store managers are reluctant to report the actual amount of theft, as it does not "fit in with the [positive] narrative" of the border fall. Already sick of the perceived entitlement GDR visitors had, taking advantages of privileges such as free admission to swimming pools and other services, many municipalities moved to change the policy to end perks to those visiting from the East. This is just one of many examples of the tone of the reporting covering the German–German transition shifting quickly, from the portrayal of the East German refugee as a victim fleeing ideological persecution or as a wide-eyed innocent tourist in the West from the early 1980s right up until the fall of the Berlin Wall, to one of indignation and distress at the prospect of West German cities, towns, and villages being overrun by eastern migrants with no real justification to flee their homeland after the border no longer held them in against their will. West Germans were not only suddenly faced with the financial burden of housing refugees and providing "welcome money" to GDR citizens visiting for the first time, but also had to contend with managing the day-to-day inconveniences that accompanied the influx of thousands of daily visitors.[3]

The shock of the consequences of the opening of the border in November 1989 – specifically, that not only did it not stop emigration from the GDR but rather seemed to encourage it, suddenly changed the portrayal of GDR refugees in popular and public discourse from victims fleeing persecution into perpetrators seeking to take advantage of the hospitality and resources available in the West. As will be seen later in this study, West Germans in the 1980s had been relatively generous with aid for "exceptional" refugees, but once asked to open their communities for the influx of thousands of refugees who arrived after the collapse

---

2 "Ende der Schonzeit" *Der Spiegel* 50, December 10, 1989.
3 Initially citizens of the GDR were entitled to "welcome money" (*Begrüßungsgeld*) of 100 DM upon first entry into the FRG. The program ended on December 29, 1989, and was replaced with an arrangement whereby GDR citizens could exchange up to 100 East German *Ostmark* (OM) into West German *Deutschmark* (DM) at a ratio of 1:1, with an option to exchange and additional 100 OM at a rate of 5:1.

of the border, became increasingly vocal in their opposition to the right of these GDR citizens to migrate to the West. Upon careful examination of historical migration patterns in Germany, it becomes evident that these constructions are strongly related to wider historical characterizations of migration and regional identities in German-speaking lands. Specifically, the persistence of shifting perceptions of regionality relates to evolving conversations concerning the persistence of fundamental differences between East and West Germans in the two decades following formal political unification.

The formulation and expression of these differences between East and West have operated on several different levels. As West German managers, professionals, and bureaucrats migrated into the so-called wild "bush-land" of the East, the image of the *Besser-Wessi* (Western know-it-all) soon joined that of the *Jammer-Ossi* (whining Easterner) in popular parlance.[4] While newspaper cartoons and popular media exploited and expanded upon these stereotypes, work such as the interview series by East German writer Katrin Rohnstock, who interviewed East and West German men and women in the immediate aftermath of the *Wende* shows how powerful and pertinent these perceptions were to the lived experience of Germans in the midst of transition.[5]

Ostalgie, a form of nostalgia for life in the GDR, emerged and flourished in the mid to late 1990s as it became clear that the millions of *Deutschmark* (DM) invested into transforming and modernizing the East German economy and infrastructure would not succeed in the ultimate goal of bringing eastern states up to par with their western counterparts. *Ostalgie* was first something unique to ex-GDR citizens, with an attempt to recreate the old structures and material culture of life before the *Wende*.[6] in the late 1990s and early 2000s it was commercialized

---

4 The term *Ossi*, commonly used to refer to an East German who came of age in the GDR, is generally considered to be derogatory when used by West Germans. More specifically, a *Jammer-Ossi* suggests an individual who whines about occupying an inferior position in society and is generally unable to function in a western democratic/capitalist milieu (although many East Germans also self-identify as *Ossi*). The western counterpart, *Besser-Wessi*, has a similar stereotypic effect, referring to West Germans who approach their position vis-à-vis East Germans with a patronizing air of superiority.

5 Katrin Rohnstock. *Stiefschwestern: was Ost-Frauen und West-Frauen voneinander denken* (Frankfurt am Main: Fischer Taschenbuch Verlag, 1996). Katrin Rohnstock. *Stiefbrüder: was Ostmänner und Westmänner voneinander denken* (Berlin: Elefanten Press, 1995).

6 Daphne Berdahl. *Where the World Ended: Re-Unification and Identity in the German Borderland* (Berkely: University of California Press, 1999).

into a sort of kitsch embodied in television specials, material goods, and a retro aesthetic consumed by both East and West Germans.[7]

Even as articles foretelling the end of the East–West divide appeared periodically in the national press throughout the late 1990s and early 2000s, East and West German caricatures embodying unbridgeable differences flourished in print, on television, and as a part of everyday discussion. Although its expression has changed during the past 30+ years, the assertion of a specific identity rooted in an association with the former German Democratic Republic decades after unification has been amplified by the persistence of economic dependence of the eastern states on federal subsidies and the continued emigration of its most educated and potentially most productive inhabitants.[8]

This book investigates the intersection of migration between eastern and western Germany and shifting conceptions of German identity through the lens of the major transformative periods of the late twentieth century – postwar, Cold War, and the post-Cold War eras. Firstly, this book relies upon statistical analysis to look at broad trends concerning directional migration, and age and gender patterns within those directional movements at any given time. As has been demonstrated by migration historians such as Steve Hochstadt and Volker Ackermann, a statistical view of regional/internal migration can reveal myriad phases of transformation involving various points in space and periods in time.[9] Although the nature of statistical analysis can seem discrete and absolute, it exists in neither a historical nor a contemporary vacuum. Examining trends in internal migration on multiple levels – local, regional, national – gives a more nuanced view of how human movement can both reflect and influence the development of large-scale historical phenomena. In this case, migration is a particularly acute starting point for examining the working out of German identity politics through periods of war, peace, division, and unification intertwined with the transformations of the past five decades.

---

7 See "Ostalgie on TV: Ein Kessel DDR [A GDR Potpourri] (August 20th, 2003)" *German History in Document and Images.* URL: https://ghdi.ghi-dc.org/sub_image.cfm?image_id=3129. Accessed June 20, 2022.

8 See Andrea Boltho, Wendy Carlin, and Pasquale Scarmozzio, "Will East Germany become another Mezzogiorno", *Journal of Comparative Economics* 24, no. 3 (1997), 241–264, as well as Wolfgang Keller, "From Socialist Showcase to Mezzogiorno? Lessons on the Role of Technical Change from East Germany's Post-World War II Growth Performance", *Journal of Development Economics* 63 no.2 (2000), 485–514.

9 Steve Hochstadt, *Mobility and modernity: migration in Germany, 1820–1989* (Ann Arbor: University of Michigan Press, 1999) and Volker Ackermann, *Der "echte" Flüchtling: Deutsche Vertriebene und Flüchtlinge aus der DDR, 1945–1961* (Osnabrück: Rasch, 1995).

Assessing the overall significance of German internal migration, this book integrates a thorough statistical analysis by age, gender, and location with an examination of political, economic, social, and cultural discussion surrounding German identity and nationalism from the end of the Second World War into the twenty-first century. While the migration of Germans between eastern and western regions after unification signaled a new phase of internal mobility, it also exposed tensions concerning the nature of what it meant to be German in this new post-Cold War iteration of the nation. Exposing the intersection of German mobility with the chaotic reconfiguration of self and states shows how complicated the already shifting nature of postwar German identities became in each period of transition.[10]

The five chapters that follow trace internal migration in Germany through war, division, and unification. Chapter 1 centers upon the immediate postwar period, the phenomenon of the "Displaced Person," and changes in legal and public perception of migrants both east and west after the formation of the two German states. Chapter 2, set in 1949–1989, examines the intersection of statehood and the conscious construction of German identities, with both westward emigration and internal migration within each Cold War State. Chapter 3 examines the pivotal period between the fall of the Berlin Wall and unification. The overall migration in this period is interesting not only concerning the sheer volume of mostly westward migration, but also for the sudden shift of the perception of East German migrants in the West as being victims of a totalitarian regime to being economic opportunists. Chapter 4 examines migration from the formal unification of the two German states, 1990–1994, and looks at the demographic mobility shift inherent in this period to being primarily young and female, but also how this gendered out-migration shaped conceptualizations of men and women in both eastern and western Germany across generational lines. Chapter 5 investigates the decade after privatization and the effect that these changes had for existing workers, as well as those transitioning into the economy. Stereotypes surrounding Germans who had been trained or educated in the GDR led to overrepresen-

---

10 Much has been written on the ideological work that went into the active construction of German identities in the two Cold War states in the postwar period. See Jeffery Herf, *Divided Memory: the Nazi past in the two Germanys* (Cambridge: Harvard University Press, 1997), an investigation of the different ways both the FRG and the GDR utilized and came to terms with the legacy of Nazism to establish political legitimacy. Also see Jan Palmowski's investigation of citizenship in the GDR, "Citizenship, Identity, and Community in the German Democratic Republic," in *Citizenship and National Identity in Twentieth Century Germany*, edited by Geoff Eley and Jan Palmowski (Stanford: Stanford University Press, 2004), 73–94.

tation of West German managers and a significant number of young females who chose to migrate to the West for better opportunities.

Furthermore, this book establishes the relationship between mobility and the multi-layered transformations throughout Europe from the postwar period to the present day. Looking at the relationship between migration and identity formation during these periods of intense structural transformation, this book argues that the patterns of transformation to and within Germany since 1989/1990 reflect the continuing persistence of different values, attitudes, and multiple facets of identity among East and West Germans through the early twenty-first century. At its core, this research pays particular attention to demographic trends, including gender and age, as indicators that uncover both eastward and westward trends in internal migration. Using theoretical models from a variety of fields including migration studies, minority group development, media and cultural analysis, and memory studies, this study offers insight into the extent to which the perception and portrayal of migrants, and the phenomenon of migration itself, can influence the processes of global, national, local, and individual identity formation.

Literature Review

This research draws upon the historiography and methodology of three fields: migration studies, modern German history, and historical memory studies. In an investigation of the historical development of internal migration and the corresponding debates concerning the nature of German identity, this book situates migration within the German historical narrative while also historicizing the cultural study of memory, identity, and material culture. By historicizing both migration and cultural studies and, thereby, widening the scope of German historiography to include narratives of mobility, this study broadens the understanding of how these three strands of scholarship can fit together into the structural and psychological makeup of modern German studies. An understanding of the historiography of each of these areas is essential to understanding the importance of how this book fits into the many fields from which it takes its methodology.

Migration studies came into their own as a discipline in the 1970s, with research on historical emigration as well as an increasing focus on global migrations of the post-industrial age. Although some significant case studies, such as that by James Jackson, have highlighted local and regional migrations, most research has focused on migration across national borders. Research on German migration has also tended to lean more toward international mobility– in particular, the emigration of Germans to North and South America in the nineteenth century and the immigration of Gastarbeiter primarily from Portugal, Italy, Greece, Yugoslavia, and Turkey to the Federal Republic in the 1960s and 1970s.[11] While this work on international and transnational migration has been indispensable to our understanding of how migration has functioned in the postwar transition from an industrial to a global economy, scholarship in these areas have tended to work best at the extremes, either as a macro-level examination of political and economic forces behind system of migration, or as micro-level case studies.[12] For example, as seen from the macrostructural level, the migration of large numbers of Turks into West Germany in the latter half of the twentieth century significantly changed the ethnic composition of many West German urban areas, while also calling into question essential legal and psychological dimensions of German identity. On the other hand, at the micro-level, investigations of individual communities and experiences of migration and cultural renegotiation have complicated debates surrounding how global transformations translate to the level of individual experience, both in terms of the migrant and their families as well as for the members of the host community.[13]

Beginning in the late 1980s, some scholars of European migration began to move beyond an international focus to challenge a basic tenet of modernization theory – namely, that preindustrial populations were mostly immobile and that

---

11 For more on German emigration see Mack Walker, *Germany and the Emigration, 1815–1855* (Cambridge: Harvard University Press, 1964). Klaus J. Bade, "German Emigration to the United States and Continental Immigration to Germany in the Late Nineteenth and Early Twentieth Centuries," *Central European History* 13, no.4 (1980), 348–377, and "From Emigration to Immigration" The German Experience in the Nineteenth and Twentieth Centuries," *Central European History* 28, no 4 (1995), 507–535. For more on female emigration see the edited volume by Monika Blaschke and Christiane Harzig eds., *Frauen wandern aus: Deutsche Migrantinnen im 19. und 20. Jahrhundert* (Bremen: Universitätsdruck, 1991). Ulrich Herbert, *A History of Foreign Labor in Germany, 1880–1990: Seasonal Workers, Forced Laborers, Guestworkers* (Ann Arbor: University of Michigan Press, 1990) gives an overarching view of the history of foreign labor in modern Germany. For the history of *Gastarbeiter* in West Germany see Rita C.K. Chin, *The Guest Worker Question in Postwar Germany* (Cambridge: Cambridge University Press, 2007), as well as the classic work by Ray C. Rist, *Guestworkers in Germany: The Prospects for Pluralism* (London: Praeger, 1978).
12 For an overview of the macro-level approach, see Stephen Castles and Mark Miller, *The Age of Migration* (New York: Guilford Press, 2009).
13 Jennifer A. Miller. *Turkish Guestworkers in Germany: Hidden Lives and Contested Borders, 1960s to 1980s* (Toronto: University of Toronto Press, 2018). Work by Karin Hunn, *"Nächstes Jahr kehren wir zurück": Die Geschichte der türkischen Gastarbeiter in der Bundesrepublik* (Göttingen: Wallstein Verlag, 2005), a collection of 14 case studies examining the lives of Turkish Guest Workers is an example of the micro-level approach, revealing the complexity of the experience of migration told through individual experiences.

migration became widespread only with the arrival of industrialization. Taking a long view of history, this relates to movements in the late twentieth century by seeing the changes in migration patterns as part of a long tradition of movement in response to different motivating factors, instead of a new phenomenon in and of itself. In terms of the East German question, the cessation of regional patterns of migration with the fortification of Cold War borders becomes the exceptional development when seen in the long term and shifting patterns – circular, chain, and other common migration patterns – which have been present in the region since the Middle Ages, albeit often altered or interrupted by war, climate, famine, or other crises. Research into the prevalence of regional and internal migration – temporary, permanent, and seasonal, short distance and long – has undercut the perceived newness of mobility in the lives of Europeans. This research has been fundamental in challenging the perception that the migrations of the late twentieth and early twenty-first century signaled a division between developing world citizens who moved and citizens of the so-called developed world who stayed.

While it is indeed undeniable that the nature of European migration changed dramatically along with the extreme structural reconfigurations that accompanied industrialization in the nineteenth century, mobility itself was nothing new. Permanent migration because of war, persecution, and demographic decline, as well as the seasonal rhythms of seasonal and circular migration shaped European lives centuries before the political, economic, and social dislocations that accompanied industrialization began to take hold. The concentration of modernization theory in the 1960s and 1970s on the disruption of so-called "traditional" societies with "modern" mass mobility obscures the important role migration has played in centuries past.[14] This historical amnesia resulted in a sharp fragmentation separating the history of European migrations from the mainstream narratives of European history.

The historical roots of German migrations have been largely obscured by the seemingly new developments of postwar labor migration into West Germany after the end of the Second World War. The migration scholar, Klaus J. Bade, emerged in the late twentieth and early twenty-first centuries at the forefront of a community of scholars whose works helped dispel the postwar myth that despite a continuous influx of ethnic German returnees, asylum seekers, and labor migrants, Germany was "not a country of immigration":

---

[14] Steve Hochstadt, "Migration in Preindustrial Germany," *Central European History* 16, no. 3 (1983), 195–224.

According to Bade,

> Facing migration problems is a new and threatening experience to many Germans. Contemporary public debate has chosen to ignore the fact that throughout German history the movement of people across borders and the consequent clash of cultures was not the exception but the norm. It has also been forgotten that many native inhabitants are descendants of foreigners who emigrated to Germany, and that millions of German emigrants were strangers in foreign countries, just as many foreigners today are strangers in the united Germany.[15]

In 2000, Bade published *Europa in Bewegung*, which examines the interconnected nature of historical mobility in the context of Europe.[16] Integrating a discussion of local and regional migration into the discussion of the more commonly examined national and international movements, Bade's work has been foundational in shifting the gaze of historical migration from the national to the regional and local. This shift in perspective has not only provided more detail to the historical record regarding the complexity and ubiquity of migration patterns but has also been important in creating a more detailed and inclusive view of different forms of human mobility and how they interact and respond to the forces of history.

While Bade has worked to expand the conception of mobility beyond national borders for the modern era, there have been other scholars that have emphasized the role of migration in shaping Europe from the preindustrial age. Jan Lucassen's *Migrant Labor in Europe* is perhaps the best-known study of regional migration in early modern and modern Europe.[17] Tracing the rise of the North Sea System, Lucassen uncovers the interconnected nature of different migration streams over 300 years by identifying not only the major "push" and "pull" areas, but also by investigating the factors that accounted for various shifts in migration patterns over time. Lucassen uses a regional analysis to view the North Sea system not only in terms of its place in the European economy but also in relative comparison to other migratory systems active during the same period. As observed by migration historian Steve Hochstadt, Lucassen's study is important in that it demonstrates that in the "development of European seasonal migration, particular systems rose and declined at various times, but the overall mobility of

---

15 Bade, "German Emigration to the United States and Continental Immigration to Germany in the Late Nineteenth and Early Twentieth Centuries," 507.

16 Klaus J. Bade, *Europa in Bewegung: Migration vom späten 18. Jahrhundert bis zur Gegenwart* (München, C.H. Beck, 2000).

17 Jan Lucassen, *Migrant Labor in Europe, 1600–1900: The Drift to the North Sea* (London: Croom Helm, 1987). For more on seasonal German labor migration to the Netherlands see also Albin Gladen, *Hollandsgang im Spiegel der Reiseberichte evangelischer Geistlicher: Quellen zur saisonalen Arbeitswanderung in der zweiten Hälfte des 19. Jahrhunderts* (Münster: Aschendorff, 2007).

labor expanded in the 19th century, particularly in central and eastern Europe."[18] Here, the comparison of different migratory systems and their development over time, unhindered by a focus on migration over national borders, allows one to discern the importance and scale of a larger regional pattern.

Taking a more comprehensive view, Leslie Page Moch's monograph, *Moving Europeans: Migration in Western Europe since 1650*, uses a regional analysis of European migration systems to trace the development of different forms of mobility in Western Europe from 1650 through the twentieth century. Although not discounting the very real and human consequences of the formalization of national borders in the late nineteenth century, Moch sees the region as revealing the most comprehensive information about the various types of movements undertaken by various populations in European society. According to Moch, the region is "best suited to the study of migration because historically, while the majority of human movement has occurred within regions, regions also vary enormously. In terms of structural and cultural characteristics, making it a particularly enlightening lens through which to examine economic and demographic change."[19] The application of a regional approach is particularly important to a study of post-unification Germany, as it redefines regional boundaries to reflect former national boundaries. As will be seen throughout this book, the five federal states that were created out of the dissolution of the German Democratic Republic retain economic and demographic characteristics, which reflect and are reflective of migratory trends well into the twenty-first century.

Scholarship specifically looking at German internal migration as regional phenomena is rather scarce but rich.[20] James Jackson's 1997 study, *Migration and Urbanization in the Ruhr Valley, 1821–1914*, uses data from local migration registers to document movement to and from Duisburg. Going beyond mere economic arguments to explain migration as a by-product of urbanization and industrialization, Jackson argues that migration was a social process. This study has been a key model for the inclusion of network theory and the consideration of agency into studies of mobility based primarily upon demographic data.

---

18 Hochstadt, *Mobility and Modernity: Migration in Germany, 1820–1989*, 9.

19 Leslie Page Moch, *Moving Europeans: Migration in Western Europe since 1650* (Bloomington: Indiana University Press), 9–10.

20 Much of the work on internal migration by historians has been done by researchers affiliated with the *Institut für Migrationsforschung und Interkulturelle Studien* (IMIS) at the University of Osnabrück. Note works by Klaus J. Bade, including *Europa in Bewegung*, as well as work by Jochen Oltmer, *Migration im 19. Und 20. Jahrhundert* (München: R. Oldenburg, 2010).

According to Jackson,

> Ordinarily persons in the Ruhr Valley were not passive in the face of massive structural change: political mobilization was only a small part of their strategy and adjustment. As social ties between sending and receiving areas intensified over time, networks of kinfolk, fellow villagers, and business associates emerged, which were built on reciprocal obligation, and which ultimately encouraged mass migration. Families who came to regard residential mobility as an effective survival strategy intensified the social process of migration.[21]

As in the Ruhr Valley in the nineteenth century, East German individuals at the turn of the twenty-first century, mostly young and female, used personal and professional networks and "regarded residential mobility as an effective survival strategy," which is evident in the continuing demographic gender and age gap between the eastern and western federal states.

German historian, Georg Fertig, also considered the importance of human agency in his examination of the historical migratory climate in eighteenth-century transatlantic migration.[22] Until 1980, internal migration had not been included in the examination of the process of mass transatlantic migration from Germany to North America. In looking back from the age of mass migration to traditions of internal migration in preindustrial Germany, Fertig identifies seven main "channels" that facilitated migration.[23] In his investigation of the variety of possibilities for mobility, Fertig shows not only that the individual had several socially acceptable opportunities to migrate, but also that these means contributed to the mass transatlantic migration in the eighteenth century through the utilization of established mobility networks.

Another regional work, Steve Hochstadt's monograph on German internal migration, *Mobility and Modernity*, has been groundbreaking in its depth of inquiry as well as in its spatial and temporal breadth. In an investigation of the evolution of migration in Germany from 1820 to 1989, Hochstadt examines population register data from the Düsseldorf region to draw larger conclusions regarding the nature of internal migration in greater Germany.

---

21 James H. Jackson Jr., *Migration and Urbanization in the Ruhr Valley, 1821–1914* (Atlantic Highlands, N.J.: Humanities Press, 1997), xvii.
22 Georg Fertig, "Eighteenth-Century Transatlantic Migration and Early German Anti-Migration Ideology," in *Migration, Migration History, History*, ed. Jan Lucassen and Leo Lucassen (New York: P. Lang, 1999), 271–312.
23 The seven channels that facilitated migration are as follows: the legal system, labor contracts, professional specialization, alms as insurance, The Protestant reformation, military recruitment, and state recruitment after the Thirty Years' War. Fertig, "Eighteenth-Century Transatlantic Migration and Early German Anti-Migration Ideology", 276–278.

According to Hochstadt, the use of available data, no matter how limited, to make broader conclusions as to the nature of the greater historical democratic trends over time is indispensable to understanding not only patterns of migration but also broader social change in Germany society:

> Broad patterns certainly operate within narrow contexts: local factors give a particular shape to general structures. It is the nature of the general structures, which currently is in question in migration research. This study seeks the general by comparing many communities: its argument is that demographic generalization is necessary to understand local phenomena. The use of aggregated data covering a large region offers the possibility of approaching big questions in European social history.[24]

The necessity of understanding the historical patterns of mobility to complicating and elaborating on the significance of larger questions of German history stressed by Hochstadt, Moch, Jackson, and Fertig has been key in the academic movement toward an integration of German history and migration studies and vital to my own approach looking at both the demographic and socio-cultural aspects of migration between eastern and western Germany. This means not only broadening the scope of inquiry spatially, but also temporally. While this monograph sets its focal point as the moment of German unification to understand both historical and contemporary ramifications and structures of migration, it will look to the past as well as to the present to understand how individual experiences of migration as well as the collective perceptions of mobility intersect to reshape the physical and psychological landscapes of contemporary German society.

Recent works by German historians have linked federal law, public policy, and migration – in particular, the plight of the refugee or asylum seeker – in historical context while also considering German public opinion regarding the migrants themselves. The 2020 monograph, *Flucht: Ein Menschheitsgeschichte* by Andreas Kossert, examines both the German-speaking and non-German refugee as being grounded in otherness.

According to Kossert,

> [After the Second World War], the millions of German compatriots from East Prussia, Bohemia or Silesia on the other side of the Oder and Neisse were simply "the refugees," and they were by no means welcome, but perceived as a threatening disturbance. The same goes for the people from Syria, Afghanistan or the African states who come to Europe today. Anyone who supports them runs the risk of being derided as a "do-gooder".[25]

---

24 Hochstadt, *Mobility and Modernity: Migration in Germany, 1820–1989*, 54.
25 Andreas Kossert, *Flucht: Eine Menschheitsgeschichte* (München: Siedler, 2020), 13.

Kossert identifies otherness as a condition of the refugee, and the status of refugee as one of "otherness," despite ethnic background. Patrice Poutrus's 2019 book *Umkämpftes Asyl: Vom Nachkriegsdeutschland bis in die Gegenwart* examines the development of the right of asylum in Germany from the postwar period through the amendment of the Basic Law in 1993 to the present. In his treatment of the intersection between law and public discourse, Poutrus shows that the asylum law debate is always about fundamental questions of the political and moral state of German society.[26] This book continues in the vein of these recent developments to consider both the structural and the discursive causes and effects of migration – and the perception and experiences of migrants themselves – in German society.

Literatures examining the formation of Cold War identities in the FRG (West Germany) and in the GDR (East Germany) in the postwar era have been important in establishing the foundation for my work examining the renegotiation of identities in the aftermath of German unification. The incorporation of the Holocaust into the reconstruction of a postwar West German identity has occupied an important and powerful position in the historiography. The politics of those memories have helped shape West German positions concerning "self" and "other" – Cold War positions that had serious consequences for German–German relations in the aftermath of unity.[27]

In terms of the historiography of national identity and unity in the GDR, there has been a push in recent years toward not only reconstructing how the state sought to build a German socialist identity from the ground up, but this investigation of the experience of everyday life also figured as a vital component of the construction and maintenance of identity in the GDR.[28] For example, Donna

---

26 Patrice Poutrus, *Umkampftes Asyl: Vom Nachkriegsdeutschland bis in die Gegenwart* (Berlin: C.H. Links, 2018).

27 See Charles Meier, *The Unmasterable Past: History, Holocaust and German National Identity*, 2nd ed. (Cambridge, M.A.: Harvard University Press, 1997); Konrad Jarausch, *After Hitler: Recivilizing Germans, 1945–1955* (Oxford: Oxford University Press, 2006); and Robert G. Moeller, *War Stories: The Search for a Usable Past in the Federal Republic of Germany* (Berkeley: University of California Press, 2001).

28 For more on the relationship between identity formation and everyday life, see Mary Fulbrook, *German National Identity after the Holocaust* (Malden, M.A.: Blackwell, 1999); Fulbrook, *The People's State: East German Society from Hitler to Honecker* (London: Yale University Press, 2005); also Fulbrook, *Power and Society in the GDR, 1961–1979: The 'Normalisation of Rule?'* (New York: Berghahn, 2009). For a consideration of material culture and everyday life, see Katherine Pence and Paul Betts eds., *Socialist Modern: East German Everyday Culture and Politics* (Ann Arbor: University of Michigan Press, 2008); Esther von Richthofen, *Bringing Culture to the Masses: Control, Compromise and Participation in the GDR* (Oxford: Berghahn, 2009); and Jan Pal-

Harsch's research on the complex negotiations involved between women and the state regarding work and family policies succeeds in removing the agency of identity formation from the realm of ideology to the experiences of everyday life.[29]

Research on German identity after unification considers both the conscious and unconscious processes involved in the construction of Cold War German identities and the renegotiations involved in the conceptualization of a united German identity. Michael Geyer and Konrad Jarausch's *Shattered Past: reconstructing German Histories* calls for the expansion of mainstream German historical narratives to include subjects such as mobility and migration, the role of women, national identity, and consumption and consumerism. Most interesting is the creation of a roadmap for the integration of these subjects into the mainstream, not merely as addenda to the main narrative, but as indispensable and inseparable components of the history to be told.[30]

Interdisciplinary scholarship on consumerism and consumption in the post-socialist age has also proven indispensable to this study. While consumerism has, at least for the past decade, been a fixture of emerging trends in West German historiography, it has been just in the past few years that it has taken hold in the realm of East German history. This development has signaled a generational shift as questions concerning the structures of dictatorship, political legitimacy, and the experience of everyday life in the GDR have given way to work that explores the unique function of consumption in the East.[31] Paul Betts's examination of the role of fantasy and consumption in shaping identities in both East and West, and the role of consumption after unification in shaping post-Wall identities has shown the symbiotic relationship between eastern and western development in, during, and after unification.[32] The border studies of the late anthropologist,

---

mowski, *Inventing a Socialist Nation: Heimat and the Politics of Everyday Life in the GDR, 1945–1990* (Cambridge: Cambridge University Press, 2007).

29 Donna Harsch, *Revenge of the Domestic: Women, the Family and Communism in the German Democratic Republic* (Princeton N.J.: Princeton University Press, 2007).

30 Konrad Jarausch and Michael Geyer, *Shattered Past: Reconstructing German Histories* (Princeton, N.J.: Princeton University press, 2003). See also Konrad Jarausch (ed.), *After Unity: Reconfiguring German Identities* (Providence, R.I.: Berghahn, 1997).

31 Benita Blessing, "Review of Paul Betts and Katherine Pence eds. Socialist Modern: East German Everyday Culture and Politics," H-German, H-Net Reviews (July 2008).

32 Paul Betts, "Remembrance of Things Past: Nostalgia in West and East Germany, 1980–2000," in *Pain and Prosperity: reconsidering twentieth century German history*. Paul Betts and Greg Eghigan eds. (Stanford: Stanford University Press, 2003), 178–208. Judd Stitziel, *Fashioning Socialism: Clothing, Politics and Consumer Culture in East Germany* (Oxford: Berg, 2005). Eli Rubin, "The Order of Substitutes: Plastic Consumer Goods in the Volkswirtschaft and Everyday Domestic Life in the GDR," in *Consuming Germany in the Cold War*, ed. David Crew (Oxford: Berg, 2003), 87–121.

Daphne Berdahl, as well as her work on consumption patterns after unification have shed considerable light on how the performance of East–West difference played out in the realm of material culture.[33] Anthropologist and media studies scholar, Dominic Boyer, also has explored the development of East–West alterities both in his fieldwork studying East and West German journalists after unification as well as in his investigation of *Ostalgie* and its role in public memory.[34]

A field that can broadly be referred to as memory studies has more recently emerged as a way to address some of the more complicated and problematic historical themes regarding both the recent and not-so recent past. Although much of the German historiographical work integrating memory studies deal specifically with the coming to terms with the "Nazi past," this intellectual labor also can be and has been applied to discussions regarding coming to terms with the memory of life in both Cold War East and West Germany, and the problematic period of the Wende, including the symbolic memory of the physical and emotional nature of the Berlin Wall.[35] Aleida Assmann's 2013 study, *Das Neue Unbehagen an der Erinnerungskultur: Eine Intervention,* engages theoretically and practically with the "culture of memory," which has pervaded German culture since the 1990s, outlining problematic areas in engaging with German memory studies, while also offering specific outlines for engagement and approach for the two areas at play in this study: GDR studies and migration.[36]

By intertwining the themes of migration, identity, culture, and memory, this book seeks to tease out elements of memory culture, which have been overshadowed by that which focus on victimhood. Although, as Assmann points out, the relationship between memory and the National Socialist regime and remembering that of the former GDR is that "the memory of Stalinism (in the GDR) cannot re-

Katherine Pence, "Women on the Verge: Consumers between Private Desires and Public Crisis," in *Socialist Modern: East German Culture and Politics,* ed. Paul Betts and Katherine Pence (Ann Arbor: University of Michigan Press, 2008), 287–322.
33 Daphne Berdahl, *Where the World Ended: Re-Unification and Identity in the German Borderland* (Berkeley: University of California Press, 1999) as well as Berdahl, "The Spirit of Capitalism and the Boundaries of Citizenship in Post-Wall Germany," *Comparative Studies in Society and History* 47, no. 2 (2005), 235–251.
34 Dominic Boyer, "Conspiracy, History and Therapy at a Berlin Stammtisch," *American Ethnologist* 35, no. 3 (2006), 327–339, Boyer, "Postcommunist Nostalgia in Eastern Germany: An Alternative Analysis," *Public Culture* 18, no. 2 (2006), 361–381, and Boyer, "Media Markets, Mediating Labors and the Branding of East German Culture at Super Illu," *Social Text* 19, no.3 (2001), 9–33.
35 Hope Millard Harrison, *After the Berlin Wall; memory and the making of the new Germany, 1989 to the present* (Cambridge: Cambridge University Press, 2019).
36 Aleida Assmann, *Das neue Unbehagen an der Erinnerungskultur: Eine Intervention* (München: C.H. Beck, 2013).

place the memory of the Nazi period" but that also the Nazi period cannot "trivialize the [experience] under Stalinism," I would argue this can be further expanded to challenge preconceptions of German–German interactions during and after the end of the Cold War.[37] Complicating positive narratives to uncover less than golden images of German unification not only highlights the nature of the German separation but also gives insight into the development of German–German relations under one state.

Methods and Sources

Methodology – Statistical Analysis

This book's foundational arguments use a comparative examination of demographic data surrounding internal migration and mobility in Germany, 1989–2004. In an analysis of migration and demographic data published by the German Federal Statistical Office (*Statistisches Bundesamt*), the primary statistical analysis concerns movement between the five new eastern states created out of the former German Democratic republic and the eleven western states of the FRG in united Germany. In the spirit of Steve Hochstadt, who argues that a mere determination of net population loss or gain due to migration hardly reveals the full extent of mobility, both eastward and westward are considered independently of "net" figures.[38]

In addition to federal migration statistics, this book also integrates economic and population studies, examining structural development and change in the eastern states following unification. A great deal of economic research on the eastern states in the first decade after unification has shed some light on the structural reasons that the so-called "economic miracle" promised in the East after the collapse of the Berlin Wall did not develop. Findings concerning changing demographic indicators, including the population age distribution, gender balance, and birth rate all give clues to factors that encourage migration amongst a certain part of the population as well as to the effects of uneven migration rates on the sending and receiving areas.

---

37 Assmann, *Das neue Unbehagen an der Erinnerungskultur: Eine Intervention*, 114.

38 Net migration refers to the total population loss or gain in an area due to movement across borders. For example, if 2000 people migrated into an area while 2500 left, it can be said that the area has had a net migration gain of 500. While useful for demographic purposes (measuring population gain or loss), the net figure obscures the true extent of mobility, which is vital to properly assess the true extent and impact of human migration patterns.

However, understanding migration and mobility does not merely serve to highlight demographic and economic trends associated with regional development. Rather, migration is also a highly social phenomenon and has had serious and profound consequences on the regional perception and portrayal of "east" and "west" in the public sphere. This study makes use of articles from national magazines and newspapers as well as local publications to illustrate the nature of the dialogue concerning East–West difference and German identity after unification. As two nation-states became one, what had been emigration and immigration became internal migration. The sharp shift between an emphasis on East German immigrants fleeing the GDR, and regional migrants "invading" western states is a measure of both physical numbers (it became easier to move after the opening of the border) and a reconceptualization of German regionality. The states of the former GDR began to be associated with perceived negative social habits and cultural tastes, dilapidated infrastructure, and economic dependence. When easterners migrated to the western states, they brought with them these negative connotations.

Methodology – Popular Discourse

One interesting facet of conducting historical research so close to contemporary circumstances is that most of the primary sources used in my work do not exist in traditional archives. In terms of public discourse, this book draws from articles and columns published by national and regional popular presses. These daily newspapers and weekly magazines are particularly astute in measuring popular tension, especially addressing popular opinion of issues such as migration and the effects of migrants on local communities. Compared against trends in demographic migratory patterns, the gap between how Germans felt about migration in the moment and what has evolved as the popular memory of each of these periods becomes evident. The recent advent of online archival databases most notably that of *Der Spiegel* a weekly (West) German national news magazine published continuously since 1946, has made the documentation and analysis of the evolution of public debates surrounding East–West migration and German identity possible. I have also made extensive use of smaller databases and archival resources at the Hans Bredow Institute in Hamburg, the Frederick Ebert Stiftung in Bonn-Bad Godesberg, as well as university libraries in Osnabrück and Münster. While some articles were first accessed in print, the accessibility of German media (including both national and local papers) has allowed for electronic access and reference. Although newspaper articles may, at first glance, appear to be limiting in terms of methodology, combined with statistical analysis and with a lens toward the public discourse surrounding migration, both national and local patterns of characterization – often in ethnic, economic, political, or gendered terms – can be discerned.

Mobility and Migration

At its very core, the narrative told through this research is that of the continual redefinition of categories of migration and mobility through times of political, economic, social, and cultural change. The chaotic mobility of the "Year Zero" (as coined by Ian Buruma) persisted throughout the Allied occupation of the German Reich, and wartime migrant categories such as "displaced persons" (foreign nationals residing within German territory at the end of the war, including those who had performed forced labor for the Nazi regime and survivors of concentration camps), "expellees" (ethnic Germans who had lost residence or ownership on/off land, which no longer counted as German territory after the war), and even "prisoners of war" (including those who had been imprisoned by both Allied and Axis powers) were legally, economically, and socially significant through the late 1950s.

After the formation of the two Cold War German states in 1949, these national identities evolved separately. The new category of *Umsiedler* (resettler) at first was casually applied to individuals who moved between the Soviet and Western Allied sectors during the occupation, and for a brief period (1949–1953), those who moved both East from the Federal Republic to the German Democratic Republic and West from the German Democratic Republic to the Federal Republic. After the Soviet repression of the East Berlin workers' revolt in 1953, and especially after the construction of the Berlin Wall in 1961, migration began to become dominantly westward, a considerable disconnect between negative local attitudes toward both *Umsiedler* and *Vertriebene* and the positive political conception of both eastward and westward migrants by the receiving states as proof of relevancy and legitimacy, within the larger context of the Cold War.

As the "economic miracle" of the 1960s and early 1970s introduced foreign labor into both the Federal Republic and, a little later, in the late 1970s/early to mid 1980s the German Democratic Republic, legal restrictions surrounding mobility (especially non-ethnically German mobility) created categories that defined certain types of movement and certain categories of people, as legitimate and illegitimate. The perceived illegitimacy of the "economic" migration of ethnically Germany *Umsiedler* and *Vertriebene* in the late 1950s and early 1960s shifted through the heightened politicized rhetoric surrounding state legitimacy during the Cold War, the construction of the physical barrier of the Berlin Wall, as well as through the public and private narratives constructing non-German mobility (especially that of Turkish "guestworkers" in the Federal Republic. After the physical barrier between East and West came down, the legitimacy of *Umsiedler* mobility, formerly grounded legally in political repression, vanished as quickly as the East German state disintegrated. As East–West migration increased, economic tropes were invoked to portray those making false or exaggerated political claims and to garner support for the CDU party's push for rapid unification.

Gender

The reconfiguration of not only national, but regional and individual identities in times of crises and stability, in the context of the development of tropes surrounding East/West difference requires a nuanced understanding of how gender was a determining factor in the likelihood and type of mobility, as well as the perceived legitimacy of a claim to protected migrant status. The gendered order of both postwar German states was a key element in the construction of West German and East German identities, not only vis-à-vis the war but in opposition to each other as well. While the West German stabilization was based upon the restoration of the male breadwinner model, the East German gender regime was founded upon the right (and need) for all women to access full time employment.

In addition, the gendering of non-German migrants, especially majority groups (ethnic Turks) from West German *Gastarbeiter* (Guestworker) and East German (ethnic Vietnamese and Mozambiquans) *Vertragsarbeiter* (Contract Workers) schemes is also indicative of categories of legitimacy and illegitimacy largely framed in terms of sex. Examining the regulation of both of these groups (in terms of movement, living conditions (often single sex), contact with Germans, legal access to family reunion, cancellation of wages upon pregnancy) is analyzed in Chapter 2.

The continued significance of internal westward migration after the end of the Cold War by age and sex well into the twenty-first century is indicative of persistent gendered stereotypes. The collapse of the GDR gender regime upon unification made women more vulnerable to unemployment as the East was forced to adjust according to West German policies. At the same time, conflicts between East and West were often expressed in gendered terms. These gendered depictions of East and West German men and women often evoked mobility (or lack thereof) as a major component. Although these stereotypes were often quite far from the reality of the relationships and experiences of East and West German men and women, the gendering of East and West that resulted has held considerable power in the reworking of German identities after unification.[39]

Identity

The concept of identity is often held up as an example of academic jargon – a term according to Rogers Brubaker and Frederick Cooper, that "tends to mean too much (when understood in a strong sense), too little (when understood in a weak sense), or nothing at all (because of its sheer ambiguity)."[40] In the historical profession, however, concrete investigations of identity have been particularly important, especially regarding the emergence of nationalism and national identity. This is nowhere more the case than when examining the historical debates surrounding German history and society in the aftermath of the Second World War. However, in terms of migration, the focus has often been solely on the effect of international migration and the integration of foreigners into German society rather than a focus on how the movement of Germans has influenced dialogues surrounding the politics of national identity.

For the purposes of this research, I use the concept of identity in order to grasp the ways in which "East" and "West" as categorizations (both self and other) have been kept alive in the more than two decades after unification.[41] This study uses the idea of the construction of identity by outside forces, by the creation of stereotypes through rhetoric used in public space and in the reification of these stereotypes through the performance and discussion of categorization. While such labels as *Ossi* and *Wessi* were first and foremost used as pejoratives, the ways that these categories have changed and been co-opted and owned over time has reflected and affected the ways in which post-Wall German identities have been reconfigured, considering shifting conceptualizations of East and West.

---

39 For the construction of West German gender regime see Robert Moeller, *Protecting Motherhood: Women and the Family in the Politics of West Germany* (Berkeley: University of California Press, 1996). For an examination of the construction of policies for working motherhood see Myra Marx Ferree, "The Rise and Fall of 'Mommy Politics,' Feminism and Unification in (East) Germany," Feminist Studies 19, no. 1 (1993), 89–115. The edited collection by Eva Kolinsky and Hildegard Maria Nickel, *Reinventing Gender: Women in Eastern Germany since Unification* (Portland: Frank Cass, 2003) provides a variety of viewpoints on the renegotiation of the perceptions of and realities faced by East German women after unification.
40 Rogers Brubaker and Frederick Cooper, "Beyond Identity," *Theory and Society* 29, no.1 (2000), 1.
41 Mark Howard, "An East German Ethnicity? Understanding the New Division in Unified Germany," German Politics and Society 13, no. 4 (1995), 49–70.

Bringing into dialogue the structural, statistical, and the everyday, this study ultimately analyzes the ways in which contact between East and West Germans after unification has influenced the development of these discussions surrounding identity. Examining the age and gender specific patterns of migration in the two decades following unification in concert with the continued portrayal of East and West Germans as different in public discourse begin to address the question of to what extent mobility, structural forces, and regional identity relate to the way in which "being" German – in both the East and in the West – has shifted throughout the twentieth and into the twenty-first century.

Chapter Overview

This book is divided into five chronological chapters, each focusing on a specific phase of interaction between internal migration and the reshaping of German identities from the postwar era to the present. Chapter 1, "'*Vertriebene*' or '*Umsiedler*'? Postwar and Cold War Migration and the (Re)Formation of German Identities, 1945–1949," investigates changes in mobility in the immediate postwar years. Displaced persons (DPs) and evacuees were treated much differently in the emerging eastern and western zones as population movements continued to develop throughout this period. The legal establishment of the Federal Republic of Germany and the German Democratic Republic in 1949 further politicized these migrants, while also allowing for formal policies regarding refugee and DP status to be established to mitigate the economic consequences of continued displacement.

Chapter 2, "*Republikflucht* and *Gastarbeiter*: Migration Regimes within and between the Two Germanies, 1949–1989," examines the extensive migratory movements that occurred in the immediate postwar era and includes not only the massive movement of refugees, but also the multi-faceted redistribution of population within Germany, rural to urban, north to south and east to west. When the statistical reality of migration is set in juxtaposition to its portrayal in the press, it becomes clear that the reality of the significance of internal migration in German history was lost in the volume of migration in the immediate postwar era.

Chapter 3, "Tearing Down One Wall While Erecting Another: GDR Refugees in the West before and after the Fall of the Berlin Wall, 1989–1990," examines the period from the start of the escalation of East–West migration in the summer of 1989 until formal unification was enacted on October 3, 1990. In stark contrast to their initial reception as "our brothers and sisters from the East" seeking shelter from political persecution, after the fall of the Wall, GDR refugees were increasingly portrayed as socially damaged, criminally corrupt, or as parasites trying to abuse the West German social system.

Chapter 4, "Emigration Becomes Internal Migration: A New German Minority and a Crisis of National Identity, 1990–1994," follows the development of internal migration between the five new eastern states and the eleven "old" western states from unification through the formal end of East German privatization in 1994. Economically, the wholesale transfer of political and economic structures from West to East and the privatization of state-owned enterprises disrupted the normal functioning of the East German labor market and resulted in skyrocketing unemployment rates in all five of the newly formed eastern states. This displacement and lack of opportunity for those educated and trained in the former GDR fueled a continuing emigration from East to West.

Chapter 5, "German Mobility and a New Generation, 1994–2004," examines the decade after the end of East German privatization and explores the intersection between shifts in internal migration and the resurgence of "East" German identity. While many experts lauded the coming of the *Aufschwung Ost* (eastern recovery) as the labor market in the East seemed to be stabilizing with the decline of East–West migration from 1994–1997, the stabilization of migration was only a temporary consequence of generational change. Examining internal migration patterns, 1998–2004, indicates that emigration again increased as the first generation to be schooled in united Germany came of age, while there was a concurrent decline in West–East migration as investment tapered off. Westward movement in this period was dominated by younger age groups, as a future in the East became harder for that cohort to envision.

The book's conclusion examines the relevance of internal migration to historical narratives and the relationship of "contemporary" developments to historical memory. As is outlined in Chapter 1, there is quite a bit of literature dealing with the reworking of historical memory in the Cold War period. The FRG and the GDR not only took divergent paths, but also sought to form their national identities as a mirror image of one another. This is reflected not only in two radically opposed political systems, but also in the ways these states sought to transform and reform themselves in the wake of fascism and echoed in the ways the state sought to relate to its people.

1 *"Vertriebene"* or *"Umsiedler"*? Postwar and Cold War Migration and the (Re)Formation of German Identities, 1945–1949

By the time Eduard Modekat and his family found themselves residents of the Sal-zufer refugee camp in West Berlin in 1953, they were not only veterans of war but also of migration. After being captured as a Wehrmacht soldier by the Americans, Modekat was sent in 1942 to Oklahoma where he and other German prisoners of war performed manual and agricultural labor, clearing trees as far north as Can-ada. In her husband's absence, Modekat's wife was swept up in the westward purge of millions of ethnic Germans from the eastern lands of the Reich in the last months of the war. In December 1944, Frau Modekat loaded the horses, the family bedding, and a sack of oatmeal into a boxcar, fleeing westward from their East Prussian hometown of Allenstein (today Olsztyn, Poland) to Neustrelitz, a small farming town in Mecklenburg-West Pomerania, located in the Soviet post-war occupation zone. After the end of the war, Modekat was released, and he made his way back to his family's new home in Neustrelitz where they had settled on a potato farm.

After this reunification, life was generally stable for the Modekat family until their farm was officially collectivized in July of 1952. An early frost in the fall of that year destroyed not only the crops in the field, but also the collective's stock of seed potatoes. Modekat was targeted and accused by the central commission of the collective of committing "industrial sabotage" by sabotaging farm equipment. After the collective denied his family food and provisions, Modekat saw no other option but to flee once again. One evening, taking a long-distance train toward Berlin, back to Neustrelitz, instead of disembarking at his designated stop, he sim-ply stayed on. Once in Berlin, Modekat used the local S-Bahn to cross into West Berlin, where he sought refuge at the Salzufer camp. A few days later, his wife and sons took the same route and joined him at the refugee camp.[1]

Whether seen as a "flight from the republic" *(Republikflucht)* or as simple "re-settlement" *(Umsiedlung)*, the story of Eduard Modekat and his family is represen-tative of the political, economic, and social underpinnings surrounding the migra-tion between the two German states in the 1950s. Modekat was not simply one of the 16,000 farmers who fled the GDR between November 1952 and February 1953 in response to the decision made by the SED at the Second Party Conference

---

1 "Sowjetzone-Flüchtlinge: Reine Torschlusspanik."

https://doi.org/10.1515/9783110716221-002

in July 1942 to push forward with the collectivization of socialist agriculture.[2] A focus on the complex migration history of the Modekat family reveals several intersecting threads to some common postwar experiences – a POW sent to a camp in North America, an ethnic German family expelled from the eastern Reich, refugees crossing the German–German border, and possibly, emigration out of Germany for good.

The significance of the migration of individuals and families depended upon which side was writing the history. While in the German Democratic Republic (GDR), Modekat would be portrayed as guilty of *Republikflucht*, one of the "old farmers" resistant to collectivization and change, in the Western Federal Republic (FRG), he would be labeled as an "expellee" (*Vertriebener)* – one of the vulnerable victims, first driven into the GDR by the Red Army, as well as a "resettler" (*Umsiedler),* and later forced to flee further West by the Soviet-style reorganization of agriculture in order to ensure the basic survival of his family.

Once he reached West Berlin, Modekat's story of persecution at the hands of the collective made him eligible for the label of a political *Umsiedler*, a distinction that in 1953 allowed him not only citizenship rights as a "German" in West Germany but also provided an opportunity for permanent emigration. While the majority of "West-Refugees" hoped to be approved for migration into West Germany, Modekat hoped to migrate even further afield. As a result of his experience laboring in Canada as an American POW during the war, he hoped to be sponsored for migration by the Canadian government; however, his request was ultimately denied.[3]

The story of the Modekat family captures the complexity of migration and mobility within and between the two Cold War German states in the first decade after the end of the war. For many displaced persons (DPs), wartime or postwar movements did not simply end at a refugee camp, or even with resettlement. As exemplified in this story, migration within occupation zones or states as well as migration between the four occupation zones (later, the two German nations) were survival strategies to counter political objection or persecution as well as to improve one's general chances for personal advancement and familial security.

---

2 The SED, or Socialist Unity Party (Sozialistische Einheitspartei Deutschlands) was the ruling party in the German Democratic Republic, from its formation in October 1949 until the first free elections in the East, after the collapse of the border between the FRG and GDR in March 1990.
3 Although the Canadian government showed active interest in refugee farmers, Modekat's petition was most likely unsuccessful. The approval of a petition for asylum, even on political grounds, was highly selective. At 45 and with at least two children (the article was unspecific on this point), Modekat was considered old and had too much baggage.

Both academic research and public discourse regarding German migration and mobility after the Second World War tends to downplay the complexity in favor of an emphasis on the international political ramifications; namely, they view migration primarily from the vantage point of the state.[4] Despite each state's intention, borders did not become impassable after the formation of each Cold War nation-state. While the political ramifications of migration between the FRG and GDR cannot be overlooked, the various migration regimes were more complex and interconnected than the simplified rhetoric of political migration that it allows.

This chapter will sketch the movement of Germans, both ethnic and state-defined, between and within the two German states from the immediate chaos of the aftermath of the Second World War through the domestic and international struggles that defined the era of Cold War. Furthermore, this chapter will question the focus of research to date on postwar German–German migration in order to expand and deepen an understanding of the various forms of migration; this will yield a more complete and interrelated picture of German migration and mobility. Important movements in this period include those of DPs, evacuees, and expellees of the immediate post war period, internal rural–urban migrations within each state, as well as the advent of international labor migration in both the FRG and the GDR. An examination of how these migratory systems and regimes coexisted in the same space and time will reveal how these systems formed multiple social and psychological categories of mobility in both postwar German states: namely that of the ethnic German victim, the East German political refugee, and the foreign labor migrant. Each of these categories were significantly gendered in public portrayal, and constantly reconfigured to set standards of legitimacy. These categories, in turn, were key to postwar formation of German identities and have had major influence on the development of German constructions of mobility, since unification.

Examining the period from the end of the Second World War (May 1945) to the establishment of the FRG and GDR as nation-states in May and October 1949, respectively, the following pages investigate the complex self and official identities individuals had to navigate in the gray space in-between war and statehood. As forced laborers, prisoners of war and refugees moved away from the broken war machine; the Allied powers redrew the borders of Germany and divided the nation, as well as the city of Berlin, into four occupied zones. Refugee camps were

---

4 For an overview of the political influences and ramifications of postwar immigration to and from Germany, see Chapter 4 in Andrew Geddes, *The Politics of Migration and Immigration in Europe* (London: Sage, 2003).

established not only for those with nowhere to return, but also for German people fleeing eastern lands that were no longer German. Migration policy in this period focused on repatriation of foreign nationals and the resettlement of expelled ethnic Germans. Although policy varied among the four occupation zones, the newly arrived ethnic Germans were often resettled in sparsely populated rural areas in order to fill gaps in the agricultural labor force, which made them more vulnerable economically and more likely to migrate further, either from the Soviet Zone to one of the western zones, or from any zone abroad.

After the establishment of statehood, with the growing volumes of internal migration streams within and between the FRG and the GDR, as well as the introduction of large scheme international labor migration in the 1960s and early 1970s, the historical reality of German mobility was removed from conceptions of "German" identity on both sides. Once East–West migration picked up again in the late 1980s, it was portrayed and legitimized in the FRG as legitimate return of German citizens on political grounds. After the collapse of the GDR, however, thousands of new citizens of the new Federal Republic of Germany continued to migrate. Once the grounds of political legitimacy were removed, it was difficult to obscure the economic reasons underscoring east–west migration. Destabilizing the definition of German "migration" as politically motivated required a major shift in public and private attitudes toward East and West German migrants in the years after unification, contributing to a serious crisis of identity that has yet to be fully resolved.

Multiple mass migrations of groups and individuals took place within and out of the European continent in the aftermath of the Second World War. Although definitive counts are impossible to come by, some estimate there were between 30 and 35 million people in Germany who could be defined as a refugee, expellee, DP, or evacuee by the time the dust had settled in 1950. While this chapter will focus primarily on the movement and redistribution of German expellees within the four German occupation zones, it is important to establish the great volume of movement that was taking place alongside the official tabulated displacement. It is in the context of this mobility that Germans found common ground with those who had been victims of their regime, while also developing a unique culture of victimhood that was formed in the aftermath of the war. German expellees, as well as those identified as evacuees, were officially recognized as victims of the war, long before victims of the Holocaust were offered compensation.[5] The focus on the historical memory of German victimhood helped to displace some of the German war guilt, and contributed to the formation of postwar German identities in both the FRG as well as the GDR.[6]

1.1 Displaced Persons

The label "displaced person" covered foreign nationals who found themselves in Germany after the end of the war, including those who had performed forced labor for the Nazi regime and survivors of concentration camps.[7] The military authority of each occupation zone administered the estimated 10–12 million DPs left in Germany at the end of the war. As of January 1945, the United Nations Relief and Rehabilitation Administration (UNRRA) took charge of repatriation in the western zones. Under the UNRRA, with the assistance of the Red Cross and military authorities, roughly half of the total DPs were repatriated within the first four months after the war.[8] By the end of 1945, only 1.7 million DPs remained in

---

5 Despite the passage of the *Bundesentschädigungsgesetz* in 1953, which set out compensation criteria for victims of the regime, most did not qualify for assistance or reparation because they lived abroad. However, assistance and reparation of West German citizens was quite extensive. The 1950 *Bundesversorgungsgesetz* set out guidelines for assistance and compensation to veterans who had been injured in the line of duty (explicitly excluding those who were found to be guilty of war crimes). The 1952 passage of the *Lastenausgleichsgesetz* (Equalization of Burdens Law) levied a property tax of 50% for those who owned considerable property in 1948, in order to compensate and provide for (1) those who had lost property or been injured as a result of war, (2) late returning POWs of the USSR, (3) those who had lost property through expulsion from the Eastern Reich, flight from the Soviet Zone, later GDR, or been considerably damaged by the Currency Reform of 1948. The 1953 *Bundesevakuiertengesetz* (Law for the Protection of Evacuees) recognized evacuees as victims of the war and outlined formal assistance for housing and employment. The 1953 *Bundesvertriebenengesetz* (Law for the Protection of Expellees) did much the same for "Expellees," with the inclusion of a "right to return" to the property they had left behind.
6 For more on German victimhood, see Moeller, *War Stories: The Search for a Usable Past in the Federal Republic of Germany* (Berkeley: University of California Press, 2001) and Elizabeth Heinemann, "The Hour of the Woman: Memories of Germany's 'Crisis Years' and West German National Identity," *American Historical Review* 101, no. 2 (1996): 364–374.
7 In October 1944, there were more than 8 million forced laborers in Germany, including 6 million civilian laborers and 2 million prisoners of war from over 20 different countries. Klaus J. Bade and Jochen Oltmer, "Flucht und Vertreibung nach dem zweiten Weltkrieg," *in Enzyklopädie Migration in Europa: vom 17. Jahrhundert bis zur Gegenwart*, ed. Pieter C. Emmer, Leo Lucassen and Jochen Oltmer (Paderborn: Schönigh, 2007), 158.
8 Bade and Oltmer (2007), 159.

the western zones; a year later, just 500,000 remained. Those who were not willing to be repatriated to their home countries, for various reasons, were either settled in countries that agreed to accept DPs to fill labor shortages (Belgium, the United Kingdom, Canada, and Australia) or, in the case of many Jewish survivors, settled in the new state of Israel.[9]

Despite this attempt to organize and repatriate foreign nationals in the occupied sectors of Germany, these numbers did not include ethnic Germans who had been expelled from other European nations, including the Netherlands, Poland, and Czechoslovakia, into the occupied zones. Those arriving in late 1946 in the Soviet and French sectors, and after April 1947 in the American sectors, were refused processing. As the window of gaining refugee status closed, a number of DPs, primarily Poles, Czechs, and other eastern Europeans, refused repatriation. The third commission to the UN, against Soviet pressure, declared:

> No refugees or displaced persons who have finally and definitively, in complete freedom and after receiving full knowledge of the facts, including adequate information from the Governments of their countries of origin, express valid objections to returning to their countries of origin . . . shall be compelled to return to their countries of origin.[10]

Although many of these "last million," as they were called, eventually settled in Germany or abroad, a few hundred, mostly single males, stayed on permanently at a few long-term DP camps. The last UNRAA-run DP camps, Föhrenheim, and Wels, were closed in 1957 and 1959, respectively.

The Soviets handled repatriation much differently than the western allies. Repatriation was universal and mandatory. According to the historian Eugene Kulischer, in his 1949 report published in the *Annals of the American Academy of Political and Social Science,*

> The Soviet approach was simple. All persons met by the Russian army were to be repatriated, willingly or by force; those who refused to return home were assumed to be collaborationists, Nazi helpers or quislings, and therefore should be extradited to their legal governments as war criminals. By January 1947 it was announced that no single displaced citizen of an Allied nation remained in the U.S.S.R. or in the Soviet occupied countries.[11]

---

9 Bade and Oltmer (2007), 158.
10 General Assembly UNHCR. *Refugees and Displaced Persons Report of Third Committee.* 13 December 1946. https://www.unhcr.org/en-us/protection/historical/3ae68bee8/refugees-displaced-persons-report-third-committee.html. Accessed August 18, 2022.
11 Eugene Kulischer, "Displaced Persons in the Modern World," *Annals of the American Academy of Political and Social Science* 262 (1949), 170.

The Soviets also insisted upon universal repatriation of their citizens from Allied-occupied territories, an expectation founded upon repatriation agreements signed between the American and British forces, and the Soviet Union, at Yalta.[12] With the cooperation of the UNRRA, 2 million prewar Soviet citizens were subject to compulsory repatriation, many against their will.[13] Targeted groups included prisoners of war and former slave laborers, as well as persecuted groups, who had fled the Soviet Union under political auspices. Upon repatriation, many were found to have fought for the German forces or to have otherwise collaborated, and were tried and punished, including 1.5 million Red Army soldiers who had been POWs in Germany, who were subsequently exiled to the Gulag.[14]

1.2 Evacuees

The intensification of the air war against Germany in 1944 and 1945 by the British and American forces resulted in mass evacuations of over 6 million citizens. The end of the bombing, however, did not mean the return of the people. An estimated 25% of housing was destroyed nationwide, but in some larger cities, notably Cologne and Wurzburg, the destruction was near total.[15] Despite massive efforts to rebuild, many evacuees simply could not return home. As of April 1947, an estimated 3–4 million evacuees still remained outside of their hometowns.[16]

---

12 For an extended discussion of the repatriation agreement see Mark Elliot, "The United States and Forced Repatriation of Soviet Citizens," *Political Science Quarterly* 88, no. 2 (1973), 253–275.
13 According to Kulischer, "(Yalta) provided compulsory repatriation of Soviet citizens (from the prewar U.S.S.R. territory not including the Baltic States, eastern Poland and Bessarabia) who were: (1) captured in German uniforms, (2) members of the Soviet Armed Forces, or (3) found on the basis of reasonable evidence to be collaborators with the enemy." Kulischer (1949), 170.
14 "The official posture (toward POWs) stemmed from the Soviet concept of proper battlefield deportment. The Red Army field manual assumed that a loyal soldier was either fighting or was dead; surrender was tantamount to treason." Mark Elliot, "The United States and Forced Repatriation of Soviet Citizens." *Political Science Quarterly* 88 no. 2 (June 1973), 258. For more on Soviet treatment of returnees see Ulrike Goeken-Haidl, *Der Weg zurück: Die Repatriierung Sowjetischer Zwangsarbeiter während und nach dem zweiten Weltkrieg* (Essen: Klartext Verlag, 2006).
15 See Jeffery Diefendorf, *In the Wake of the War: The Reconstruction of German Cities after World War II* (New York: Oxford University Press, 1993), 125–127. Cologne was particularly hard hit, with 70% of its housing stock destroyed. Even after the massive mobilization of resources after the war toward reconstruction, urban housing fell short. In Cologne, although by 1954 there were two and a half times as many dwellings as in 1945, it only reached 69% of the 1939 level.
16 Gregory F. Schroeder, "Ties of Urban Heimat: West German Cities and their Wartime Evacuees in the 1950s," *German Studies* Review 27, no. 2 (2004), 310.

The immediate circumstances for long-term evacuees were dire. While their material situation resembled those of expellees and DPs, they were often forced to compete for the sparse aid resources available, with groups that had been explicitly targeted for aid by the military occupation authority. A 1946 report from the south German *Süddeutsche Zeitung* painted a catastrophic picture of the humanitarian situation, with this appeal to Christian charity:

> If one were to describe the misery of one refugee family in detail, then most certainly many good readers would come forward and write to the editor to offer assistance. What would happen, however, if we published a list from the desk of the Bavarian State Commission for Refugee Matters, which holds the laconic heading "Most Urgent Requirements for the Needs of Refugees"? There, one would within the stark numbers, that in 1946 in Bavaria, 470,000 people that were driven from their homes, do not own mattresses, and 850,000 have no blanket. 500,000 refugees use a straw sack for a bed, while 700,000 do not have a pair of useable, manufactured shoes. One million cannot call one dinner plate their own, while one and a half million do not have one coffee cup. 20,000 families need an oven, 150,000 men and 480,000 women and girls have no underclothes. 285,000 children are missing necessary pieces of clothing.[17]

Only after the end of the occupation and the foundation of the Federal Republic in 1949, could formal attempts to help evacuees reintegrate into society be offered. The Law for the Protection of Evacuees (*Bundesevakuiertengesetz*) of 1953, which was fervently promoted by evacuee interest groups, formally recognized evacuees as victims of the war and offered formal assistance with housing and employment.[18] Recognition at this point was not merely a formality, but rather an attempt to deal with the very real problem of evacuees who had still not been reintegrated into society, either in their hometowns or elsewhere. Those who qualified for assistance mainly consisted of the unemployable and elderly evacuees who faced the most barriers in the competition for aid, housing, and employment in the occupation years. Political economist, Karlheinz Kugler, described the situation in Wurzburg as such: "The time for the resettlement of evacuees in terms of 'self-help' has come to an end. Those evacuees who could help themselves, have, as a rule, already done so. The resettlement of evacuees with the full help of the establishment therefore must begin now."[19] While cities such as Frankfurt, Wurzburg, and Munich

---

17 Werner Friedmann, "Der Berg des Elends," *Süddeutsche Zeitung,* November 19, 1946.

18 See Katja Klee, "Luftschutzkeller des Reiches: Evakuierte in Bayern 1939–1953: Politik, Soziale Lage, Erfahrungen," *Schriftenreihe der Vierteljahrshefte für Zeitgeschichte* 78 (München: R. Oldenbourg, 1999), 273–78.

19 Karlheinz Kugler, Die Umsiedlungsproblem der Würzenburger Außenbürger (1952) cited in Klee (1999), 273.

which had a large number of evacuees in "exile" offered assistance to help facilitate the return of their citizens in exile, as of 1963 (the last year federal statistics were kept on evacuees), almost 50,000 of the over 500,000 registered evacuees were still waiting to return to their hometowns.[20]

By far, the largest migrant group in the immediate postwar period was that of the ethnic German *Vertriebene*, or expellees. Between 1944 and 1949, over 14 million ethnic Germans (out of a total estimated population of 18 million) either fled or were deported westward by the advancing Soviet army. There were roughly three phases of expulsion; the first lasted from late 1944 to early 1945 as ethnic Germans fled the advancing Red Army. From the early spring through July of 1945, "wild" expulsions took place in the lost German territories in Poland and Sudetenland (later Czechoslovakia). By the third period, which lasted through 1949, expulsions had become roughly "organized and orderly" under the protocols of the Treaty of Potsdam. By 1949, a total of 12.5 million expellees had sought refuge in occupied Germany.[21]

Although the Potsdam Treaty called for an equal distribution of expellees amongst the four zones, settlement was quite uneven, with the French occupation zone receiving less than 1% of all settlers. From 1944 to 1949, approximately 4.3 million expellees settled in the Soviet Occupation Zone, while the total count in West German zones in 1950 put the number of expellees at 8 million (7%) of the total population.[22] From the establishment of the two German states in 1949, two different strategies were implemented in efforts to provide material support and to encourage social integration of the expellee population.

1.3 Resettlers in West Germany

The immediate postwar years were chaotic for expellee populations in the western zones. From 1945 to 1948, expellees faced dire material situations, since they competed for resources with evacuees and DPs. By 1950, more than 8 million expellees had settled in the three western Allied zones, making reconstruction

---

20 Schroeder, "Ties of Urban Heimat: West German Cities and their Wartime Evacuees in the 1950s," 308.

21 A number of 500,000 settled in Austria, 300,000 were deported to the USSR under repatriation laws and hundreds of thousands did not survive the journey. Bade and Oltmer, "Flucht und Vertreibung nach dem zweiten Weltkrieg," 258.

22 Gerhard Reichling, *Die Deutschen Vertriebenen in Zahlen: Umsiedler, Verschleppte, Vertriebene, Aussiedler 1940–1985* (Bonn: Kulturstiftung d. Dt. Vertriebenen, 1995), 17.

a priority.[23] In contrast to the Soviets, who focused on the repatriation of DPs in order to make room for the material reorganization of East German resources in order to optimize reparations, a focus on reconstruction (as well as the logistical problems of administering three zones) meant that economic help in the Allied zones was slow to reach the expellee population.

Both the Allies and Soviets settled expellees primarily in rural areas.[24] Klaus Bade and Jochen Oltmer identify three main "expellee-states" in the western zones; Schleswig-Holstein, where 837,500 expellees made up 31.6% of the population, Lower Saxony had 1,475,500 expellees, constituting 22.9% of the population; and Bavaria with 1,657,800 expellees, or 18.4% of the state population.[25] In particular, the Emsland in western Lower Saxony was seen as an ideal destination point for refugees because of the relative lack of destruction during the war and the abundance of land in dire need of improvement.[26]

The British military authority, which wanted to avoid a concentration of refugees in the eastern half of the state, planned to transport expellees to the sparsely populated districts of Aurich and Osnabrück, as well as to the northern East Frisian Islands. In the case of expellees who were transported to Lower Saxony, the eastern side of the state was preferred by expellee farmers, who preferred the dry fields of the East over the swamps of the Emsland, as well as by workers who hoped to find work in the industrial districts of Hannover.[27] Those who were called to be transported westward, frequently chose either not to go or left shortly after arrival. According to one government official speaking in 1951, the prospects for resettling a great number of expellees westward were slim:

> Our past experiences have shown us that directing refugees into the camps we have selected for them is not so easily achieved. It should have been, for example, the western part of

---

23 Gerhard Reichling, "Die Heimatvertriebenen im Spiegel der Statistik," *Schriften des Vereins für Sozialpolitik* 6, no. 3 (1953), 34–42.

24 Philipp Ther, "The Integration of Expellees in Germany and Poland after World War II: A Historical Reassessment," *Slavic Review* 55, no. 4 (1996), 89.

25 Klaus J. Bade and Jochen Oltmer, "Einführung: Einwanderungsland Niedersachsen – Zuwanderung und Integration seit dem Zweiten Weltkrieg," in *Zuwanderung und Integration in Niedersachsen seit dem Zweiten Weltkrieg*, ed. Klaus J. Bade and Jochen Oltmer (Osnabrück: Universitätsverlag Rasch, 2002), 14.

26 Most of this land was waterlogged and required extensive work to become productive. Bade and Oltmer (2002), 13.

27 Bernhard Parisius, "'und ahnten, dass hier die Welt zu Ende ist.' Aufnahme und Integration von Flüchtlingen und Vertriebenen in westen Niedersachsens," in *Zuwanderung und Integration in Niedersachsen*, ed. Klaus J. Bade and Jochen Oltmer (Osnabrück: Universitätsverlag Rasch, 2002), 41.

Lower Saxony that would have been the next area to be settled with refugees; but only a small percentage of those that are put on the march into the special trains in the direction of Aurich and Osnabrück arrive at their intended destinations. Many of the refugees, against the explicit orders given to them, select a destination of their own discretion.[28]

The greater difficulty – integration in rural areas – contributed to the tendency for expellees to migrate again, within western Germany. While rural areas were targeted for resettlement because of the lower population density, employment and housing were in short supply.[29]

> Refugees who are settled in one of the 700 camps [in Schleswig-Holstein], miles away from the few industrial islands near the peasant or fishing villages remain forever victims of structural unemployment. Graduating boys are not even offered apprenticeships. 53 percent of the refugees in Schleswig-Holstein and 42 percent in Lower Saxony have no regular employment.[30]

In the early 1950s, there were reports of the formation of "trek associations" in the reception states with the highest number of evacuees. The largest of these associations, founded in Schleswig-Holstein, signed up 34,000 refugees to make a potential migration across West Germany in order to protest the slow pace of resettlement policies. As Rudolf Brenske, the leader of the Bavarian Trek Association, told *Der Spiegel*,

> We will not set foot inside a barrack; if we must, we will sleep in the central market of each city. The objective of each trek group is the market. There we remain as long as we must in passive resistance until we can secure proper living quarters. If the city refuses us entry we will behave like an infantry battalion, we will swarm around in small groups and slowly seep inside.[31]

Although none of these planned treks actually took place, the threat of thousands of refugees marching across West Germany seemed to have some impact on the speed with which resettlement took place, and by the mid 1950s, resettlement ceased to be a politically contentious issue.[32] Of the more than 5 million who settled in the three main reception states of Bavaria, Lower Saxony, and Schleswig-

---

28 Hans Joachim Malecki, cited in Parisius (2002), 42.
29 Daniel Levy, "Integrating Ethnic Germans in West Germany: The Early Postwar Period," in *Coming Home to Germany? The Integration of Ethnic Germans from Central and Eastern Europe in the Federal Republic*, ed. David Rock and Stefan Wolff (Oxford: Berghahn Books, 2002), 27.
30 "Ich bete zum Satan," *Der Spiegel*, February 20, 1952.
31 "Ich bete zum Satan."
32 Ian Connor, "German Refugees and the Bonn Government's Resettlement Programme: The Role of the Trek Association in Schleswig-Holstein, 1951–3," *German History* 18, no. 3 (2000), 348–350.

Holstein from 1950 to 1955, over 1 million had been officially resettled in one of the six remaining states of the FRG by 1963.[33]

1.4 Resettlers in the German Democratic Republic

The Soviet Occupation Zone and the later German Democratic Republic targeted the resettler population as a mechanism to justify the redistribution of housing and land. With the establishment of the Central Office for German Resettlers (*Zentralverwaltung für deutsche Umsiedler*) in September 1945, the Soviet authorities pursued an aggressive policy of redistribution. However, as was generally true throughout the population of the SBZ/GDR, the younger, working-age population received the most assistance.[34] Meanwhile, since the need to support resettlers was given as a primary reason for moving ahead with social restructuring and land redistribution, expellees were often the target of hostility in the immediate postwar years.[35] In an interview conducted by the historian Alexander von Plato in the late 1980s, one expellee remembers public attitudes in the early days of the GDR:

> I personally did not [have any problems], but generally the times were not completely problem free. We were referred to every now and then as intruders. I can imagine it goes much the same way now in the FRG for those that have recently fled. In any case, you go over, take away their work and people have no sympathy for why you have come. At the time, that is how it went for us. People arrived and were unloaded with nothing on their person – nothing at all, except for lice if one was lucky . . . That is the way they [West Germans] must feel about those [East Germans] who go over now.[36]

---

33 *Statistisches Jahrbuch für der Bundesrepublik Deutschland – 1965* (Wiesbaden: Statistisches Bundesamt, 1965), 214.

34 Esther Neblich, "Das Umsiedlerproblem der Jahre 1945–1955 in der SBZ/DDR am Beispiel des Oberen Vogtlandes," in *Agenda DDR-Forschung*, ed. Heiner Timmermann (Berlin: LIT Verlag, 2005), 248.

35 See especially the discussion over the "Umsiedler Neubauern" in Michael Schwartz, *Vertriebene und Umsiedlerpolitik: Integrationskonflikte in dem Deutschen Nachkriegs-Gesellschaften und die Assimilationsstrategien in der SBZ/DDR 1945 bis 1961* (Oldenbourg: Oldenbourg Wissenschaftsverlag, 2004), 707–709.

36 Wilhelm Meinicke and Alexander von Plato, *Alte Heimat – Neue Zeit: Flüchtlinge, Umgesiedelte, Vertriebene in der Sowjetischen Besatzungszone und in der DDR* (Berlin: Verlag Anst. Union, 1991), 197.

Negative public attitudes, such as these as well as the short-term nature of aid programs, relegated resettlers in the GDR to the bottom of the social hierarchy. The lack of opportunity for social mobility and the closed nature of the SED party system made non-professional expellees a permanent underclass in the GDR. These factors contributed to the high rate of emigration of expellees into West Germany through the 1950s.[37]

After the foundation of the two Germanys in 1950, attention in both countries shifted from issues of initial settlement and covering basic needs to integration. Key to the difference in integration policies in both East and West is the language used to address ethnic German migration. Whereas the *"Umsiedler"* in the SBZ/GDR were referred to as "resettlers" in order to avoid offending the GDR's Soviet benefactors, and the memory of violence was played down in favor of a new beginning, the *Vertriebene*, or expellees, of West Germany embodied German victimhood in the years immediately following the end of the war. Unlike the label of *Umsiedler* used in the Soviet Zone and later in the GDR, which transformed postwar flight into a benign "move," *Vertriebene*, people of the "expulsion" embraced German victimhood. As a 1946 editorial in the West German weekly *Die Zeit* argued:

> They have been called "refugees" here in Germany, but that word is false. It makes it sound as if these people went willingly to escape some sort of pressure, like the "refugees" of the seventeenth century who fled France after the Edict of Nantes, in order to live according to their beliefs in another land, or like emigrants of the time of the French revolution, or under the Nazi regime in Germany, who left their fatherland, in order to wait for political change. They are not refugees, but expellees. These are people who the war shoved out of their apartments and who may not return to their homeland, as well as others, who after the war are required to leave even though their ancestors have resided in those places for centuries.[38]

The significance in labeling these migrants as expellees, as opposed to refugees, is key to understanding the development and treatment of German–German migration on both sides during the Cold War. As will be seen in the following section, the political language and rhetoric that accompanied the push toward integration, especially in the case of West Germany, contributed to the general discussion surrounding the German as "migrant" during the Cold War. As the migration of ethnic German expellees and native Germans (*Einheimische)* increased from the GDR

---

37 Schwartz, *Vertriebene und Umsiedlerpolitik: Integrationskonflikte in dem Deutschen Nachkriegs-Gesellschaften und die Assimilationsstrategien in der SBZ/DDR 1945 bis 1961*, 714.
38 "Ohne Heimat," *Die Zeit*, September 5, 1946.

to the FRG, a language of migration was developed that contributed to the separation of the political (legitimate) migrant from an economic (illegitimate) migrant.

Meanwhile, the labeling of *Vertriebene* as formal victims of the war, and the continuing influence of expellee interest groups that exerted considerable political pressure on their behalf, combined with a modest level of social mobility, softened the path to integration for expellees as a whole. Although on average expellee families experienced a lower standard of living than "native" families, by 1965, they were no longer seen to be an "impoverished" group within the FRG.[39] By the time the FRG started to import a large volume of foreign labor, public discourse surrounding the migration had shifted its attention away from expellees. As Daniel Levy argues, "The expellee problem had become the foreigner problem."[40] However, it was not just the *Gastarbeiter* that had captured the attention of the media; rather, the discourse had split. On the one hand, the "otherness" of the *Gastarbeiter* was posted against the background of the economic miracle; on the other hand, the East German refugee, as a political being, was being cemented as a core component of the postwar German identity.

---

39 Levy, "Integrating Ethnic Germans in West Germany: The Early Postwar Period," 27.
40 Levy, "Integrating Ethnic Germans in West Germany: The Early Postwar Period," 28.

2 *Republikflucht* and *Gastarbeiter*: Migration Regimes Within and Between the Two Germanies, 1949–1989

The worries about us refugees were over when we left the camp," writes a young man about Sandbostel near Bremen, the largest youth camp in the West, which was his gateway to the Federal Republic. "When I went into freedom [in the West], it was clear to me that one cannot be welcomed with open arms and that a palace will not be made available to one immediately. But I was hoping for better help." Although he reports that he has now found a good position as a driver, he exclaims: "I had to swim to keep from sinking. That's why I can easily understand it when a few comrades end up behind bars or find their way back to the GDR.[1]

In a 1955 newspaper article about the prominence of young refugees from the GDR to the FRG, the experiences of this young man were set as typical for those arriving in the West. Although they were often portrayed in the West as political refugees, in this period before the western economic miracle, GDR refugees were often given very little support to integrate into the western society. The dissonance between the portrayal as victims and the reality of a lack of support given to GDR refugees would serve as an important Cold War trope and would develop in even sharper contrast after the Berlin Wall.

This chapter examines the migration regimes within and between the two Germanies during the Cold War. The first section of this chapter will investigate the period of 12 years between the establishment of the two Cold War German states and the construction of the Berlin Wall in 1961. As occupation and statehood stabilized the chaos of mass East–West migration in the immediate postwar years, the borders between the FRG and the GDR remained quite porous. While the western economy stabilized and grew, the GDR undertook a massive restructuring of the society, which resulted in a general feeling of unrest amongst those displaced by these measures. From 1950 to 1961, over 3.5 million people migrated from the GDR to the FRG, from both the top (doctors, lawyers, and professionals), and the bottom (expellees and common workers) categories of the East German society. Eastward migration paled in comparison, with slightly more than 500,000 moving eastward to the GDR. Aside from a few who migrated out of ideological reasons (such as the playwright Bertolt Brecht), it can be surmised that the majority were cases of familial reunification, including mostly pensioners, who wished

---

1 Else Schülter, "Enttäuscht sie der Westen?" *Die Zeit* July 28, 1955.

https://doi.org/10.1515/9783110716221-003

to be reunited with their family in the East.[2] Although the westward flow was somewhat reduced by a law against *Republikflucht* (flight from the German Democratic Republic), migration continued mostly unrestricted until the sealing of the border between East and West Berlin, with the sealing off of U-Bahn and S-Bahn lines and the construction of the Wall in 1961.

Both official and unofficial political maneuverings in the GDR and the FRG, as well as the public outlet of the press, shaped public opinion concerning migration and migrants in this period. While the West German press and government did their best publicly to play up the political motivations for migration, there was still public concern over resources and space for these "refugees." The GDR, on the other hand, used the public presentation of *Westrückkehrer* (those who had returned from the West) and negative portrayals of life in the FRG to discourage further emigration. While these public rhetoric surrounding migrants did little to discourage actual movement, the portrait of migration as having both political motivations and consequences helped to obscure other motivations, and influenced the portrayal of the so-called legitimate migration.

The final section of this chapter will address the period from the construction of the Berlin Wall in 1961 to the escalation of emigration in the fall of 1989. While the political discourse surrounding migration had its roots in the period before the closing of the East–West border, the aura surrounding migration between the two Germanys was cemented with the construction of the Berlin Wall in 1961. Once the border into West Berlin was sealed, East–West migration trickled almost to a standstill. Both the FRG and the GDR recruited significant foreign labor migration to fill gaps in the workforce, further complicating how migration – both German and non-German – were conceptualized in popular discourse. Consequently, migration from the GDR to the FRG was being even more closely associated with political dissidence, which would push the migration history of the late 1940s and early 1950s even further into the realm of political lore. The experience of the Cold War itself, and especially the construction of the Berlin Wall, resulted in the further perception that German mobility was an exception rather than the historical rule. Whereas for centuries, mobility had been quite a normal behavior for Germans, the migration of GDR citizens to the West was viewed as a singular phenomenon – a political action undertaken in order to escape the control of an unnatural state, and regain a measure of "German-ness."

---

2 *Statistisches Jahrbuch für der Bundesrepublik Deutschland – 1964* (Wiesbaden: Statistisches Bundesamt, 1964), 347–362. While some data is available from the westward flow from the West German statistical office, demographic data with the exception of age has not been established for the eastern flow.

Prevailing attitudes that constructed authentic migration as only being carried out under political circumstances was further reinforced in West Germany during the 1960s and 1970s, with the arrival of tens of thousands of non-German *Gastarbeiter* from southern Europe, eastern Europe, and Turkey, which exaggerated the division between "foreigners" as those who moved and "Germans" as those who stayed, while in the GDR, emigration to the West was a criminal offense and those who defected through "escaping" to the West were branded as traitors.[3] Outside of the minimal amount of immigration that occurred from the FRG to the GDR, the migration of Germans was set in opposition to the control of the state. The arrival of contract workers (*Vertragsarbeiter*), from Vietnam, Mozambique, Angola, and Cuba in the 1970s and 1980s established a legal foreign labor force within the GDR. However, the experiences of *Vertragsarbeiter* were quite different than those of *Gastarbeiter* in the West. *Vertragsarbeiter* were under the firm control and monitoring of the state. They were separated from the East German community at large and discouraged from socializing with East Germans in any way. The entrenchment of the attitudes of East Germans toward migrants and migration in both the East and the West in the 40 years of German division was to have a major effect on attitudes toward German internal migration, once the borders opened.

While exposing the complexity and variety of migration narratives behind the statistics covering the highly politicized cross-border migrations of this period, this chapter will also address the ways in which East–West migration was portrayed and presented in the public realm. Set within the wider picture of the growth and visibility of international migration since the 1960s, this examination of the mobility of Germans and the rhetoric surrounding these movements, exposes how tentative and frail the conceptions of "German" identity had become. Both German states, formed out of the rubble of the war and carefully composed in political, economic, social, and cultural opposition, struggled not only to rebuild, but to redefine what being "German" would mean in the postwar world.

A combination of political maneuvering and renegotiation of identities through periods of transformation is revealed in an examination of both West and East German discourse surrounding migration and identity. Care was taken to draw out possible propagandistic statements on both sides as well as to engage the nature of the propaganda as an active and semi-conscious tool in the reconstruction of postwar German identities. As will become evident in subsequent chapters, the 40-year

---

3 Attempts to control departures, of course, were not particular to the GDR. For more on the politics of emigration see Nancy L. Green and François Weil eds., *Citizenship and Those Who Leave: The Politics of Emigration and Expatriation* (Champaign-Urbana, IL: University of Illinois Press, 2007).

history and portrayal of the migration of Germans between the FRG and GDR is intimately related to how East Germans and West Germans have viewed each other since the end of the Cold War. The fabled "wall in the head" (*Mauer im Kopf*) is still alive and well, its foundation strengthened and complicated by the complex histories of German migration and mobility that have outlived the fall of its physical manifestation – the Berlin Wall.

2.1 *Flüchtlinge* and *Vertriebene* in the FRG and the GDR, 1953–1961

Mass migration from the GDR to the FRG in the 11 years before the sealing off the East–West border, symbolized by the construction of the Berlin Wall, is often approached from a wholly political point of view. While it is undeniable that many defections occurred because of political persecution, a majority of those who "fled the Republic" did so on material rather than ideological grounds. Whether it was a physician who had lost the right to private practice, a farmer whose agricultural estate was broken up through land redistribution, or an expellee who needed to provide for the basic needs of his family, political and social motives for migration were bound up in material and economic concerns.

The integration of expellee populations was approached in a radically opposite way in the GDR. The GDR, which had used the expellees as part of an excuse for radical restructuring of land distribution, declared integration complete in 1951. This declaration, however, did not reflect real-world success. Although many expellees had been given stakes in new agricultural collectives, these were often not enough to scrape by with more than a basic living. Expellees and their families were shut out of opportunities for social advancement. As a result, expellees, as the most limited and vulnerable portions of the society, made a disproportionate number of all emigrants from the GDR to the FRG from 1953 to 1961.[4]

In addition to expellees, a large portion of migrants "fleeing the Republic" (*Republikflüchtlinge*) in the pre-wall era consisted of professionals and other skilled workers who found themselves displaced or unhappy with the reorganization of society. A report printed in the West German newsmagazine *Der Spiegel* points to a distinct pattern of emigration that was directly related to Soviet and East German attempts at social and economic reorganization:

---

4 As shown in Graph 1, expellees comprised between 21% and 30% of all migration from the GDR to the FRG between 1953 and 1960, while comprising between 17% and 26% of the total population.

From 1945–1947 came mostly owners of large businesses and industries that had been deposed by Soviet reorganization. In 1948, smaller business owners and light industrialists, especially from Saxony and Thuringia, after the hunt for capitalists was revived by textile commissioner Fritz Lange. In 1949 came numerous owners of large commercial firms, after the creation of national wholesale head offices for the retail trade. In 1950, (after the foundation of the German Democratic Republic) many fallen ministers of the SBZ people's parties, Eastern CDU ministers, district administrators and mayors . . . . in 1951 and 1952, an increasing number of physicians was counted, who had been obligated to give up their private practices in favor for public health centers. Likewise, pharmacists whose pharmacies were also nationalized, and owners of theaters, who saw their theaters communalized. By the end of the year, the exodus of the farmers had begun. The iron stirring the cauldron of the transformation had now reached the depths of the social pyramid.[5]

While political and economic grounds were often entwined, there were some other non-material motives for migration. As a pamphlet published by the West German Senate for Refugee matters reported, after mass propaganda appeared in the GDR in the early 1950s announcing compulsory military service for the National Army and labor duty in the Soviet Union, the number of males between the ages of 14 and 24 appearing at refugee camps in West Berlin increased by 37.5%.[6]

Emigration in this period was highly dependent upon age cohort, and as a result, as we will see in the discussion of the mass migrations after German unification, migrations had profound implications for social structure and future regional productivity. While the gender balance struck around 50/50 (with females out-numbering males approximately 52% to 48%), between 1949 and 1961, more than 75% of all migrants were under the age of 40.[7] In addition, more than 30% of those who migrated from 1949 to 1953 were classified either as a housewife or a dependent child. This, future West German Chancellor Willy Brandt argued, signaled an emigration of potential productivity of future generations for the GDR:

> From a sociological point of view, it is not an "export of misery", but about a mass exodus in which the able-bodied dominate. Nothing indicates so far that the stream of people is coming to a halt. [In addition], No responsible [West] German will refuse their compatriots from the Soviet zone acceptance in[to] their own country.[8]

---

5 "Sowjetzone-Flüchtlinge: Reine Torschlußpanik."
6 Senate of Berlin, ed. "Refugees Flooding the Island of Berlin: Senate Report" (Berlin: Senate of Berlin, 1953).
7 *Statistisches Jahrbuch für der Bundesrepublik Deutschland* – 1965 (Wiesbaden: Statistisches Bundesamt, 1964), 98–117.
8 Willy Brandt, "Die Bedeutung der Massenflucht aus der Sowjetzone," *Gewerkschaftliche Monatshefte* 4, no. 4 (1953): 224–228.

While the reasons for departure could be viewed as fundamentally material, the consequences for the GDR of the continued emigration of the most productive parts of its population to their Cold War doppelganger, the FRG, were certainly political on both sides. In the GDR, migrants were portrayed as *Republikflücht-linge*, enemies of the state, who had fled the GDR, either by choice or by force. In the early 1950s, the SED went to great lengths to discourage the general population from considering fleeing to the FRG. In 1953, SED Commissioner for *Republi-kflucht* Gerhard Eisler went "on tour" to several GDR cities with a dozen citizens who were reported to have fled over the border but decided to return to the GDR. As Eisler proclaimed to the West German newsmagazine *Der Spiegel*:

> These people have come back. They lost their heads, but they realized pretty quickly that only the castoffs of the GDR collect themselves in West Berlin, those who have not heard the call of the hour to fight for Germany. It will be for all of those who flee, like their predecessors, the Russian Kulaks, spies and cowards. They will end up in the bordellos, penitentiaries and foreign legions of western Europe. Restless they will roam from miserable quarter to miserable quarter, always moving further westward.[9]

While the GDR was trying its hardest to discourage its citizens from seeing if the grass was any greener on the other side, West Germans were performing some damage control of their own. In the early 1950s, before the economic miracle had taken hold, the increasing number of emigrants from the GDR was seen as an economic threat, more so than the migration of *Vertriebene*, who, by definition, had a political motive for migration (they were "driven" from their homeland). The early migration of GDR citizens into the FRG was regarded with considerable negativity, especially in the light of material conditions in West Germany, which still included at that time a great housing shortage and significant unemployment.

This situation was to change with the passing of the Federal Refugee Law, or *Bundesvertriebenengesetz* (BvG) on May 15, 1953. While the previous statute defined the parameters for refugees from the Soviet Zone (*SBZ-Flüchtlinge*), the BvG made no distinction between refugees, effectively lumping *Vertriebene* and *SBZ-Flüchtlinge* into the same category. Furthermore, as material conditions in the West improved and tensions with the GDR increased, refugees became important political capital in the emerging Cold War.

The year 1957 can be seen as a turning point on both sides. While the West German government pushed for eventual unification, it became important to stress the illegitimacy of the political regime in the GDR. As argued by Volker Ackermann, this resulted in a playing down of non-political reasons for migration from the GDR to the FRG, to the point where it even tried to suppress the publica-

---

9 "Sowjetzone-Flüchtlinge: Reine Torschlusspanik."

tion of an Infratest study by the *Frankfurter Allgemeine Zeitung*, which indicated that most who fled the GDR upon arrival gave non-political grounds for flight (*unpolitische Fluchtgründe*) and, furthermore, that 29% of those who came did so to "improve their economic situation."[10] In July of the same year, an amendment to the BvG expanded the grounds for flight to include a "serious conflict of conscience." The evolution of grounds for acceptance of GDR refugees makes it clear that the political struggles of legitimacy between the FRG and GDR were being fought in the realm of migration.

Three months after the amendment to the BvG, the GDR voted a passport requirement into law (*Passgesetz*), which in addition to increasingly restrictive visa requirements and the introduction of educational and economic punitive measures for the relatives of those who "fled" the republic, formally outlawed *Republikflucht* increased punishment for those who had been caught, and introduced measures to facilitate the confiscation of property of those who emigrated illegally. As can be seen in Graph 1, the passage of this law contributed to the reduction of East–West migration by one-third between 1957 and 1958. However, the legislation did not get to the root of the problem, namely the porous border between East and West Berlin, which would not be closed until the construction of the Berlin Wall in 1961.

In addition to pressure from the West German government to play down economic reasons for migration from the GDR, there were also debates within the media concerning the exaggeration of the escalation of migration from the GDR to the FRG. In 1958, *Der Spiegel* ran an article accusing media mogul Axel Springer of using his newspaper monopoly in northwest Germany (*Die Bild, Die Welt* and *Hamburger Abendblatt*) to induce a "news oversupply" concerning "Zone refugees," to further his own political aims.

While migration rates in July and August of 1958 were in fact lower than in previous years, the Springer papers announced such headlines as "Alarming Escape from the Zone," and "Why do you want to come to West Germany?" The *Berliner Zeitung* exclaimed in response to the "news oversupply" in the northwest, "Suddenly they woke up. Suddenly they all cry, as if the refugees had just come from the Zone yesterday."[11] In this case, the "fear of the closing gate" (*Torschlußpanik*) was not caused by the mounting restrictions on movement by the GDR government, but rather was at least partially manufactured by the West German media.

---

10 Volker Ackermann, *Der "echte" Flüchtlinge: Deutsche Vertriebene und Flüchtlinge aus der DDR, 1945–1961* (Osnabrück: Universitätsverlag Rasch, 1995), 35.
11 "Sowjetzone Fluchtlinge: Reine Torschlußpanik."

Migration from the GDR to the FRG (including Berlin), 1953-1960

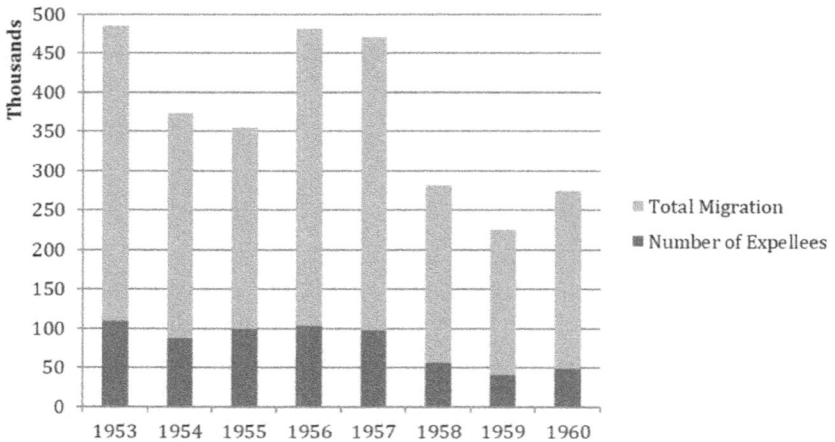

Graph 1: "Migration from the GDR to the FRG (including Berlin), 1953–1960." Source: *Statistisches Jahrbuch für der Bundesrepublik Deutschland-1963* (Wiesbaden: Statistisches Bundesamt, 1964), 68.

Although the massive flight from the GDR to the FRG tends to get most of both the popular and scholarly attention, a considerable number of FRG citizens chose to move to the GDR each year. From 1950 to 1961, approximately 400,000 people migrated from the FRG to the GDR.[12] These migrants were very important as tools of propaganda for the SED, and in addition to taking migrants who had returned from the West on a public speaking tour, the GDR also issued periodic press releases detailing the numbers of migrants and the reasons for their defection.

In 1960, *Der Spiegel* reported on the outrage of the West German media over reports in the *New York Times* and the *New York Daily Mail* (the former written by the famous Walter Lippmann) concerning the increase in the number of West Germans choosing to defect to the GDR. Although *Der Spiegel* emphasized the propaganda that had been dealt out by the SED in order to make the movement appear larger than it already was, the report did concede that there were a total of eight reception centers in the GDR, which were designed to receive West "refugees," including a special center for members of the intelligentsia. *Der Spiegel* re-

---

12 400,000 by West German estimates, figures from the statistical offices of the German Democratic Republic report a figure of around 600,000.

ported, "The reception center for the intelligentsia, found in Ferch near Potsdam, is reserved primarily for doctors and technicians from the West. These [migrants] are particularly precious to the authorities in the Soviet Zone considering the drift of many their colleagues in the reverse direction and are therefore accommodated in a comfortable forest mansion."[13]

Despite the measures taken to outlaw *Republikflucht* in 1957 and the energy put into creating propaganda that showed people moving in the opposite direction, illegal migration to the FRG continued to be a real concern. Indeed, stopping the "bleeding out" of the GDR became seen as the key to stabilizing the country internationally, economically, and socially. As long as members of the professions and intelligentsia kept fleeing to the West, the GDR could not hope to even out socially nor economically.

Mounting internal pressure to match the standard of living of the West as well as repeated external pressures by the West German government to recognize the legitimacy of fleeing the GDR meant that something drastic had to be done in order to stabilize the situation. When an amendment to the BvG was passed in June 1961, officially recognizing economic reasons as grounds for flight, the last formal barrier was removed for the resumption of mass migration from the GDR to pre-1958 levels. With the closing of the porous border between East and West Berlin, less than 2 months later in August 1961, mass emigration stopped. However, the few who did succeed in crossing the border were more politicized than ever before, making the flight to the West a dramatized spectacle that constitutes one of the key images of the Cold War era. The ultra-politicization of migration and migrants from 1961 to the opening of the borders in 1989 was to have serious consequences for German–German relations and the perception of German–German migration after unification.

2.2 The Politics of Emigration after the Berlin Wall, 1961–1989

The construction of the Berlin Wall and the physical isolation of West Berlin from the surrounding GDR were highly successful in dramatically reducing the volume of illegal emigration. Nevertheless, an average of 20,000 GDR citizens a year managed, either through legal or illegal channels, to migrate to the FRG. While the dramatic bleeding out of the GDR had stopped, emigration became even more political and was used as a tool by politicians and the media as evidence of the submodern conditions in the East. The closing of the border cemented the place of the *Umsiedler* in the West German public discourse. The motives of GDR refugees

---

13 "Zonenflucht: Es Stand in der Welt," *Der Spiegel*, September 10, 1958.

were no longer questioned; rather, they were assumed (and expected) to be ideological.

The drastic decline in westward migration after the construction of the Berlin Wall as seen in Graph 2 shifted West German coverage of *Umsiedler* from a discourse surrounding volume and intent to highly sensationalized reporting including violence experienced by those at the hands of East German authorities whilst attempting to cross the border, the defection of GDR celebreties to the West such as the actor Manfred Krug, and the comedy and tragedy of the adjustment of refugees to life in the West. While sympathy for the unemployed (especially unemployed non-German migrants) ran thin, in 1978, *Die Zeit*, a major West German newspaper, published a call for help for "Gisela P." who fled the GDR 6 months prior with her 16-year-old son, and could not find work in her profession as a professional cosmetician. Readers were asked to make a deposit into her bank account in order to help purchase warm clothes for herself and her son for the winter.[14]

Migration between the GDR and the FRG, 1957-1987

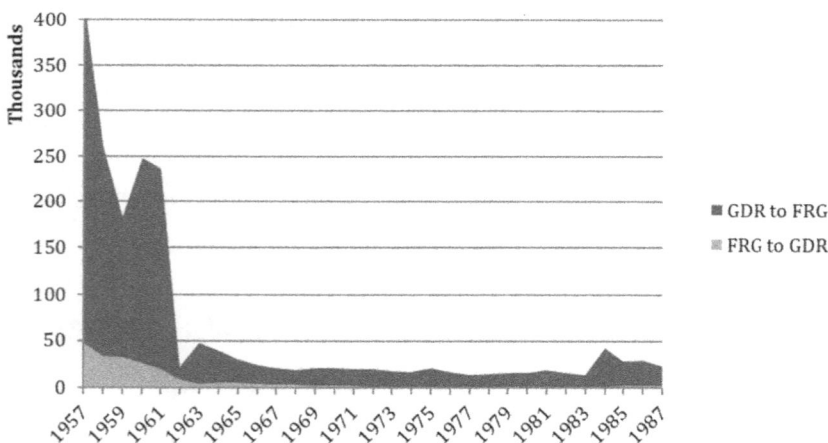

Graph 2: "Migration between the GDR and the FRG, 1957–1987." Source: *Statistisches Jahrbuch für der Bundesrepublik Deutschland – 2000* (Wiesbaden: Statistisches Bundesamt, 2002), 92–94.

The inability of GDR refugees to survive in their new surroundings was also a common theme. A 1979 article in *Der Spiegel* reported that a large number of

---

14 "Barbara bittet," *Die Zeit*, October 6, 1978.

those who make it to the FRG, end up homeless, alcoholic, mentally ill, or as a criminal. Much like the media coverage after unification, the faulty society of the GDR was blamed for the inability for East Germans to adapt to the West German system.

From *Der Spiegel*,

> [Once the East Germans have sobered up to the realities of West German society], many Germans from the East react helplessly. Some expire into stubborn resignation; others succumb to the underworld of loan sharks. There are some refugees who do not dare to enter a shop "because they will only smack me on the ear." There are others who squander away their cash for their living allowance on taxi fares, because they "want to see the West."[15]

This inability to function in West German society is framed as an insurmountable flaw. In essence, East Germans have been irrevocably broken as a result of existing in the perceived dysfunction of life in the GDR. This theme would become an important part of the East–West dialogue after unification, not only in the caricatures of the East Germans flooding into the west in their two-stroke Trabants, clearing out West German shops of their entire stock of bananas with their DM 100 *Begrüßungsgeld* (welcome money). These characterizations would also be at the heart of a deeper rift between East and West, long after unification is realized, as many East Germans were dispossessed of their positions in the labor market because they were trained or educated in the GDR.

2.3 Foreign Labor Migration in Postwar West Germany

Although the FRG gained industrial jobs in the northwest because of the postwar economic revival, migration in West Germany from the end of the war through the 1960s consisted both of interregional migration from the north to the south, as well as intraregional urban to suburban movement. From 1955 to 1973, West German citizens moved away from the urban center to new suburban settlements. In 1967, for example, the total volume of internal migration in West Germany (interregional plus intraregional) equaled 4.3% of the population. Of these migrants, 1.7% moved to another state, with the majority to the south.[16] Ironically, despite most of the job creation occurring in the industrial centers of the northwest before the oil crisis put a halt to economic growth in 1973, the majority of

---

15 "Wie die Motten: Viele DDR-Bürger, die in der Bundesrepublik kommen, scheiten," *Der Spiegel*, December 31, 1979.
16 RK. Vedder, L.E. Gallaway and G.L. Chapin, "The Determinants of Internal Migration in West Germany," *Weltwirtschaftliches Archiv* 106, no. 2 (1967), 315.

the interstate migration of Germans remained southward. This trend was to pick up more steam after the oil crisis, as unemployment grew in the heavy industrial areas of the northwest and as a new high-tech industrial center merged in the states of Bavaria and Baden-Württemberg.[17]

Changes in migration to West Germany after the war helped to shape the need and nature of labor migration. Until 1961, many vacancies had been filled by migration from the GDR, as well as small-scale contract labor from Italy. The construction of the Berlin Wall in 1961 however, cut off the stream of labor migrants from the GDR that had been arriving steadily since the war. Although the rate of growth of the postwar German economy would have required recruiting skilled and unskilled foreign labor even without the sealing of the German–German border, the sudden halt of an average of 300,000 migrants from the East aggravated the situation. Although there were more than 1 million unemployed workers in Germany, most were "unable or unwilling" to move to the new industrial centers to do the hard labor required of the new industrial economy.[18] After an initial success in negotiating a bilateral labor agreement with Italy in 1955, the Federal Republic decided to expand access to foreign labor. In the economic boom of the 1960s, the West German government recruited *Gastarbeiter* (guest workers) in order to fill vacancies in the growing industrial labor force. In 1960, contracts similar to that made in 1955 were signed with Spain and Greece. From 1961 to 1968, contracts were signed with Turkey, Morocco, Portugal, Tunisia, and Yugoslavia. From the construction of the Wall in 1961 to the end of foreign recruitment with the worldwide oil crisis in 1973, the FRG brought more than 14 million foreign *Gastarbeiter* to Germany.[19]

The recruitment ban that was instituted in the wake of the worldwide oil crisis in 1973 ended the notion that *Gastarbeiter* were really mere "guests" who would come and go according to the needs of the Federal Republic. Of the 14 million who came between 1961 and 1973, approximately 11 million returned to their country of origin, leaving approximately 3 million migrants who settled permanently in Germany, with many choosing to bring their families both before and after the family reunification act passed by the Bundestag in 1994.[20] At the time of the recruitment

---

17 Jörg Decressin, "Internal Migration in West Germany and Implications for East-West Salary Convergence," *Review of World Economics* 130, no. 2 (1994), 161.
18 Deniz Götürk, David Gramling and Anton Kaes, *Germany in Transit: Nation and Migration, 1955–2005* (Berkeley: University of California Press, 2007), 10.
19 Klaus J. Bade and Jochen Oltmer, "Mitteleuropa: Deutschland," in *Enzyklopädie Migration in Europa: vom 17. Jahrhundert bis zur Gegenwart*, ed. Pieter C. Emmer, Leo Lucassen and Jochen Oltmer (Paderborn: Schöningh, 2007), 164.
20 Klaus J. Bade and Jochen Oltmer, "Mitteleuropa: Deutschland," 164.

halt, a total of 605,000 Turks resided in Germany, already making up the largest foreign population in the country. Thus, Germany was faced with the social problem of a large number of non-Germans as long-term residents, despite declarations to the contrary that Germany was *kein Einwanderungsland* (not a country of immigration).[21] As Rita K. Chin described the situation, "Germany had to figure out how to deal with being a non-immigration country with a whole lot of immigrants."[22]

The refusal to officially recognize the reality of immigration resulted in contradictory and confused policies that made efforts toward integration, sporadic and generally unsuccessful. For example, family unification laws were relaxed in 1974, which resulted in a mass of family members migrating to Germany. Yet, throughout the 1970s and 1980s, the right to family unification was paired with (largely unsuccessful) incentive programs for returning to one's country of origin. One such measure, the "Act to Promote the Preparedness of Foreign Workers to Return," was passed in 1983 with the support of all the major political parties. Only 500,000 of the 4,500,000 who were included in this measure accepted the offer.[23] The political tension between attempts to relax citizenship requirements in 2004 and to implement measures toward integration on one hand and the denial of the reality that Germany was indeed an "immigration country" on the other, impeded integration and contributed to the stark divide between the *Einheimische* (native born) and *Ausländer* (foreign born), which has persisted well into the twenty-first century. The foundational generation who stayed through the oil crisis continued to utilize chain migration to add new migrants from Turkey to a very willing (in terms of demand, not law) labor market. The addition of additional ethnic Turkish groups from Cyprus, the Balkans, and North Africa, as well as the appearance of second, third, fourth, and fifth generations brought the estimated number of Turkish Germans to over 7,000,000 in 2020.

Understanding migration as not just a physical action but as a geographical phenomenon is also fundamental to analyzing the tension between the "guests" who stayed for generations, and continued issues concerning foreign migration, refugees, and contested spaces in unified Germany.[24] Recent work by Sarah Thomasen Vierra has used geographical space as a category of analysis in battles over legitimacy and belonging (in Vierra's study – the workplace, neighborhoods,

---

21 A phrase first attributed to Chancellor Helmut Kohl, first set forth in the immigration policy of his regime in 1982. Ulrich Herbert, *Geschichte der Ausländerpolitik in Deutschland: Saisonarbeiter, Zwangsarbeiter, Gastarbeiter, Flüchtlinge* (München, C.H. Beck, 2001), 249.

22 Rita C.K. Chin, *The Guestworker Question in postwar Germany*, 100.

23 Rita C.K. Chin, *The Guestworker Question in postwar Germany*, 128.

24 See the work of geographer Doreen Massey, "Places and their Pasts," *History Workshop Journal* no. 39 (Spring 1995), 182–192.

schools, and religious spaces) to detail the continued and regularly renewed tension over the reconsideration of German identity.[25]

2.4 Migration and the German Democratic Republic After the Berlin Wall

After the Berlin border was sealed with the construction of the Berlin Wall, *Republikflüchtlinge* in the GDR were treated more often as outright enemies of the state rather than victims of western propaganda about a capitalist material paradise. With the porous border between East and West Berlin shut down, mass emigration of the populace faded as a concern for the state. Meanwhile, pensioners were often given permission to either travel or emigrate and political dissidents, when not imprisoned, were often encouraged or, outright, forced to leave.

As in the pre-wall period, however, there was some effort given to publicize (and propagandize) the return to the GDR of those who had emigrated illegally to the FRG. In 1985, *Der Spiegel* reported that a list of over 200,000 names had been published in the national SED newspaper *Neues Deutschland*, of those who had fled westward and returned to the GDR. However, only 113 of those could be verified as having returned, and a number were proven by *Der Spiegel* reporters to still be living in the West.[26]

Internal migration in the GDR was primarily a movement to the newly constructed suburbs of large city centers and new socialist towns. The volume of internal migration also declined steadily after the culmination of reconstruction in the 1950s. The most likely candidates for new dwellings were workers, more specifically those who had been approved and granted an apartment in one of the *Neubauten* (new buildings), which were primarily located on the outskirts of large urban or industrial areas.[27]

The GDR relied upon contract labor in the industrial force, albeit to a lesser extent than the FRG. Beginning in 1966, *Vertragsarbeiter* (contract workers) from the socialist countries of Vietnam, Mozambique, and Cuba were employed in light

---

25 Sarah Thomsen Vierra. *Turkish Immigrants in the Federal Republic of Germany: Immigration, Space, and Belonging, 1961–1990.* Publications of the German Historical Institute Series (Cambridge: Cambridge University Press, 2018).

26 "Nichts wie Weg: mit einer psychologischen Kampagne will die DDR Ihren Bürgern die Lust auf die Ausreise nehmen," *Der Spiegel,* March 11, 1985.

27 Siegfried Grundmann and I. Schmidt, "Zur Binnenwanderung in der DDR," *Zeitschrift für Erkundeunterricht* 42, no. 7 (1990), 235–241.

and heavy industry. By 1989, over 90,000 workers were employed in the GDR.[28] Unlike the *Gastarbeiter* in the West, who experienced informal segregation from mainstream West German society, *Vertragsarbeiter* were separated from the general population and controlled under strict supervision. Contact with people outside the workplace was only allowed under special circumstances. Workers were housed in company barracks and not allowed to leave the premises without permission. Violating these rules would have serious consequences. A worker who became pregnant, for example, would be subject to immediate deportation. In addition, contracts were written between the GDR and the sending government. Often, pay was withheld to the individual until all work had been completed in order to ensure compliance.[29]

Although the scale of immigration was much smaller, the lack of contact between GDR citizens and *Vertragsarbeiter* was to have dire consequences after German unification. The frustration of the transition to the West German system was accompanied by high levels of unemployment with the installation of refugee quotas for the eastern states in the first years after unification and resulted in the eruption of violence against foreigners. The discomfort of the East German population with non-Germans was seized upon by the West German press as another example of the "backwardness" of GDR society in comparison to the Federal Republic. This, in turn, had a significant influence in the formation of the neo-Nazi image of East Germany, in the years after unification.

When the Wall fell in 1989, the rhetoric attaching the idea of political migration with East German migration disintegrated as well. This necessitated a serious reconsideration of a postwar identity that separated itself not only the past from the present, but East from West, with a post-wall identity that realized the complexity of reunified German society. These tensions were played out not only in the initial contact between East and West, but also in the contact between the "other" West (the west of the non-German worker and refugee) and the isolated East.

---

28 Siegfried Grundmann and I. Schmidt, "Zur Binnenwanderung in der DDR," 235–241.
29 Jeffery Peck, Mitchell Ash, and Christian Lemke, "Natives, Strangers and Foreigners: Constituting Germans by Constructing Others," in *After Unity: Reconfiguring German Identities*, ed. Konrad Jarausch (Providence: Berghahn Books, 1997), 88–90.

3 Tearing Down One Wall While Erecting Another: GDR Refugees in the West Before and After the Fall of the Berlin Wall, 1989–1990

> In August 1961 Erich Honecker oversaw the construction of the Berlin Wall, pulled up over-night from concrete paving slabs. Do we intend now to establish a concrete wall in our heads in front of the scattered Germans from the East, who come to us after so many years?[1]

In August 1988, more than a year before the actual collapse of the German-German border, Theo Sommer, Editor in Chief of the West German weekly national newspaper *Die Zeit*, issued the above plea to his readers. In the spirit of ethnic solidarity, Sommer called upon the West German people to come together to support the increasing number of GDR – (*Übersiedler*) and Ethnic German (*Aussiedler*) refugees arriving in West Germany.[2] Specifically, Sommer called upon West Germans to open up psychologically to the arrival of the Germans from the East, to not build up a "concrete wall in our heads," which would make integration more difficult, if not impossible.

Rehashing a common phrase of the Cold War era, "Refugees are Germans too!" (*Aussiedler sind auch Deutsche*), Sommer's front-page call to arms foreshadowed a major shift in public attitude toward and media portrayal of German migration and mobility. In a little more than a year, although the physical Wall dividing East and West would fall in Berlin, the mental "wall in the head" clearly not only still existed, but also had been fortified by the experience. The certainty with which both political and public rhetoric affirmed Cold War pleas to accept all "Germans" in the west as political victims ethnically bound to the homeland (*Heimat*) of the Federal Republic was replaced with official ambiguity and public bitterness. As the escalation of emigration in August 1989 strained the West German infrastructure and economy, attitudes of charity soon turned sour, as the public called to solve the emigration problem by supporting calls for unification. However, after the legal questions of German citizenship and aid were settled with formal unification in October 1990, the division between East and West persisted. As a result, attitudes toward interregional German migration changed from that of support to protest and also helped shape eastern and western stereotypes that still hold considerable damage more than two decades after unification.

---

1 Theo Sommer, "Mehr Angst als Vaterlandsliebe," *Die Zeit*, August 12, 1988.
2 The term *Übersiedler* refers to refugees emigrating from the GDR. *Vertriebene* were refugees of German ancestry who were expelled from the "Eastern Reich" and into either the FRG or the GDR.

https://doi.org/10.1515/9783110716221-004

At the time Sommer's article was published, the collapse of the border was still in no way imminent and according to most experts at the time – highly unlikely. However, the image he created of a "wall in our heads" would become one of the most common phrases used to describe the lack of psychological unity between East and West Germans. Born of postwar occupation, cemented with German division, and cultivated through the 40 years of ideological opposition, the idea of the insurmountable *Mauer im Kopf* ("wall in the head") has kept debates surrounding differences based upon Cold War dichotomies alive. The migration of Germans between East and West – or rather, the reality of the contact of two German peoples through migration, as well as the perception and portrayal of German migration before, during, and after unification have played important roles in the development of attitudes surrounding German identity and mobility.

The transformation of the image of the German migrant from political victim to economic parasite examined in the previous chapter was only one of many issues that were worked out in the processes surrounding German unity. After decades of restricted movement and little exposure to outsiders of any kind, the newly minted East German citizen of the Federal Republic was suddenly faced with the stress of having to negotiate a new life. The shock of having to go to the West to find work, to accept a new western boss at the firm, or having a camp for asylum seekers installed down the street exacerbated a general crisis of identity, which accompanied the breakdown and absorption of GDR political, economic, social, and cultural life into the structures of the West.

In West Germany, migration affected identity in more subtle ways. For 40 years, many West Germans had considered their East German friends and relatives as political victims of a totalitarian regime. In general, emigration during the Cold War was morally justified because its motivation was political. As thousands streamed across the border into the West in the fall of 1989, West Germans were suddenly forced to reconcile the picture they had constructed of ordinary East Germans during the Cold War with the reality of economically motivated migration. East German mobility after unification, especially when juxtaposed against the growing numbers of foreign migrants and asylum seekers, forced West Germans to reconsider the validity of their own postwar identities in the context of a united Germany.

This chapter examines the period from the expansion of East–West migration in the summer of 1989 to formal unification on October 3, 1990. At the beginning of this period, coverage of the escalation of emigration from the GDR was still expressed primarily in political terms. The press constructed refugees as sympathetic characters by focusing on political persecution as the primary reason for emigration. However, as more migrants began to arrive and took up more space in West German cities, towns, and villages, GDR refugees began to be cast in terms of incompatibility and difference. The perception of an East German inability to fit into the

West German system, to even perform the basic tasks of everyday life, such as to take a bus or to shop for groceries, would evolve into a commonly repeated theme after unification. As will be explored in subsequent chapters, the formation of these stereotypes would become detrimental to the treatment of East German men and women as political, economic, and social beings in unified Germany.

Despite the euphoric images of East and West Germans joyfully celebrating that are firmly established as the historical memory of the day the Berlin Wall fell, the opening of the German-German border resulted in an escalation of negativity toward the East Germans who came West to stay. As hundreds of thousands began to clog reception centers in many West German cities, public frustration emerged with the first cracks in the reasoning behind the right of anyone with German blood to return to their German homeland. While before the fall of the Berlin Wall in November 1989, GDR refugees were in general welcomed with open arms and given preferential treatment over "ethnic" Germans from the Eastern Bloc, by the time the GDR held free elections in March 1990, attitudes toward GDR refugees had soured considerably. The evolution of the coverage of GDR refugees in national, regional, and the local press indicates that as West German space and resources became increasingly strained, the East German "brothers and sisters" were portrayed more often as socially damaged, criminally corrupt, or as parasites trying to abuse the generous West German social system. While at the beginning of this period, coverage of the escalation of "escape" from the totalitarian regime of the GDR in this period was still expressed primarily in political terms, the refugee's story of persecution by the SED regime typically was set as the central point of the report or article. However, as more migrants began to arrive and less space became available, GDR refugees were increasingly portrayed in terms of incompatibility and difference.

The debates surrounding GDR refugees in 1989 and 1990 also destabilized a core element of postwar West German identity by putting the interests and security of the welfare state in direct conflict with aid for refugees contingent on their German blood. As months passed after unification and emigration from the GDR continued en masse, it became clear to politicians and the public alike that the only solution to the conflict between the right to return and the problems posed by thousands of GDR refugees in the West was rapid unification. However, the cessation of aid after the vote for unity did not put a stop to the negative perception of GDR refugees. The rapid change in the perception of GDR refugees that occurred between the fall of the Berlin Wall and German unification was founded upon contact and negative perceptions of migration.

3.1 GDR Refugees in the Federal Republic, 1962–1989

As discussed in the previous chapter, the Cold War dynamic between the Federal Republic of Germany and the German Democratic Republic was shaped by the significant and steady migration of young skilled workers from East to West. The overnight construction of the Berlin Wall in August 1961 effectively stopped the so-called bleeding out of people from the GDR by sealing the last large gap in the border between East and West. With the closure of the border gap in Berlin, the illegal emigration of GDR citizens dropped off dramatically. While in 1960, over 200,000 citizens of the GDR sought emergency assistance as refugees in the FRG, by 1962, that number dropped considerably to just over 20,000, holding steady at an average of around 25,000 a year until the mid 1980s.

Although the number of GDR refugees after 1961 seems low compared to the numbers in 1953–1961, those who did migrate became symbolic both politically and culturally. As a 1961 report in the weekly West German newsmagazine *Der Spiegel* claimed shortly after the erection of the Berlin Wall:

> No city in the FRG of the so-called "GDR" has as many inhabitants as people that have fled the "Zone." Almost three million men, women and children have fled from one Germany to another Germany since there has been two Germanys. First came the elderly, after that only the young. If the storm of people continues to flow as it has since last July, then the Zone will have lost a generation, much like Germany did after the Thirty Years War.
>
> The refugees, who have convinced the world of the previously unbelievable claim – that Germans love freedom – have handed the SED its heaviest blow. They have endangered the diplomatic position of Moscow in the fight for Germany, which weakened the formation of the Soviet Zone army and delayed Ulbricht's economic plans. The "Workers and Farmers State" has turned into a state with neither workers nor farmers. Ulbricht has turned the "refugee state" of Berlin, where thousands of people each day vote with their feet, into a state ruled by a wall.[3]

Although most of those who sought refuge in the Federal Republic did not perform the daring escapes popularized in Cold War era novels and movies, GDR refugees were legally and socially treated as political victims with a right to West German citizenship and support.[4] While sensational stories of escape have held pride of place in the popular memory of the Cold War, the majority of GDR refugees came either legally through an officially approved exit visa (normally granted to people

---

3 "Ulbrichts Wall-Stadt," *Der Spiegel*, August 9, 1961.
4 See the film Night Crossing (German title: *Mit dem Wind nach Westen*), the story of two families who made two attempts to cross the border using a handcrafted hot air balloon. The second attempt succeeded, and Disney turned the story of the families into a popular feature film starring John Hurt and Beau Bridges in 1981.

past retirement age) or were political prisoners freed by ransom payment paid to the GDR. Beginning 1963, the FRG regularly paid ransoms to the GDR for the release to the West of prisoners who had been incarcerated on grounds of trying to escape to the West or for other expression of political opposition. The size of the ransom paid per prisoner (which was paid out both in western currency and raw commodities) gradually increased from an average of DM 1000 in the 1960s up to a high of DM 160,000 per prisoner in 1977. While the average ransom declined slightly in the 1980s, it is estimated that in 1963–1989, the FRG paid an estimated DM 1 billion to the GDR for the release of over 34,000 prisoners.[5] Although these numbers are significant and affected everyday life in the GDR from the 1960s on, it did not or could not compare to the pressure that east German migrants would put on the faltering state in 1989.

3.2 GDR Refugees in West, Summer and Fall 1989

While the summer of 1989 is typically referred to as the date from which mass emigration from the GDR took hold, an increase in emigration can already been seen in late 1988. Several factors, both internal and external, coincided to result in an increased rate of emigration from the GDR. The GDR granted exit visas not only to retirees but also to known political dissidents as an "internal safety valve," which functioned to quell domestic unrest.[6] As applications for exit visas dramatically increased in the 1980s especially among the young professionals whom the GDR so desperately needed to retain, it became increasingly difficult to control dissent through controlled migration.

The inability to effectively curb unrest contributed to an increase in the frequency and size of mass protests throughout the Eastern Bloc in the late 1980s. Protest movements were primarily organized thorough the Evangelical Church. Although the Church and its members had initially faced harsh repression, the SED tolerated its existence after the formation of the *Bund der Evangelische Kirche* (BEK) in 1969. Under the BEK, churches in the GDR formally broke away from the western Protestant organizing body, while formally acknowledging the limited

---

5 *The GDR Annual Report* (London: Amnesty International, 1989), 105–117.

6 The most famous case is the expulsion of folk singer and artist Wolf Biermann from the GDR in 1976. An outspoken critic of the SED, Biermann was branded a "class traitor" in 1965 and subsequently banned from public performance or displacing his work in the GDR. In 1976, Biermann's GDR citizenship was revoked while on tour in the Federal Republic. Many prominent GDR intellectuals and artists, including author Christa Wolf and popular actor Manfred Krug, openly criticized Biermann's expulsion.

role of the "Church in Socialism." The church experienced a degree of autonomy from the state unparalleled by any other organization.[7] As a result the BEK emerged as the center of dissident activity in the GDR during the 1970s and 1980s.

Alongside these internal organizations, in the late 1980s, dissident movements began to express themselves throughout the Soviet Bloc. As Mikhail Gorbachev's policies of *Glasnost* and *Perestroika* emerged in the mid 1980s, Eastern Bloc nations began to test the limits of the Soviet spirit toward reform. Organized by the Pan-European Union president Otto von Habsburg and Ferenc Mészáros of the Hungarian Democratic Forum, a peace demonstration advertised as the "Pan-European Picnic" was held on the Austrian-Hungarian border near Sopron, Hungary on August 19, 1989. As a symbolic gesture agreed to by both Austria and Hungary, one border gate between Burgenland, Austria and Sopronkóhida was opened for three hours as the site of a peace demonstration. Around 3 p.m. in the afternoon, East Germans began to assemble, tore down the gate, and ran to the Austrian side. Not wanting to cause a border crisis, Hungarian, Austrian, or the 80,000 Soviet soldiers in Hungary did not intervene. By the end of the "picnic," a total of 661 East Germans had crossed the border into Austria – although thousands had gathered in anticipation and missed the window during which the border had been open. The largest emigration of East German citizens since the construction of the Berlin Wall had occurred and helped open the watershed that followed.[8]

The expression and organization of these dissident peace movements in the GDR culminated in the "Monday Demonstrations," which began on September 4, 1989, at the *Nikolaikirche* (Church of St. Nicholas) in Leipzig as a meeting offering a "prayer for peace." These informal weekly meetings quickly evolved into peaceful mass protests for extensive reforms including freedom of speech and above all, the end to travel restrictions. Fueled by word of mouth and reports broadcast on West German television, the movement quickly grew. On October 9, over 70,000 people filled Karl Marx Square in Leipzig; 2 weeks later, the number surpassed 300,000. However, despite the site of the crowd and an increasing police and military presence at the protests, large-scale violence did not erupt in Leipzig. In a 2009 interview with *Deutsche Welle*, Christian Fuehrer, the then pastor at the

---

7 The BEK was most active in protesting compulsory military training and in support of environmental causes. For a detailed accounting of the evolution of church organization regarding the formation of dissident movements see Karl Cordell, "The Role of the Evangelical Church in the GDR," *Government and Opposition* 25, no. 1 (2007), 48–59. Also see Steven Pfaff, "The Politics of Peace in the GDR: The Independent Peace Movement, the Church, and the Origins of the East German Opposition," *Peace and Change* 26, no. 3 (2002), 280–300.

8 See György Gyarmati, Krisztina Slachta: Das Vorspiel für die Grenzöffnung: Das Paneuropäische Picknick in Sopron am 19.August 1989. Sopron, Budapest, 2014.

Nikolaikirche, gave his explanation for the lack of violence as he described the tension between the crowd and the police:

> Around 6000 to 8000 people were crammed into the churches in central Leipzig, and a total of 70,000 people had gathered in the city. Everyone was holding a candle, a symbol of non-violence – you need to hold a candle with both hands to keep it from going out, which makes it impossible to throw stones. Later, a member of the SED Central Committee said: "We had everything planned. We were ready for anything – except candles and prayers." The police had not been briefed for this possibility. Had we thrown stones, they would have known what to do. They would have attacked. But the tanks had no choice but to withdraw without a single shot being fired, and that's when we knew that the GDR would never be the same again.[9]

Within weeks of the beginning of the Leipzig Monday Demonstrations, regular mass protests were held in large cities throughout the GDR. These protests climaxed on November 4, just five days before the fall of the Berlin Wall, when over 500,000 people gathered on Berlin's Alexanderplatz to hear speeches by leading DGR intellectuals including writers Christa Wolf and Stefan Heym calling for extensive democratic reforms. However, it was clear that democratic reforms at this point did not mean the abandonment of the GDR in favor of an open call for unification, especially not on terms dictated by West Germans. In fact, the speeches at the Alexanderplatz demonstration reflected the urgency of the problem of mass emigration and its consequences for the effectiveness of the people to enact reform. In a particularly impassioned speech, Christa Wolf called for people to stay and help forge the path toward the "third way," a reform of socialism within the GDR:

> Indeed, the language is bursting out of the bureaucratic and newspaper German in which it has been wrapped for so long, and recalling its emotional, expressive vocabulary. One such word is "dream." Let us dream with an alert sense of reason: Imagine there was socialism, and no one ran away! But we continue to see pictures of those leaving, and we have to ask ourselves, "What is to be done? And the answer echoes – "Do something!" It is a start when demands become rights – and obligations. Fact-finding committees, constitutional court, administrative reform. There is a lot to be done, and all of it during our spare time. We still need time to read the newspaper! We won't have any more time to pay official homage or to attend prescribed demonstrations.[10]

The official line of the West Germans echoed that of Christa Wolf, namely, that changed needed to occur from within the GDR and that for change to happen, peo-

---

9 Julia Elvers-Guyot, "Peace Prayers Helped Bring Down the Wall, Says Leipzig Pastor," *Deutsche Welle Online* (July 1, 2009), https://www.dw.com/en/peace-prayers-helped-bring-down-the-wall-says-leipzig-pastor/a-3805080. Accessed July 12, 2020.
10 "Christa Wolf, Christoph Hein and Steffi Spira at the Berlin Demonstration (November 4, 1989)," in *United Germany: Documents and Debates, 1944–1993*, ed. Konrad Jarausch and Volker Gransow (Providence: Berghahn Books, 1994), 70–71.

ple needed to stay. Shortly, securing the release into West Germany of more than 15,000 GDR emigrants, who had sought asylum at the West German embassies in Budapest from the Hungarian government, West German Chancellor Helmut Kohl expressed his belief that although "We Germans belong together" and that "the will for the unification of the (German) nation has a deep moral power," that change would ultimately have to come from within the GDR. As reported in the national West German newspaper *Süddeutsche Zeitung,*

> Addressing the movement form the GDR, Kohl stated that it was neither the wish nor inten-
> tion that as many GDR citizens as possible would come to the Federal Republic. However,
> living conditions must develop in the GDR so that people can remain "in their traditional
> homeland." This is also an "hour of thoughtfulness." People in the GDR will have to be able
> to experience the process of *Perestroika,* that they witness now only on television, within
> their own homeland.[11]

Ultimately, however, neither the arguments of East German intellectuals nor West German politicians could prevent mass emigration. To summarize, internal political and economic instability in the GDR, combined with increasingly fre-quent mass demonstration created an atmosphere that promoted mass emigra-tion. However, it was an eternal factor – the withdrawal of external military and border support of the Eastern Bloc by the Soviet Union, which turned the trickle of people going over the border into a tidal wave. GDR citizens applied for asylum at the West German embassies in Prague, Warsaw, and Budapest. In the wake of the Pan-European Picnic described earlier in this chapter, in August of 1989, Hun-gary declared the withdrawal of patrols from the Austrian border. Within 2 weeks, 13,000 GDR citizens traveled through Austria into the Federal Republic via Hungary in addition to the 15,000 released into West German custody after nego-tiation with the Hungarian government. By November 6, over 25,000 GDR citizens had fled to the FRG via the Prague Embassy alone.[12]

The increasing numbers of emigrants seeking shelter in West Germany over-loaded the reception centers for GDR refugees, ethnic German refugees, and asy-lum seekers. On the eve of the fall of the Berlin Wall, 86 official emergency accommodation centers (*Notaufnahmelager*) had been established throughout West Germany.[13] While there were a small number of previously established ref-

---

11 "Kohl: Eine Entscheidung der Menschlichkeit," *Süddeutsche Zeitung,* September 11, 1989.
12 Evron M. Kirkpatrick, "A Chronology of Events: The Collapse of the German Democratic Re-public and steps toward German Unity: May 1989 – January 1991," *World Affairs* 152 (1990), 195.
13 There were two main official refugee reception centers. The *Notaufnahmelager Marienfelde,* near the Tempelhof district in Berlin opened in 1953 and operated until 2003 when it was turned into a museum site. The other official center is the *Notaufnahmelager Gießen* in the state of Hesse, which was opened in 1946 and is still currently in operation.

ugee reception centers in operation from the early days of the Cold War, most emergency accommodations were quite informal. Tent cities were erected on the outskirts of Munich, and in each of the 11 western federal states, *Pensionen* (hotels), gyms, schools, and apartment spaces were being cleared out to make room for the new arrivals. A September 12 report in the *Hamburger Abendblatt* outlined the preparation for refugees across West Germany:

> Berlin is offering 2500 places in trailers, sport halls and exhibition halls. In North Rhine-Westphalia there are more than 10,000 places. Approximately 4000 places are offered alone in the refugee camp Unna-Masse. Baden-Württemberg has offered to take on 5000 emigrants, utilizing spots in apartments and dorms. Bavaria has already rented 230 private hotels; 13,000 spots in transitional housing are already taken. Lower Saxony is holding 700 spots in a police school. Hesse has 20 sport halls with around 2500 spots ready in order to take their portion of 10 percent of the emigrants. Saarland must take 500 people, who they plan to house in a country boarding school. In Rhineland-Palatinate 1000 places for in a transitional camp stand ready. As in Hamburg, all is ready is Schleswig-Holstein. In total there are around 1600 places for the refugees to spend their transition in single-family homes, hotels, and pensions as well as in military barracks, in which 300 beds will be open during the four weeks break between basic training sessions.[14]

In terms of refugee reception, each of the 11 West German federal states had an obligation to take on a percentage of all refugees according to their relative population size. However, how this obligation was fulfilled was not federally administrated and as a result, each state was left to decide how to accommodate newcomers.[15] In addition to housing, many states also offered immediate financial assistance to GDR emigrants. For example, in Berlin, each refugee was given DM 15 a day. In North Rhine-Westphalia, emigrants were given a one-time payment of DM 500. Bavaria provided 200DM per person while Schleswig-Holstein gave emigrants 100DM per child and DM 150 per adult.[16] However, after this initial outreach and aid, benefits were cut drastically after the borders were opened in November 1989.

As late summer turned into fall, the number of GDR refugees arriving in West Germany continued to climb, in addition to the arrival of increasing numbers of ethnic Germans from Eastern Bloc countries. While in September there was thousands of spots open for potential emigrants, by November this was no longer the case. On the afternoon before the fall of the Wall, the *Hamburger Abendblatt* reported that the emergency camps were "bursting at the seams." The situation was the worst in Bavaria, which because of its position bordering Aus-

---

14 "Unterbringung ist vorläufig gesichert," *Hamburger Abendblatt*, September 12, 1989.
15 "Lastenausgleichsgesetz in der Fassung der Bekanntmachung vom 2. Juni 1993," BGB1. I S. 845 (1995), 248.
16 "Unterbringung ist vorläufig gesichert."

tria served as the primary reception site for those arriving via Eastern Europe. Space quickly became sparse, as the *Hamburger Abendblatt* reported of one Bavarian camp: "The situation became so precarious that new arrivals had to switch places over and over again: Some had beds to lie in while others had only chairs. A good portion of the refugees had no choice but to stand."[17]

Similar situations occurred with frequency after the opening of the border, which exacerbated conflicts between eastern "refugees" and western "native" inhabitants. Before the fall of the Wall, refugees from the GDR were generally well received; many West Germans answered the call for donations of material goods or even opened up their homes to help support these emigrants. However, at the same time, there was also an increase in the number of ethnic German migrants from East Bloc countries, particularly from Poland and the Soviet Union. As was the case in the immediate postwar period, this led to tension between GDR and ethnic German refugees because they frequently competed for the same resources. A report concerning conflicts between GDR refugees and ethnic German refugees in an emergency campsite in Hamburg-Eidelstedt captured the mounting tension:

> "I would rather be in a German-only camp," complains Michael, a young GDR-refugee. Emigrants from Poland have manipulated the power supply line to his caravan, causing his electronic alarm clock to fail. As a result, he has overslept. "With my new job, I cannot afford [to oversleep] in the Federal Republic." He says. Does it only seem like a little thing? Indeed, however many of these little things add up to a tense situation. An employee of the Samaritans Alliance (ASB), an organization charged with looking after the refugees in the camp, describes the relationship thusly: "If a car with a Polish license plate appears on the campground, many [GDR refugees] clench their fist in their pocket in anger."[18]

While GDR-refugees and ethnic Germans were housed together in Hamburg-Eidelstedt, in Bremen they were kept quite separate both in terms of living space and regarding the allocation of donations:

> In former armed forces barracks, the two groups of Germans live separately from each other. Ethnic German emigrants from Poland and the Soviet Union bunk in the right tract half, GDR refugees on the left. "In the beginning we tried to get by without strict separation," says social worker Nikal Büyükatilla, "but this led to tensions. Whether the children are too cheeky, the kitchens too dirty, the music too loud, the others were always to blame."[19]

Tension between groups did not just arise out of the circumstances of cramped living spaces. Similar to what has been seen concerning conflicts amongst emi-

---

17 "Notaufnahmelager überfüllt," *Hamburger Abendblatt,* November 9, 1989.
18 Jens Glüsing, "Deutsche unter sich: Aus- und Umsiedler schätzen einander nicht," *Die Zeit,* October 13, 1989.
19 "Halle-Budapest-Bremen-wieder da!" *taz-bremen,* October 3, 1989.

grant groups in the postwar period these clashes formed in the anticipation of the end of the Cold War were drawn sharply upon ethnic lines. Resentment escalated quickly if one group was seen to have gained some advantage over the other. In Hamburg-Eidelstedt, competition for resources was often fierce:

> Really chaotic scenes occur at the entrances of the camping site when helpful Hamburgers deliver food and clothes. Groups of emigrants, expecting the donations, assemble at the gate and snatch the baskets and bags from them before the others have a chance. "Whoever comes first, catches the biggest fish," says a friendly older Polish emigrant with a shrug, "[In order to receive donations] the GDR refugees have to be there [at the gate] too. We are, in the end, all German."[20]

Although GDR refugees and ethnic German refugees both had a legal "right to return" as outlined in the Basic Law, they were neither viewed nor considered in the same manner. GDR refugees often held an advantage over ethnic Germans in terms of allocation of donations and supplies; moreover, they were better able to communicate in German. In Hamburg-Eidelstedt, although both GDR refugees and ethnic German refugees were housed together in the same camp, partly as an attempt to prevent the so-called ghettoization of emigrants, clear preference was given to GDR refugees both in terms of donations and housing:

> To avoid the wrangling at the entrance, the Samaritan Alliance advises the donors to select the specific families they want to help. This creates bad blood [between the GDR refugees and the ethnic German refugees] because many donors expressly want to give items "only for use by GDR refugees." In terms of apartment mediation, the competition always goes in favor of the GDR refugees.[21]

These conflicts were not limited to Hamburg. 120 km to the West in the city of Bremen, preference and purpose for donations from the community was even more explicit:

> Many [West German families] have brought in what they no longer need but will do the refugees some good. In the barracks that just a few weeks ago housed soldiers, skirts, trousers, coats, duvet covers ("quite new, only used once!") pile up beside table lamps and cartons with canned food and fresh fruit. Even an old bread machine is there. However, a condition applies to all donations: Only for use by GDR refugees, do not award to "Poles" or "Russians."[22]

This explicit hierarchy of preference contributed to conflict between the refugee groups, since GDR refugees were given priority by aid workers over ethnic Germans and other asylum seekers. According to one Samaritan Alliance (the aid or-

---

20 Glüsing, "Deutsche unter sich: Aus- und Umsiedler schätzen einander nicht."
21 Glüsing, "Deutsche unter sich: Aus- und Umsiedler schätzen einander nicht."
22 "Halle-Budapest-Bremen-wieder da!"

ganization providing assistance to refugees in Bremen), the imbalance was so great between the two groups that, "for the amount the GDR refugees receive as gives during their first 15 days . . . emigrants from Poland and the Soviet Union must work for years."[23] However, this preference was to end once the Berlin Wall fell in November 1989, after which GDR refugees were increasingly treated with suspicion and even disdain as migration into West Germany continued.

The shock to German identity, both East and West, which would come with the fall of the Wall, was mitigated and played out in discussions exploring the anxiety that accompanied the rush of newcomers. As floods of East Germans came West after the opening of the border, and as many came not just to visit but also to stay, West Germans soon tired of the spectacle of hospitality. The euphoria of the moment when the borders were opened was replaced with tension over what the unmitigated westward migration of East Germans would do to the West German welfare state that had been so carefully crafted in the aftermath of the Second World War. As it became apparent that the migration would not taper off, it became obvious to the ruling conservative Christian Democrats in West Germany that in order to turn the political situation in the GDR to their advantage, as well as to quell the growing unrest from the West German public, rapid unification offered a solution that would stabilize the situation.

3.3 Migration from the Fall of the Berlin Wall to Unification, November 1989 to October 1990

> The Wall will still stand in 50 or even 100 years, if the reasons for its existence are not removed. Erich Honecker, January 12, 1989

Although the sheer volume of migration had been steadily increasing from the time the Hungarian government dismantled its militarized border with Austria in August 1989, no one could predict the complete opening of the border between East and West Berlin that took place on the evening of November 9, 1989. As the above statement from Erich Honecker, First Secretary of the Central Committee of the SED indicates, as of early 1989 those in power in the GDR still asserted (at least publicly) that the wall would continue to exist indefinitely. In the eyes of the regime, the situation only had the potential to change with the removal of the external treat of so-called western corruption.

As the events of the following summer unfolded, however, it became obvious that the biggest threat to the Wall and the larger border it symbolized would be a

---

23 "Halle-Budapest-Bremen-wieder da!"

lack of support from Communist allies and the power of the East German people to continue to "vote with their feet." After it became clear that the Soviet Union was not willing to use force to keep the East German people inside the GDR, in Hungary, Czechoslovakia, or in East Berlin itself, it also became increasingly evident that the power of the SED itself was in jeopardy. On October 18, just 11 days after examining that "Socialism will be halted in its course neither by ox nor by ass," at the celebration of the GDR's 40th anniversary, Erich Honecker was forced to resign his post as both head of state and head of the SED.

The turning point in the story of the border collapse would come just a few weeks later in a rapid series of dramatic events. A combination of the growing strength of popular protest, epitomized at Alexanderplatz on November 4 and instability within the ruling apparatus itself, forced the resignation of the government on November 7. This was followed by the resignation of the entire Politburo on November 8. Unable to devise a way to quell the increasingly popular unrest and emigration, the newly appointed Politburo, under new General Secretary Egon Krenz, decided to allow limited border crossings with permission in the form of a visa on November 10. However, when party official Günter Schabowski, who had not been informed of the plan beforehand, was handed a note during a live press conference stating that private travel to the West would be allowed, he read the note aloud. When pressed by journalists, he added that this would be "effective immediately" (not at 4 a.m. the next morning as the Politburo had intended) and also confirmed that the Berlin border crossing was included in the order.

A sense of chaotic euphoria followed shortly thereafter, as thousands of East and West Berliners streamed to the Wall and many crossed the border for the first time in their lives, or at least for the first time in 40 years. However, as the euphoria from the moment of transgression passed, uncertainty and discomfort began to set in. Face to face meetings between West and East German relatives were tinged with awkwardness, as many had only had contact through yearly letters and *Westpakete:* boxes of western coffee, chocolates, and other goods sent by West Germans to their East German relatives, usually around the holidays.

As the West German government offered *Begrüßungsgeld*, welcome money of DM 100 to every GDR citizen who came for their first visit to the West, West Germans, particularly those living in border areas, quickly began to tire of the endless stream of *Trabis* with their characteristic cloud of exhaust as well as the seemingly backward spending habits of the *Ossis*.[24] One point of contention was a

---

24 *Trabi* is a reference to the Trabant, the most common automobile in the GDR. Its two-stroke engine was notoriously smoky – after the fall of the wall, many West Germans complained about the smog that would accompany the line up at the border crossing.

lack of common sense in terms of shopping, in particular, the irresponsibility of choosing name brands over discount offerings. As a report in the *taz-berlin* noted just days after the fall of the wall:

> Edeka in Wedding: Six roll-on deodorant sticks in the shopping cart – that must be enough for one year, around 50 marks per armpit. In addition, Pampers and Serena, seven assorted soaps from Lux to Irish Spring. Empty spaces in the shelves are the rule, as are typical *Westpaket* wares in East German carts: Nutella, Nesquik, instant pudding, Muesli, Cornflakes, Ritter Sport, Coke. All kinds of foil: baking paper, aluminum, and Melitta toppits. Scotch Britt scrubbers for the coming cleaning. No-names [generic brands] are absolutely forbidden.[25]

These first impressions of East Germans would quickly develop into stereotypes that would position East Germans as incompatible with the West German way of life. Combined with the almost automatic dismissal of professional qualifications gained in the GDR (especially for academics and civil servants), this resulted almost immediately in the displacement of East Germans from positions of power and influence, and would in turn have an impact on both East–West migration (as unemployed East Germans looked West for jobs or retraining) and West–East migration (as West German managers moved in to take over leadership positions in the East) after unification.

However strange the behavior of East Germans seemed in the first weeks after the opening of the border, for West Germans, the most immediate concern in the period between the fall of the Wall and the vote for unification was the continued migration of East Germans into the West. In November alone, close to 150,000 GDR citizens registered in the West. Although the number fell significantly to just under 65,000 in December, an average of 50,000 people a month arrived to stay from December 1989 through March 1990.[26]

The continual arrival of East German refugees after the border was opened had a significant and rapid impact on their reception in the West. Whereas just a few months before West Germans had been happy to donate and find space for a GDR family, in the months after the Wall fell, the welcome had decidedly cooled. In March 1990, residents of Bremen took matters into their own hands by refusing to allow their neighborhood sport hall to be converted into another shelter for GDR refugees:

> The mothers could not believe their eyes when they attempted to drop their children off at the Fröbelstrasse Gymnasium in Bremen-Vegesack: Craftsmen were in the process of moving chipped boards onto the parquet. "Not anymore!" they told the surprised women and chil-

---

25 "Sichtvermerk – Lilapause im Kalten Krieg," *taz-berlin*, November 13, 1989.
26 Siegfried Grundmann, *Bevölkerungsentwicklung in Ostdeutschland: Demographische Strukturen und räumliche Wandlungsprozesse seit 1945* (Opladen: Leske und Budrich, 1998), 170–174.

dren, "GDR-refugees will soon arrive." [For the parents] . . . this was the last straw, and the protest began: Angry parents, pedagogues and sportsmen took up residence in the sport hall; a desperate action by residents frustrated by the loss of the use of their own public facilities.[27]

With no end in sight to the inflow of refugees, residents of Bremen feared that their infrastructure would be overloaded, breeding a bitterness that may even lead to "civil war":

The inhabitants of Bremen fear that the infrastructure will break under the weight of the inflow. The annoyance of the population can turn into hatred unless this development stops. "With our own initiative, we want to prevent a state [that would be similar] to civil war," said a speaker for the occupants of the sport hall. Some newcomers from the East have had some quite disagreeable experiences in North Bremen. "Some Trabis had their tires punctured in the middle of the night," complains a GDR refugee who is accommodated in a sport hall in Hechelstrasse.[28]

Further west in Saarland, accommodations and resources were so sparse that an agreement was made by the city council of Lehrbach to transport 250 GDR refugees in an immigrant district of Farebersville, a small industrial town in the neighboring French province of Lorraine. In addition to paying for the costs of transportation, Lehrbach agreed to pay to house these Germans from the east in France for a minimum of six months. Here again there is a clear change of tone both in the behavior of officials and the nature of the report. Before opening of the borders, it was likely that an appeal to ethnic German solidarity would have been made to make room for our "brothers from the East." After the fall of the wall, however, it was now "perfectly justified" to send GDR refugees to France in order to establish ". . . a German colony in the midst of a *cité* where one hears no German, rather Arabic, Turkish or French."[29] Ethnic solidarity gave way to the need to manage the problem of the GDR refugees, a tense situation that began to wear on the native population of Lehrbach as well as among the refugees. Despite the prospect of moving into a mixed community of immigrants in France, GDR refugees seemed eager to apply:

In Lehrbach, many GDR refugees have announced that they are ready for relocation. Life in the mass emergency shelters tugs at the nerves . . . The partitions between the beds offer no private sphere. On the other hand, Farebersville lures with furnished twin-bedded rooms and communal kitchens.[30]

---

27 "Armut und Enge," *Die Zeit*, March 16, 1990.
28 "Armut und Enge."
29 Joachim Widemann, "Raus aus den Hallen: Das Saarland schichte Übersiedler nach Lothringen," *Die Zeit*, March 2, 1990.
30 Joachim Widemann, "Raus aus den Hallen: Das Saarland schichte Übersiedler nach Lothringen."

Turks, Moroccans, Sicilians, and Poles had first settled in the area surrounding Farebersville in the 1960s and 1970s when housing was quickly constructed for workers in local coal plants. By the 1980s however, the coal supply had been nearly exhausted, and now much of the housing lay empty, as workers had moved on. Due to the multi-cultural composition of the living quarters, refugees were not assigned to relocation at whim. There were strict precautions taken to screen out alcoholics or antisocial elements who might not fit into the largely immigrant neighborhood. Red Cross assistants screened potential emigrants in Lehrbach for problems:

> The French are anxious to avoid aggravating the newcomers. News has travelled ahead of the GDR refugees that they are [prejudiced] against Poles and Turks. Therefore Kleinhentz [the mayor of Farebersville] demanded that the Saarland "filter the Germans before their arrival." The Red Cross assistants are now doing this in Lehrbach. The choice criteria: They must be athletic and have no problems with alcohol. "Sport will eliminate all prejudice," the mayor hopes aloud.[31]

This screening process is important to note not simply because the French reception center demanded it of the Germans, but because it reflects the general sense of how GDR refugees were portrayed as people. Whereas before conflicts between GDR refugees and ethnic German refugees were chalked up to competition between two foreign groups, in the post-Wall period, the GDR refugees were pitted against "native" West Germans. Very soon after the collapse of the border, distinctions in the press between the "good" and "bad" GDR refugees became common with the implication that the "good" refugees had tended to come before the fall of the Wall and that the "bad" population flooded in after the border was open. In Lehrbach, this distinction was especially made explicit: "Recently, the police have increased patrols through the area. Employees complain that many alcoholics as well as criminals, have come in the last wave [of emigration]."[32]

In June 1991, *taz-bremen* reported on the phenomenon of a population of East German career criminals, who had appeared to have traded their "eastern prison for a western prison."[33] Many of these reports implied those who came after the fall of the Wall as mere opportunists, "fleeing" the East not to escape any real hardship, but rather to take advantage of the generosity of the western system.

This period also saw the beginning of a commentary on the moral deficiencies of GDR refugees. A story published in *Der Spiegel* describes the efforts of parents to escape responsibility for their children by emigrating to the West:

---

31 Joachim Widemann, "Raus aus den Hallen: Das Saarland schichte Übersiedler nach Lothringen."
32 Joachim Widemann, "Raus aus den Hallen: Das Saarland schichte Übersiedler nach Lothringen."
33 "Vom Ost-Knast in den West-Knast," *taz-bremen*, June 8, 1991.

Some GDR refugees, wanting to make their new start in the golden West with no baggage, leave their children behind – sometimes alone in an apartment. In this manner, an 8-year-old girl and her 11-year-old brother in Magdeburg were left to fend for themselves for three days with noodles and packaged soup. Upon discovering the children, a relative wrote the mother, who replied that she would pick up the orphans once an apartment had been found in the West.[34]

From this West German perspective, individual deficiencies were not to blame for such behaviors, but were indications of the larger result of unnatural socialization under totalitarian communism. In other words, the dependence of the people of the GDR on the state as caretaker led to a disassociation of parental responsibility. Herbert Tatus, leader of the area youth welfare and home education committee on the East Berlin City Council, explains the indifference as such, "Those fleeing parents have said to themselves: The State has always provided a lot for the children, so it will continue to do so now if I leave."[35]

The story of a man who emigrated to the West but stopped child support to his child he left in the East also invokes the image of the state as caretaker. Here again, the concept of the state as the facilitator of parental abandonment is present. In other words, the decision of the GDR-refugee to abandon a child is based on the reasoning that the state is fundamentally responsible:

Now and again Owe Fuchs sends greetings to his friends and relatives in Oschersleben, a district of Magdeburg. One time there was a postcard from Augsburg, another time the machine builder sent greetings from Hannover and Ireland. There is a reason for these quick changes of location: Fuchs left behind his 8-year-old daughter Susanne, who lives with her divorced mother back in the GDR. He is ordered to pay 160 GDR marks a month for maintenance, however Katrin Fuchs, 28, has not seen a penny from her ex-husband, who went to the Federal Republic at the beginning of January with his new partner and their daughter. All attempts to find their place of residence has failed . . . for now, the abandoned woman relies upon the state: it will pay what the father fails to provide.[36]

From the perspective of the West, 40 years under the influence of the socialist welfare state of the GDR has created a situation in which children are "thrown away like garbage," causing lasting psychological damage and future problems of responsibilities. These arguments foreshadow further discussions that will develop over the course of the next two decades concerning fundamental differences between East and West Germans in terms of moral values and familial ties.

Above all however, this story served to confirm the western fear that GDR refugees were falsifying information in order to qualify for benefits they did not

---

34 "Wie Sperrmüll," *Der Spiegel*, March 12, 1990.
35 "Wie Sperrmüll."
36 "Wie Sperrmüll."

deserve. A common argument both before and after the fall of the Wall concerned the strain of the East German refugees on the West German social system. While parents of children left behind by GDR refugees called for West German offices to do more to identify cases in which support must be paid, the West Germans claimed that they were being overrun with false claims for support. As a report in *Der Spiegel* in March 1990 observed,

> In the GDR, criticism against offices in the Federal Republic is growing. According to an educator at the Erfurt Home for Children, offices don't ask [GDR refugees] for documentation of support, only how their children are being cared for. However, this does not help in practice. "Many GDR refugees simply say that they have lost their identity card," says Hans Heuser of the refugee camp Gießen. The acquisition of new documents means that they can hide the fact that they have left their children behind in the GDR. "Like social garbage," Horst Horrman, Minister of Education and Arts in Lower Saxony explains, "many children in the GDR are simply thrown away."[37]

The continuing stream of GDR citizens emigrating to the West overwhelmed attempts at emergency accommodation, straining relationships both inside camps and within local communities. In addition to increasing social pressure caused by the simultaneous influx of ethnic German refugees and asylum seekers, GDR refugees, while previously supported by the West German public, were increasingly portrayed not as "brothers from the East," but rather as a parasitic strain on West German society. As a result, the emigration problem became a focus of local politics in major receiving areas. In April 1990, for example, Hamburg halted the allocation of apartments to GDR refugees and an increasingly hard line was taken against those trying to cheat the system. As reported in *Der Spiegel*,

> The Hamburg Social Service office wants to deal with GDR refugees [trying to cheat the system] drastically, especially those trying to be clever. The Hanseatic town wants to give neither bed nor butter bread to those who have kept their apartments in the East as a sort of safety net to fall back upon. According to Brigitte Eberle of the Social Service office, "[If anyone is caught retaining a residence in the East] . . . then he will just have to lie out on the street [immediately losing any housing in the West] – Bam!"[38]

While city councils such as Bremen-Vegesack described earlier in this chapter supported citizens' protests concerning the allocation of public facilities to house and supply GDR refugees, states also quickly entered pleas to reduce or halt acceptance and aid to emigrants from the GDR. Bremen started refusing to accept GDR refugees in the middle of March 1990. Instead of receiving accommodation and support, prospective GDR refugees were instead greeted with "one red slip of paper inform-

---

37 "Wie Sperrmüll."
38 "Schluss mit Lustig," *Der Spiegel*, March 26, 1990.

ing the newly arrived in a friendly, but certain manner . . . that Bremen cannot take up their care. The homeless refugees are simply advised to return to the GDR."[39] In the Saarland, the Federal State that had arranged to send GDR refugees to France, from April 1990, new arrivals were "given just one more free ticket, one way, 2nd class back to the GDR."[40]

The refugee problem figured significantly on the national political stage as well. The year 1990 was a national election year in West German, with emigration and unification quickly emerging as the focus of the election. The ruling Christian Democrats (CDU), led by Helmut Kohl, was convinced of the benefit of speedy unification and did not want to undertake any measures that might alienate a future electorate in the East. The opposition Social Democrats (SPD), on the other hand, found itself firmly on the other side of the issue, calling to end gifts and benefits to GDR refugees in order to stem the seemingly relentless in-migration.

Unsurprisingly, the fight in the Bundestag to end benefits for GDR refugees was led by the representatives of the states that had already undertaken measures to stop reception. Oskar Lafontaine, Prime Minister of the Saarland and Klaus Wiedemeier, Prime Minister of Bremen, spearheaded the campaign to cut of incentives for further immigration from the East. Lafontaine, the SPD candidate for Chancellor in 1990, in a speech to the Bundestag in January 1990, proclaimed the views of his electorate: "The population increasingly feels that it is socially unfair that GDR citizens, without having paid 1 Mark here [in the West] in social insurance fees or taxes, can simply come over and fully enjoy all of these social benefits."[41] Calling for a slow approach to unification, Lafontaine was blasted in the press and by the opposition party as "an enemy of the Germans" as well as the "Schönhüber" of the SPD, while the CDU campaigned on a political and emotional platform of reuniting two peoples that should have been one all along.[42] Elections in both the GDR and the FRG would ensure the CDU vision of unification would be victorious.

The first and only free election in the GDR was held on March 18, 1990 and resulted in a coalition victory for the East German faction of the CDU. The CDU and Party of Democratic Renewal received 41.7% of the votes; the SPD (formerly the SED, renamed the "Party of Democratic Socialism" in the wake of the collapse) received 21.9%, while the German Social Union and other liberal parties gained 12.2%. With its position in favor of speedy unification confirmed, the CDU passed

---

39 "Schluss mit Lustig."
40 "Schluss mit Lustig."
41 Klaus-Peter Schmidt, "Falscher Neid: Nur wenige Rentner aus der DDR belasten bisher die Rentenversicherung der Bundesrepublik," *Die Zeit*, January 26, 1990.
42 "Schluss mit Lustig," A reference to right-wing politician Franz Schönhüber, former SS officer, and founder of the populist *Die Republikaner* party.

a law just two days after the election that would end benefits to GDR refugees by July 1, the date of the currency reform.[43]

The path to unification after the free elections in the GDR was swift. Although there were several political parties in the GDR that called for unification via the construction of a new constitution considering both Germanys, the victory of the CDU on March 18 was basically a vote for the more rapid path toward unification. In August 1990, the *Volkskammer* voted for unification with the West under Article 23 of the Basic Law, which instead of a renegotiation resulting in a new constitution simply extended the structures and laws of the Federal Republic eastward to cover the territory of the GDR. The unification treaty signed on August 31 designated that the five newly formed federal states of the former GDR would become states of the Federal Republic of Germany.[44] On September 12, the Allied victors officially signed off on unification with the "two plus four" treaty.[45] On October 3, 1990, Germany was formally unified.

At this point, Germany may have been structurally united, but the consequences of unification played out quite differently in the East than in the West. While West Germans bore the brunt of hefty monetary transfers to the East, everyday life in the West remained unchanged. However, the West German political, economic, social, and cultural structures were transferred to the East without compromise.

Professionally, socially, and personally, migration played a key role in the transfer of structures and the transformation of everyday life for East Germans. After unification, East German managers, professionals, and academics were removed from their positions en masse, either forced into early retirement or simply fired. As a result, many were compelled to migrate westward to either take a new position or to retrain for a new profession. Gender was a major factor in the decision to migrate in this period, with more East German woman then men making the choice to go West in order to stay employed. As many of the benefits of working motherhood in the GDR began to disappear with restructuring, many women were either forced out of the employment market or chose to delay childbearing in order to remain employable in either the East or the West.

---

43 Deutscher Bundestag, *Entwurf eines Gesetzes zur Aufhebung des Aufnahmegesetzes* (Bonn: Deutscher Bundestag, 1990).

44 On July 22, 1990, the GDR parliament (*Volkskammer*) voted to territorially reorganize the 14 administrative districts (*Bezirke*) into 5 federal states (*Bundesländer*). Upon unification on October 3, 1990, the 5 states of Brandenburg, Mecklenburg-West Pomerania, Saxony, Saxony-Anhalt, and Thuringia joined the 11 western federal states to form the Federal Republic of Germany.

45 The "two-plus-four" agreement, officially the "Treaty on the Final Settlement with Respect to Germany" was signed on September 12, 1990, by the United States, France, the United Kingdom, and the Soviet Union in Moscow, and renounced the rights of all four allied occupation powers to claim territory in eastern and western Germany, including Berlin.

Many of the East Germans who kept their jobs now found themselves under West German oversight, as thousands of managers and professionals either moved or commuted East in order to restructure the factory, form, or office in the West German manner. When East Germans did not meet the expectations of their West German overseers, they were dismissed using the terms developed in the debates surrounding migration in the period between the fall of the wall and unification. Instead of East and West Germans being two peoples who "belong together and should grow together," a gulf of misunderstanding developed. The emerging conversation over the nature of "Germanness" after unification emphasized the seemingly insurmountable differences between East and West in united Germany, and in effect, pushed them even further apart.

4 Emigration Becomes Internal Migration – A New German Minority and a Crisis of National Identity, 1991–1994

"You need to wear a gas mask over there [in eastern Germany]," claimed an 18-year-old [West German]. "The smoke from the brown coal factories and the Trabis make it hard to breathe . . . everything there is so rundown and muddy, it is almost as if there are no real Germans there at all."[1]

In January 1991, as part of a special issue examining the relationship between East and West Germans in the first year after unification, the West German weekly newsmagazine *Der Spiegel* published an article summarizing the findings of a national opinion poll conducted by the Emnid Institute. The analysis of the responses of 488 West Germans and 1897 East Germans summarized their impressions of the landscape, infrastructure, people, and social structure *da drüben* (over there). This article exposed the extent of differences between the East and the West, a gap that had apparently widened since unification just 3 months prior. While political unification had sought to equalize East and West Germans, for many, unification had merely emphasized the seemingly insurmountable differences after four decades of separation.[2]

Reading the impressions of individual East and West Germans of the "other Germany" side by side, the differences become undeniable. Generally speaking, East Germans held positive impressions of the West. After 40 years of division, when everyday life in the GDR with its chronic shortages in the availability and variety of manufactured goods was commonly defined against an idealized vision of the "golden" West, for the most part, West Germany lived up to eastern expectations. The most common East German response to the survey lauded the superior quality and variety of material goods and the experience of western popular culture, including the presence of "cultured restaurants" and the availability of exotic wares, such as tropical fruits, sleek cars, and colored condoms, all of which had been available only to a select elite with access to foreign currency in the

---

1 Wolfgang Gust, "Kopfschmerz von Geholperter: Wolfgang Gust (Hamburg) über spontane Antworten auf offene Fragen," *Der Spiegel*, January 1, 1991.
2 The opinion poll was administered by the West German opinion research agency, Emnid. Emnid originally distributed over 4000 questionnaires, 2097 to West Germans and 2209 to East Germans. *Der Spiegel* speculated that the low response rate of the West Germans could be attributed to the fact that a greater proportion of East Germans had visited the West after the opening of the German–German border in November 1989.

https://doi.org/10.1515/9783110716221-005

GDR. These positive impressions were balanced with criticism of the plight of the homeless and the poor, embodied by the "misery at the railway stations," and the shock of "seeing poverty in such a land."[3]

In contrast, West German discourse took a decidedly negative tone when reporting first impressions of the former GDR – both the land and its inhabitants.[4] While East German responses tended to refer to specific incidents or examples to illustrate the difference, West Germans tended to characterize the gap between East and West initially as surprising, and somewhat unbridgeable. West German responses overwhelmingly focused on the character of the East German people as a group, and their general failure to reach a constructed threshold of "Germanness." "Those [East Germans] lack any will to achieve," reported a 51-year-old West German man to the survey. A 40-year-old West German woman had an even cruder view of the relationship between the East and the West, exclaiming, "the (ex) GDR-citizen nestles up to the seemingly rich West German as if they are trying to milk a cow.[5]

Rather than focusing on specific details of the East–West interaction, West German critiques stressed the presence of malfunction and disorder in East Germans and East Germany as the focal point for discussions of difference. However, West German responses tended to go beyond mere commentary on the relationship between the East and the West. Rather, these remarks called into question the capacity of the ex-GDR citizens to think, feel, behave, and essentially be, German. As the quotation that opens this chapter describes, West Germans found eastern Germany in such a dilapidated condition after unification that to many, it was not evident that any "real" Germans lived there at all. Picking up on the mounting hostility, many East Germans reported feeling increasingly unwelcome by West Germans, after unification. One East German described the situation: "With the first visit [we were received] with friendliness and curiosity, with the second, only discontent and impoliteness."[6]

The results of the Emnid opinion poll reflects the thickening atmosphere of mistrust and skepticism between East and West Germans, and begins to uncover one of the main barriers faced in the attempt to rework the two antagonistic post-

---

3 Gust, "Kopfschmerz von Geholperter."
4 The opinion poll consisted of two open ended questions distributed to all respondents. One question asked the respondent to report what they found particularly "good" about the East or the West and the second question asked them what they found particularly "bad." According to the article, 20% of West German respondents found "nothing good" about eastern Germany while 25% of East German respondents found "nothing bad" about the West.
5 Gust, "Kopfschmerz von Geholperter."
6 Gust, "Kopfschmerz von Geholperter."

war German identities into the idealistic image of unity projected on November 9, 1989. On October 3, 1990, after 40 years on opposing sides of the Iron Curtain, East and West Germans officially became *ein Volk* (one people). However, the quick transfer of western political and economic structures to the East did not so easily solve the problems that had taken hold in the 11 months between the fall of the Berlin Wall and the formal unification. While politicians and the public alike had seen rapid unification as a remedy to the increasing civil unrest caused by the continuing influx of GDR refugees, political unification halted neither migration nor social conflict. Even after the formal right to benefits and shelter was removed, thousands continued to move from the former GDR into the West, as the eastern economy faltered and unemployment soared.

While the change in status of the GDR refugees from *Übersiedler* (German emigrant) to *Binnenwanderer* (internal migrants) altered the burden of the state itself to provide for their care and integration, it did not alter either the cause or the reality of large-scale East to West migration. As the official status of East German migrants changed, West German attitudes and portrayals of East–West migration and East Germans shifted as well. Immediately before unification, the GDR refugee movement was portrayed as a flood that would soon overload the resources of the many already overcrowded West German cities and towns. After unification, however, East German migrants came to be seen less as an immediate threat to public civil stability than as awkward interlopers, who while technically "German," were condemned to struggle to learn the rhythms and rituals of everyday life in western Germany as a result of the so-called corrupting experience of more than four decades of life in the GDR.

Although the five new eastern states were officially joined to the eleven western states as one nation, in many ways, eastern Germany was perceived as "another country." The negative western perceptions concerning the backwardness of East Germans continued to evolve as more and more West Germans traveled into the eastern states, witnessing firsthand the dilapidated infrastructure and poor air and water quality that had come with decades of a focus on heavy industry in the GDR. The neglected condition of the landscape itself was often attributed to the fault of the East German people – further evidence that the *Ossi* simply did not possess the same professional drive, personal accountability, and moral compass that had emerged as a characteristic of the *Wessi* in the economic miracle and recovery of the postwar West.

Immediately after unification, contact between the two groups was often hierarchical and helped to develop an atmosphere of judgment and mistrust as East German society was reconfigured to fit into the West German model. West German managers and professionals sent into the East as a part of transition or takeover teams often acted as if they were going on a so-called safari and given

Buschgeld (bush money) to compensate for the perceived difficulty in undertaking an assignment *da drüben* (over there). East Germans, who migrated westward, often took either entry level, blue-collar work or took jobs in an established professional field, well below their qualification level. Combined with the stress of adjusting to the West German way of conducting business, *Ossis* were often portrayed as lacking common sense and savvy within the workplace. These experiences and attitudes contributed to a discourse of difference between East and West Germans that painted the former citizens of the GDR as a different people altogether; a pseudo-German group that lacked the defining qualities of a "true" German, namely ambition, cleanliness, orderliness, and common sense.

This chapter will examine the intersection between the redefinition of the German identity and the patterns of internal migration between the eleven "old" western federal states and the five "new" eastern states, from unification in October 1990 to the end of economic privatization, with the closure of the *Treuhandanstalt* in 1994.[7] While the initial economic shock caused by the wholesale restructuring of the "employment society" of the GDR to fit the West German "capitalist risk" model resulted in widespread unemployment in each of the five new eastern states, it was portrayed as a temporary situation that would be remedied once the economy in the East had stabilized. However, the "blossoming landscapes" promised by Helmut Kohl on July 1, 1990, never materialized and the market did not grow as predicted.[8] As it became clear that there would be no "economic miracle" in the East, the combination of this initial displacement of workers and a continued lack of new opportunities fueled a continuing emigration of skilled workers from the East, well into the twenty-first century.

The loss of a high proportion of the most productive portion of the population resulted in a skill gap that further discouraged investment possibilities in the East, long after the initial period of high emigration. In addition, a considerable percentage of westward migrants were both young and female, which according to demographic research, has been a major factor in the decline in the birthrate, especially in rural areas. The effect of the prolonged emigration of productive females over the last two decades has contributed to the perpetuation of structural

---

7 The *Treuhandanstalt* (*Treuhand*) was the government agency responsible for selling public land and assets in order to restructure and privatize more than 8500 state owned enterprises. Initially formed by the GDR *Volkskammer* on July 17, 1990, oversight was transferred to the united German government upon unification.

8 Kohl's famous prediction of "blooming landscapes" in the East as a result of unification first came in a television interview on July 1, 1990. Helmut Kohl, "Blooming Landscapes." German Historical Documents and Images, http://ghdi.ghi-dc.org/sub_document.cfm?document_id=3101. Accessed July 13, 2020.

weakness and demographic decline in the eastern states that has, in turn, pre-vented growth, and made the region unattractive to both domestic and foreign investment.[9]

Patterns of internal migration in the 20 years following unification reflect the long-term economic instability and unemployment in the eastern states caused by rapid and wholesale structural transformation. Rather than a unification of two halves into a new unified whole, western systems were transferred to the new Eastern states. Because the East was simply remade in the image of the West, this transformation made the qualifications of entire sectors of the eastern workforce obsolete and resulted in a large eastward migration of western expertise to fill the gap. While this seemed at first to somewhat compensate for the displacement of East German professionals, many of these western managers did not move to a new house and family to settle in the East. Therefore, this West to East migration did not compensate structurally for the loss in the native eastern productive population.

For the most part, West German managers did little to establish dialogue with their eastern colleagues, resulting in a widening of the social gap between East and West, rather than drawing closer together through the shared experi-ence of work or community. As commuters, most West Germans in the East did not contribute significantly to the locality. When newly established or reorgan-ized enterprises in the East failed after the initial injection of capital (as many did in the middle and late 1990s), many of these West German managers simply re-turned to the West, creating a further professionalization gap in the eastern states.

As can be inferred from the brief summary above, the development of inter-nal migration in the period, between unification in 1990 and the end of the formal structural transfer and privatization process in 1994, had serious consequences for the formation of East and West German stereotypes in united Germany. These stereotypes were primarily defined in relationship to employment and work but were also formulated in terms of age and gender. The emergence of these stereo-types in conjunction with the increase of internal migration trends by both gen-der and age, reflect the economic stagnation in the eastern states that would ultimately discourage investment, which in turn resulted in a resurgence in the westward migration rate after 1997.

---

9 See a 2007 report by the Berlin Institut, which argues that emigration of people who were young, qualified, and female left in large numbers, has caused a population imbalance where men outnumber women by a rate of 25% or more in rural areas. Steffen Kröhnert and Reiner Klingholz, "Not am Mann: Von Helden der Arbeit zur neuen Unterschicht?" (Berlin: Berlin Insti-tut für Bevölkerung und Entwicklung, 2007).

The western-dominated nature of unification influenced both East–West and West–East internal migration patterns. In turn, these migration patterns helped to form the core features of East–West stereotypes. The initial unemployment shock in the East sent many into the West in search of employment. In the initial period, many East Germans sought to work for less than the West German rate. This led to an association of East German workers as *Lohndrücker*, or "scabs," ready to undermine the West German labor market. As East German women lost most of the social support they relied upon in the GDR, a disproportionate number of women found themselves unemployed. This resulted in a higher proportion of women seeking jobs in the West through migration.

The West–East migration stream was also a gendered experience. In the 4 years after unification, migration was dominated by middle aged, primarily male professionals, who came to the East to take over management positions in East German companies. Put in a position of power over East Germans as a group, a dichotomy quickly developed, setting West German and East German males in opposition. In particular, the characterization of West German males as ambitious and East German males as passive/docile, contributed to the attitude that East Germans were "incompatible" with the competitive, performance-driven environment of the East.

After unification, patterns of internal migration became even better defined in terms of both age and gender. There was a much higher rate of labor market participation among women in the GDR (nearly 83% in 1990) than in West Germany, where the participation rate hovered between 56–60%, upon unification.[10] After unification, privatization and structural transfers disproportionately affected female workers, who were more likely than men to become unemployed. In addition, women also lost state support for child rearing and publicly funded childcare, which had both been introduced in the GDR in the 1960s and 1970s to support women's participation in the labor market. Without state support, women of childbearing age began to look westward in order to remain in the labor market or were forced out of the job market altogether. In these terms, East German women were often portrayed as more flexible in terms of their attempts to stay in the labor market, in comparison to East German men. However, they were often also cast as lacking as real women in terms of their seeming lack of maternal impulses. Their perceived unwillingness to mother their own children, in favor of putting them in a crèche, tied the behavior of East German women to the damage done to the East German family structure under socialism. As a western critique, this dysfunction

---

10 Gerd Wagner et al., "An der Schwelle zur Marktwirtschaft: Ergebnisse aus der Baiserhebung des Sozioökonomischen Panels in der DDR im Juni 1990," *Beiträge zur Arbeitsmarkt- und Berufsforschung* 143 (1990), 143.

within the home was tied to a moral breakdown within the East German society, rooted in the experience of life in the GDR, which served to further separate the East Germans from the so-called real Germans.[11]

Male East German migrants were less visible than female migrants, partly because men in higher positions were more likely to be retained (albeit often at a lesser position) or (re) hired through the restructuring and privatization process. However, many men were also forced out of their chosen professions, into temporary retraining or work creation schemes, or out of the labor market altogether. In contrast to both, East German women, whose visible migration portrayed a willingness to adapt to the western model, and judged against the competitive drive for success of West German men, the immobile *Ossi* male became increasingly stereotyped as immobile and complacent – in other terms, as broadly incompatible with the West German way of life.[12]

The formulation of gendered stereotypes, based upon perceived mobility and adaptation after unification, had consequences for the portrayal of West Germans as well. West–East migration, after unification, was overwhelmingly male, and consisted primarily of managers and entrepreneurs who migrated in response to the need for western expertise in the structural transfer and reorganization of eastern Germany. West German women, while typically not migrants themselves, came to be defined, by proxy, against both West German men and East German women. In the reunified Germany, West German women were assumed (and therefore portrayed) as more maternal and more materialistic than East German women. West German men, like those who commuted to the East, were encouraged to leave their families in order to satisfy the consumer desires of the West German women. In turn, East German women were portrayed as more masculine and independent, as well as paradoxically more natural than West German women. The formation of these gendered conceptions of East and West, fundamentally related to gendered migration trends, would prove to have a lasting impact on perceptions of East and West Germans, long after the initial period of structural transfer and redistribution had run its course.

Aside from the effect on population structure, the distinct age structure of both eastward and westward migration, after unification, had further consequences after privatization in 1994. The lack of investment in the East further encour-

---

11 See Hannelore Scholz, "East-West Women's Culture in Transition: Are East German Women the Losers of Unification?" *Journal of Women's History* 5, no. 3 (1994): 109–116. Also see the volume edited by Eva Kolinsky and Hildegard Maria Nickel, *Reinventing Gender: Women in Eastern Germany since Unification* (Portland: Frank Cass, 2003).

12 For more on East German masculinities see the collection edited by Katrin Rohnstock, *Stiefbrüder: Was Ostmänner und Westmänner voneinander denken* (Berlin: Elefanten Press, 1995).

aged the young and the talented to look toward the West for their futures. The continued emigration of this segment of the population influenced a further crystallization of East–West stereotypes. As a new generation came of age in the late 1990s, a cultural generation gap opened up in the East between the young who had largely either gone West temporarily or permanently for training, university or work, and the older generation, who had been socialized in the GDR and remained in the East.

4.1 Internal Migration in United Germany, 1989–1994

Figure 1: "German Federal States after Unification," *Geoatlas* ©Graphi-Ogre 2004. http://www.geoat las.com.medias/maps/countries/germany/ge2z94y/germany_po.pdf.

The formal unification that occurred on October 3, 1990 was preceded by the geopolitical reconfiguration of the former German Democratic Republic, from 14 *Bezirke* (administrative districts) into five new federal states. Upon unification, East and West Berlin were combined into a unified city-state and the five new eastern states joined the eleven western states to form the Federal Republic of Germany.[13]

Geopolitical unification was the final step in the process of reclassifying the movement of GDR refugees (*Übersiedlung*) of the Cold War era into the internal migration (*Binnenwanderung)* of united Germany. As examined in Chapter 3, the legal status and burden of support for GDR refugees was a central issue in the rush toward unification. The widespread halt of monetary support and free shelter for GDR-refugees by state and local governments after the first and only free elections in the GDR was intended to discourage further emigration into the West and to assuage the growing public negativity toward emigrants who had already arrived.[14]

Although numbers declined significantly from the summer/fall of 1989, neither migration from the East nor the problems it created were solved with legal unification. While a mixture of political and economic factors influenced the mass emigration from the GDR during the Cold War, the collapse of the East German economy resulted almost immediately in the creation of a large wage gap and high unemployment between the eastern and western states. These immediate shocks, combined with the long-term process of the deprofessionalization of GDR qualifications and the privatization of native industries, allowed emigration rates to the western states remain significant, after unification. The volume of westward migration is especially significant when comparing the total volume of emigration with the declining population in the East. While the total population in united Germany grew from 79,365,000 in 1990 to 81,422,000 in 1994, the population in the eastern states fell from 16,111,000 to 15,564,000 during the same period.[15]

---

13 As seen in Figure 1, the five eastern states established in 1990 were Brandenburg, Mecklenburg-West Pomerania, Saxony, Saxony-Anhalt, and Thuringia. Unless otherwise noted, Berlin is not included in migration data after 1990. After unification the city-state of Berlin was counted neither politically or statistically as belonging to the eastern or western state grouping. As a result, data on movement between East Berlin and West Berlin are absent, and migration from another federal states into or out of Berlin are not included in tabulations of eastward or westward movement.

14 The elections held in the GDR on March 18, 1990 resulted in an overwhelming victory for the CDU and Party of Democratic Awakening (Alliance Parties). Led by Lothar de Maiziere, the Alliance worked closely with Helmut Kohl's CDU in the West toward speedy unification under Article 23 of the Basic Law. For a more detailed account of the election process, see David Childs, "East Germany's First Free Elections," *Parliamentary Affairs* 43 no. 4 (1990), 482–496.

15 "Bevölkerungsentwicklung," *Statistisches Jahrbuch für der Bundesrepublik Deutschland – 2002* (Wiesbaden: Statistisches Bundesamt, 2001), 76–82.

Even before privatization had begun to dismantle the economic framework of the GDR, East German labor was already in the process of moving westward. Even in areas with relatively high unemployment (and theoretically a large pool of potential employees), it was hard for many West German companies to find workers willing to work, particularly in construction and in the industry. In November 1990, *Der Spiegel* reported that some West German companies were pushing out part-time workers (primarily women) in favor of East Germans who were willing to work full time. In northeastern Bavaria, which traditionally had been the center of the German glass and ceramics industry, a district labor office official reported that many factories were taking advantage of the surplus of the willing labor across the border in the eastern state of Thuringia in order to increase production:

> Many companies run three shifts, but nevertheless cannot handle all their orders. Thus, they have suggested to the part-time women either to work full time, or not at all. Substitutes are at the ready. Every month in the labor office in the district of Coburg, around 2000 Thuringians apply for work. "Hundreds of them," reports labor official Robert Rauth, "offer to work for less than the going rate."[16]

Although there were instances of individuals actively seeking to work under the table on the black market, East German workers in West German manufacture were hired as the result of contracts negotiated directly between West German and (former) GDR firms. For industrial workers from the former VEB Intron in Dömitz, this entailed a daily 140-kilometer (round-trip) commute to the Matsushita factory in the West German town of Luneburg:

> In the early morning, at half past four, the chartered bus stands in the Mecklenburg town of Dömitz to fetch people to go to work. The first shift in the Matsushita factory in Luneburg begins at 6:45 a.m. Around six in the evening the workers arrive home again. Day after day, 50 residents of Dömitz, predominantly women, make the long journey to Luneburg where they mount components for video recorders and television sets. They earn 6.50 DM an hour. In addition, a benefits package of 300 DM a month is included as well. All together, they gross 1400 DM a month for a 60-hour workweek (including the bus journey).[17]

East German labor was easily accessible through an established framework – that of the *Gastarbeiter/Vertragsarbeiter* of the postwar economy. These agreements between former GDR employers and western businesses satisfied a need for full-time industrial labor, while creating a significant profit for East German companies who had lost their original market. Before unification, the GDR manufacturer Intron had manufactured spark plugs exclusively for the East German Trabant

---

16 "Es rumpelt in den Betrieben," *Der Spiegel*, November 26, 1990.
17 "Es rumpelt in den Betrieben."

automobile. With the introduction of both new and used western cars into the eastern market, demand for the Trabant fell off and these parts were no longer needed. Instead of collapsing immediately, the former VEB Intron survived temporarily as a GmbH, selling the labor of its people.[18] While the workers themselves made just DM 6.50 an hour plus benefits, the Japanese company Matsushita transferred DM 23 per head per hour to Intron, resulting in a considerable profit for the company.[19] While former GDR structures were able to temporarily bend to western and global market demands, it was often at the cost of their own solvency, and it weakened the economy in the long run.

Between the opening of the borders and unification, these lending contracts were considered legal if the new companies did not pay less than the rate of pay in the region.[20] As a result, industrial and manufacturing jobs, were for the most part, temporarily safe. However, from unification on October 3, 1990, all companies that rented labor were required to apply for a license in the federal state where they operated. The state would then investigate the company and forward their application to the federal labor office for final approval. This process, however, was highly inefficient. For example, in the western state of Hesse, which shares a border with the eastern state of Thuringia, over 400 companies had applied for the lending license on the eve of unification. However, a backlog had resulted in only 17 applications being forwarded to the federal labor office in Berlin for approval.[21] This would prove fatal for many former VEB entities trying to survive the economic transactions.

Due to this clunky and inefficient system, approvals were slow, allowing illegal labor rental companies to proliferate in the West. Most commonly, these illegal companies operated either as facilitators of contract work (in which contracts were granted to East German companies for a fixed price without specific terms being set for labor) or as retraining schemes in which the workers in question were supposedly completing qualifications, and thereby not subject to federal labor law. The result was an opportunity for abuse, forcing East German workers to choose between working in the West or becoming unemployed. In the case of the employees of the assembly plant IHO, based in Leipzig, the workers were not

---

18 *Volkseigenebetriebe* (VEB) was the official title given to state owned enterprises in the GDR. *Kombinate* were conglomerations of VEBs responsible for fulfilling state dictated plans and quotas. *Gesellschaft mit beschränkter Haftung* (GmbH) is the designation for a limited liability company.

19 "Es rumpelt in den Betrieben."

20 Deutscher Bundestag, "Gesetz zur Regelung der Gewerbsmäßigen Arbeitnehmerüberlassung," *Arbeitnehmerüberlassungsgesetz –AÜG* (BGBl I: 1995).

21 Roland Kirbach, "Illegale Beschäftigung: Mitarbeiter zweiter Klasse," *Die Zeit*, October 19, 1990.

even told they were to work in the West until the day they showed up and were put on a bus to work in a sheet-metal plant in the western state of Saarland:

> The workers of Leipzig industrial assembly company IHO already had a disagreeable labor situation: they were contracted to perform assembly work in a rundown nuclear plant in Greifswald. However, one day in July, instead of working in Greifswald, thirty skilled metal workers found themselves on a 19-hour bus journey to the Saarland city of Homburg to work for the West German company Dillinger Stahlbau GmbH. Their employer had delivered them without further ado to the West, without informing the affected persons beforehand; they were only able to inform their families at home only once they had arrived in Saarland.[22]

The wage gap between East and West that fueled both emigration and the formation of these labor rental schemes did not significantly change after unification. While West Germans shied away from lower paying jobs, the lack of quick wage convergence provided a ready pull factor that satisfied both West German employers seeking full-time labor and East Germans in search of a better wage. As reported in the national newsmagazine *Stern* on September 26, 1991, West German industry and construction still looked to the East to fill a chronic shortage of labor:

> In the Sula Factory, a manufacturer of sweets in Metelen near Münster, ten workplaces are waiting to be filled. Despite an unemployment rate of 7.7 percent in the district of Münster, no one applies or even inquiries about these job that pay from 18 to 20 DM an hour. Company-head Thomas Suwelack: "I have had to recently had to advertise for jobs in eastern Germany."[23]

Part of the appeal of going West to look for work was the continuing wage imbalance between East and West. Although the decision to go with a 1:1 conversion rate was made in order to keep labor in the East, the fluctuations caused by rapidly converting the market created more long-term structural problems than they solved.[24] As argued by Christoph Buechtemann and Jürgen Schupp, "With the decision for a 1:1 conversion rate, which from one day to the other turned a hitherto sheltered, low productivity economy into an open high-wage economy, the makers of the transition treat strongly pressured by prospective East German voters

---

22 Roland Kirbach, "Illegale Beschäftigung: Mitarbeiter zweiter Klasse."
23 Harald Schröder, "Jagd auf die Schmarotzer," *Stern* 40, October 6, 1991.
24 G. Akerlof, et al., "East Germany in from the Cold: The Economic Aftermath of the Currency Union," *Brookings Papers on Economic Activity* 1 (1991): 62–80.

and West German unions alike, set the stage for the subsequent demise of the run-down (by western standards) uncompetitive East German economy."[25]

While the currency union had been proposed in order to bring wages in East Germany up to western standards quickly and to boost the value of individual savings of East German citizens, in actuality, it precipitated the demise of native industry. From July to December 1990, the total net industrial production in the former GDR dropped by almost 50%.[26] This left many factories fully staffed, but without any production orders. Thus, many former GDR companies were faced with a choice of either participating in labor rental schemes in which they profited from the labor of their employees or going out of business altogether.

The dip in production seen after the currency union was especially pronounced in the sector of consumer goods, and precipitated a great deal by the rise in demand for western products by eastern consumers.[27] The sarcastic portraits of East Germans "filling up the parking lots and buying up all the yogurt" contained more than a hint of truth as 40 years of separation from a consumer economy, more than encouraged East German consumers to set aside their old brands to "Test the West."[28]

The chain of revolution in eastern Europe and the breakdown of the Soviet Union, which took away the main East German export market, further exacerbated the drop in home consumer spending for East German goods.[29] The resulting economic vacuum not only encouraged western companies to take advantage of rising East German employment but also created an opportunity for western goods to satisfy the culture of consumer longing that had been cultivated over 40 years of *Westpakete* and indirect access to West German advertising.[30]

---

25 Christoph Buechtemann and Jürgen Schupp, "Repercussions of Unification: Patterns and Trends in the Socio-Economic Transformation of East Germany," *Industrial Relations Journal* 23, no. 2 (1992), 91.

26 Christoph Buechtemann and Jürgen Schupp, 95.

27 Deutsche Institut für Wirtschaftsforschung, "Konsum," *Wochenbericht* 58, no. 47 (1991), 655.

28 Wolfgang Bickerich, "Es ist ein anderes Leben," *Der Spiegel*, September 24, 1990.

29 For a detailed explanation of the external factors for collapse of former GDR industry, see Gareth Dale, *Between State Capitalism and Globalization: The Collapse of the East German Economy* (Berlin: Peter Lang, 2004).

30 During the Cold War, West Germans would often send care packages to their East German relatives filled with Western products including coffee, clothing, and other goods. In addition, except for the area around Dresden, cheekily referred to as the "valley of the clueless," most areas of the GDR could receive West German television and radio signals. For more see Michael Meyen and Uwe Nawratil, "The Viewers: television and everyday life in East Germany," *Historical Journal of Film, Radio and Television* 24, no. 3 (2004), 355–364.

Figure 2: On the day following the fall of the Berlin Wall, students from the West Berlin district of Wedding greet East German visitors with a homemade banner, sporting a popular advertising slogan used to sell *West* brand cigarettes, "Test the West!" Berlin, Bornholmer Straße – Grenzöffnung. November 10, 1989. Source: *Das Bundesarchiv*; photo by Hans Peter Lochmann.

As can be seen in Figure 2, phrases such as "Test the West" indicate that both sides had a shared language of consumerism which helped them to communicate immediately after the border fell.

While both internal and external factors caused an initial shock to the "employment" society of the GDR, the federal role in selling of former state assets and industries further shook up the employment situation in the eastern states. The privatization process was initiated when the first freely elected government of the GDR enacted the *Treuhandgesetz* (Trust Agency Law) on June 17, 1990.[31] Under this law, privatization was supposed to occur as "quickly and comprehensibly as possible." Formal privatization began with monetary union on July 1, 1990. All publicly owned entities then became companies, and those companies were in turn under the ownership of the Treuhand. The Treuhand was entrusted with the responsibility for preparing companies for sale (or if they were not competitive or saleable, liquidating them) and vetting potential buyers. Under the terms of

---

31 "Gesetz zur Privatisierung und Reorganisation des volkseigenen Vermögens (Treuhandgesetz)," *Gesetzblatt* (1990).

the unification treaty, the Treuhand was transferred to the control of the united government of the FRG.[32]

The organization and administration of the Treuhand influenced the development of internal migration in both directions after unification. A lack of desire in the East for eastern goods, out of date equipment, inadequate telecommunications, and outdated infrastructure, combined with the collapse of the largest potential export market in eastern Europe, attracted far fewer investors than had been predicted. This contributed to the massive loss of employment in the eastern states, which hovered at around twice the rate in the West throughout the 1990s. In August 1992, an article in *Die Zeit* reported that the number of jobs in the East German economy had fallen by 64% between 1989 and 1992.[33]

While the attractive force of higher wages and employment in the West fueled westward migration, the "selective selling" of former GDR companies to West German investors encouraged the eastward migration of West German professionals, managers, and entrepreneurs. While the Treuhand focused upon modeling the East German economy on the image of the West, little was being done to encourage the formation of the middle-sized businesses that had been the core of West German postwar economic success.[34] This essential component, the *Mittelstand*, was virtually non-existent in the GDR, whose economic structure had centered around a vertical organization of VEBs, which were further grouped into *Kombinate*, industrial conglomerations, which were responsible for fulfilling state-dictated quotas and industrial goals. As Jörg Roesler argues:

> The Treuhand did not show any readiness during its first year of existence to support the creation of small firms in the east of Germany by selling the Treuhand enterprises to East Germans. Only when the Treuhand learned that the medium and small-scale enterprises created by the deregulation of the former Kombinate would not find a buyer, did it begin to favor management buyouts by the managerial personnel of the employees. The successful MBO group was usually not the former top managers of the old firm, but rather those who had acted in second or third place previously.[35]

32 Upon unification, the *Treuhand* became a federal agency of the Federal Republic overseen by the Minister of Finance. *Vertrag zwischen der Bundesrepublik Deutschland und der Deutschen Demokratischen Republik über die Herstellung der Einheit Deutschlands (Einigungsvertrag)* BGB1. H.S. 897 25 v. 28.9.1990.
33 "Wirtschaftsbericht," *Die Zeit*, August 7, 1992.
34 For more on the role of the *Mittelstand* see Heike Belitz, *Aufbau des Industriellen Mittelstands in den neuen Bundesländern* (Berlin: Dunker & Humblot, 1995).
35 Jörg Roesler, "Privatization in Eastern Germany, Experience with the Treuhand," *Europe-Asia Studies* 46, no. 3 (1994), 510.

This initial bias against allowing or encouraging East German management buy-outs resulted in a dramatic decline in overall employment rates in the eastern states. The large *Kombinate* were, at first, sold off to West German or foreign firms. However, outside investment was not as forthcoming as had been hoped, and many prospective investors were wary of entering into such an unsure situation or were tempted to wait out the market.[36] This not only led to a general increase in the unemployment rate as companies were downsized and reformed, but also resulted in a large scale displacement of older East German managers, facilitated by the relaxation in qualifications for early retirement.[37]

The decline of the East German market far outpaced the rate of deconsolidation and privatization, since both West German and foreign firms were reluctant to commit to immediate investment. By the time the Treuhand started to approve East German management buyouts, the GDR first-tier management typically had already left the company, either bought out in early retirement schemes or pushed toward alternate employment options in the West. For example, before the revolutions of 1989, security specialist Wolfgang Weyer had been the Chief Safety Officer of a large hardware manufacture in Schwerin. After the *Kombinat* was consolidated and Weyer was laid off, he opted to take the entrepreneurial path, ultimately entering into a partnership with a West German engineer who had been searching for a connection to the eastern market. However, although he was hired on account of his regional expertise, this choice took him out of the East German labor market, and entailed a daily commute from his home in the eastern state of Mecklenburg-West Pomerania to his office in the western state of Lower Saxony.[38]

---

36 Jörg Roesler, "Privatization in Eastern Germany, Experience with the Treuhand," 508.

37 Immediately after unification a specific early retirement scheme was implemented for East Germans in order to encourage the withdrawal of older workers from the labor market, giving unemployed East Germans 55 and older from the obligation to search for a job while claiming benefits. Instead of receiving unemployment benefits, early retirees received "pension transition allowances" (*Alterübergangsgeld*). More than 3.5 million East Germans took advantage of this program between 1990 and 1994. Karl-Ulrich Mayer, Martin Diewald and Meike Solga, "Transitions to Post-Communism in East Germany: Work life Mobility of Women and Men between 1989 and 1993," *Acta Sociologica* 42, no. 1 (1999), 38. For more information concerning the strategy behind early retirement schemes targeted toward East Germans see also Barbara Koller, "Ältere – Eine Manoverermase des Arbeitsmarkts? Ältere Arbeitsnehmer in den neuen Bundesländern zwischen Vorruhestand und Erhöhung des Rentenzugangsalters," in *Die Arbeitsmarkt- und Beschäftigungspolitische Herausforderung in Ostdeutschland*, ed. E. Wiedemann, et al. (Nuremburg: Beiträge zur Arbeitsmarkt und Berufsforschung, 1999).

38 Wolfgang Gust, "Machen aus Angst alles," *Der Spiegel*, January 1, 1991.

The simultaneous shrinking of the size of the East German managerial class combined with the growing West German influence resulted in a more permanent displacement of native professionals. Early retirement schemes permanently decreased the number of older managers in the workforce. Economist Heinrich Best estimated that from 1990 to 1995, around two-third of the leadership positions that had existed in the GDR in 1989 had been eliminated. Furthermore, of the total number of managers left in the eastern states in 1995, as many as 25% had lived in West Germany before 1990.[39] The combination of a decrease in mean retirement age for East German managers and the decrease in available management positions due to privatization resulted in a firm western hold on management and decision-making in eastern Germany in the aftermath of unification.

Unemployment and emigration not only affected the industrial and manufacturing sectors in the East. Academic, intellectual, and research positions were also hit hard by the "shock therapy" of system transfer. For example, medial establishments in the East became very short staffed as the exodus of physicians that had been mounting in the late 1980s continued and expanded after the border was removed. A hallmark of the brain drain that spurred the construction of the Berlin Wall in 1961, the number of East German physicians seeking asylum in the West had grown in the mid 1980s, with an estimated 4000 doctors illegally emigrating from 1985 to 1988.[40]

The exodus of healthcare professionals came to a head in 1989 with the exit of approximately 4500 physicians, dentists, and nurses, anxious to take advantage of the opportunities for better wagers, facilities, and working conditions. Dr. Detlef Scholz, for example, an Internist at the Weißensee hospital in East Berlin, emigrated to the West, shortly after the borders were opened, where he quickly found work at a health spa in Bavaria. In an interview published in *Der Spiegel*, Dr. Scholz remarked jokingly that he was merely fulfilling his duty as a physician by following his patients to the West: "When hundreds of thousands of East Germans go to the West, the doctors have to go too. Otherwise, they leave their patients in the lurch."[41]

The loss of medical professionals did not cease once it became clear that the open border between East and West would become permanent. In May 1990, *Der Spiegel* reported that an estimated 13,000 doctors, dentists, and nurses had gone to the West since the beginning of the year. In the Weißensee clinic, Dr. Scholz was certainly not the only member of the hospital staff to leave for the West. In the months before the report published in *Der Spiegel*, the hospital had lost its chief

39 Heinrich Best, "Cadres into Managers: Structural Changes of East German Economic Elites before and after Unification," *Historical Social Research* 30, no. 2 (2005), 18.
40 "Junge, du bist ein Esel," *Der Spiegel*, January 15, 1990.
41 "Junge, du bist ein Esel."

anesthesiologist, a surgeon, another internist, an ear, nose and throat specialist, the director of cardiology, and several nurses. Although there was moderate demand for eastern medical professionals in the West, those who emigrate often took work in non-medical fields, many well below their qualification level. The wage imbalance that had fueled the bulk of the westward migration after the fall of the Berlin Wall did not leave healthcare professionals immune to its pull. As one state official reported, "At the end of the month, licensed physicians hired [in the West] as truck drivers, musicians, and waiters held more in their pockets than their clinical colleagues [back in the GDR]."[42] At Weißensee, even the building superintendent had gone West to work as a medical waste disposal driver, reportedly making more than his boss, the Chief of Medicine, back in East Berlin.[43]

The result was a continuing exodus of healthcare professionals throughout the early 1990s, since the healthcare systems in the eastern states was restructured from a system centered around physicians based in polyclinics and hospitals (who still made home visits), to the western system founded upon the establishment of private practice.[44] The shortage of physicians would persist throughout the 1990s into the 2000s and become an ever more visible problem as the demographic consequences of unification began to take hold. As the younger generation (especially those with the potential to become healthcare professionals) chose to move West or even further abroad for training and employment, the rapidly aging East German population was left with a shortage of doctors. These trends in turn gave rise to an increase in the immigration of eastern European physicians, particularly from Poland and the Czech Republic, in the new millennium.

The restructuring of fields across the board resulted in the shakeup of established professionals, and in many cases, the wholesale replacement of leadership positions in the East with western expertise. On the whole, universities had a difficult process of transition. All institutions of higher education underwent the process of *Abwicklung*, in which existing departments were dismantled and then reconstructed in western terms. Under the terms of *Abwicklung*, which had been set out under article 13 of the unification treaty, all positions had to be evaluated and if kept, reposted for open application. Only those academics who could prove themselves to be both "politically uncompromised" as well as academically quali-

---

42 "Zurückgekommen ist keiner," *Der Spiegel*, June 4, 1990.
43 "Junge, du bist ein Esel."
44 While as of December 3, 1989 only two percent of physicians worked out of private practice in the GDR, by December 31, 1994, 97% were self-employed. For more on the reorganization of the East German medical system after unification see Martina Merten and Thomas Gerst, "Vom Westen viel Neues," *Deutsches Ärzteblatt*, no. 10 (2006), 451–454.

fied were eligible for reappointment.[45] As a result, they were put in direct competition with much better funded western scholars.

This process was overseen by the *Wissenschaftsrat* (Academic Council) and resulted in the eventual wholesale dissolution of the Research Academies, which had employed more than 24,000 academics and researchers in 60 different institutions. In addition, it resulted in the reduction of academic posts in universities and colleges by an estimate of 20,000, of which 5000 were professors.[46]

This rule affected various disciplines differently. While those in the hard sciences (engineering, mathematics, and natural sciences) came out of the situation relatively politically untainted, those in history, law, and economics were the most ideologically suspect, and consequently, many entire departments were dismissed. According to Anke Burkhardt and Dorit Scherer, approximately 85% of the 8000 full-time academic positions lost in the *Abwicklung* were in the humanities and social sciences.[47] When the Berlin City Council decided in 1991 to dissolve three departments and two institutes at the Humboldt University in Berlin, it was the ideologically charged areas of law, economics, education, history, and philosophy that were cut without recourse.[48]

The process of *Abwicklung* consisted of a wholesale restructuring of higher education and a reduction in the total academic positions by one-third. When reconstituting departments, especially in the humanities and social sciences, often, either a junior colleague or a West German was chosen over a senior East German scholar to fill the position. By 1997, the balance of West German to East German professors in higher education was quite striking – an estimated 45% of all professors appointed to positions in eastern universities and colleges of applied sciences (*Fachhochschulen*) hailed from the West.[49]

---

45 Anne Brocklehurst, "Brain Drain Troubles East's Universities," *New York Times*, October 8th, 1992. See also the *Wissenschaftsrat* 6 (7:90:21) cited in Rosalind M. O. Pritchard, *Reconstructing Education: East German Schools and Universities after Unification* (Berlin: Berghahn Books, 1999), 168.

46 According to Rosalind Pritchard, many of the professors who lost their original positions were rehired by Universities of Applied Sciences (*Fachhochschulen*). Most of the permanent reductions affected mid-level academics who had not yet completed postdoctoral theses and not employed as full professors. Rosalind M.O. Prichard, "Was East German Education a Victim of West German 'Colonisation' after Unification?" *Compare* 32, no. 1 (2002), 53.

47 Anke Burkhardt and Dorit Scherer, "Wissenschaftliches Personal und Wissenschaftlicher Nachwuchs," in *Hochschulen in den neuen Ländern der Bundesrepublik Deutschland*, ed. Gertraude Buck-Bechler et al. (Weinheim: Deutscher Studien Verlag, 1997, 337.

48 Dieter E. Zimmer, "Abwicklung als kurzer Prozess: Die Berliner Humboldt-Universität als Beispiel," *Die Zeit*, February 1, 1991.

49 Burkhardt and Scherer, "Wissenschaftliches Personal und Wissenschaftlicher Nachwuchs," 333.

Although, there are no official figures indicating how many of these West German professors moved with their families to the East and how many commuted, anecdotal evidence suggests that quite a large percentage of western professors chose to maintain their permanent residence in the West. In 1998, an article in *Die Zeit* stated that out of all the positions in the Department of Law at Viadina University located in the eastern city of Frankfurt-Oder on the Polish border, all 14 professors hailed from the West. Furthermore, six of these 14 professors commuted weekly between Frankfurt-Oder and the West. Referred to as *"Di-Mi-Do-Professoren"* (Tuesday-Wednesday-Thursday professors), these commuters were seen as existing outside of the framework of eastern society as members of the so-called *Wossi-Bürgertum.*[50] According to Jürgen Bolten, a western professor and co-founder of the *Institut für Interkulturelle Wirtschaftskommunikation* at the University of Jena, the younger the new faculty member, the more likely they are to commute: "[Bolton] has been with this Institute since it was founded [shortly after unification] and has been exclusively surrounded by colleagues from the West. According to his observations over this time, only those faculty members over the age of 50 move [to Jena] as permanent residents, while the younger [professors] frequently commute."[51]

The prominence of young West German commuter professors corroborated fears that East German universities were being made into a dumping ground for professors who had not yet made it in the West. Ingo Koloa, a western professor of Romance Studies at the Technical University in Dresden, explained the situation in his department, in which three out of five professors make the weekly commute from the West to the East: "Four out of five positions are at the C3 [junior] level. As a result, many professors spend their energy looking for C4 [senior] positions in the western market."[52] Despite the impression that East German higher education was colonized by the West, it was mainly an emotional reaction to the necessary process of Abwicklung; the continuing dominance of commuter professors into the late 1990s supports the claim that many western academics saw positions at East German universities as a so-called way-station in their career rather than the endpoint. The trend toward professional commuting would increase well into the new millennium, long after the rate and intensity of West to East migration would drop off.

---

50 The term *Wossi-Bürgertum* refers to the establishment of a West German professional class transplanted to the East who were characterized as taking financial advantage of a job opportunity in the East without becoming invested enough to participate in the everyday life of the community. This term carries different connotations than the label of *Besser-Wessi*, which implies a more stereotypically arrogant and not necessarily mobile West German.

51 Klaus-Peter Schmidt, "Sie lehren im Osten und Leben im Westen. Für viele Hochschullehrer sind die neuen Bundesländer nur eine Durchgangsstation," *Die Zeit*, January 23, 1998.

52 Klaus-Peter Schmidt, "Sie lehren im Osten und Leben im Westen."

Although both eastward and westward migration streams developed as a result of different motivations, and with their own gender and age characteristics, some useful generalizations can be inferred. First of all, the initial shock of the change in economic structure sent the East German labor market into a tailspin. This resulted in immediately high unemployment for East Germans while simultaneously creating a need for West German expertise in the newly structured market economy. The most salient characteristic of this economic imbalance was the lack of wage convergence between the East and the West. This extreme wage imbalance first resulted in the success of a labor rental economy in which former GDR companies utilized the capital of their work force in order to survive the transition. As seen in Graph 3, while the initial narrowing of the wage imbalance between East and West served to reduce the initially high levels of East to West migration, convergence slowed considerably after 1992.[53]

Internal Migration in United Germany, 1991-1994

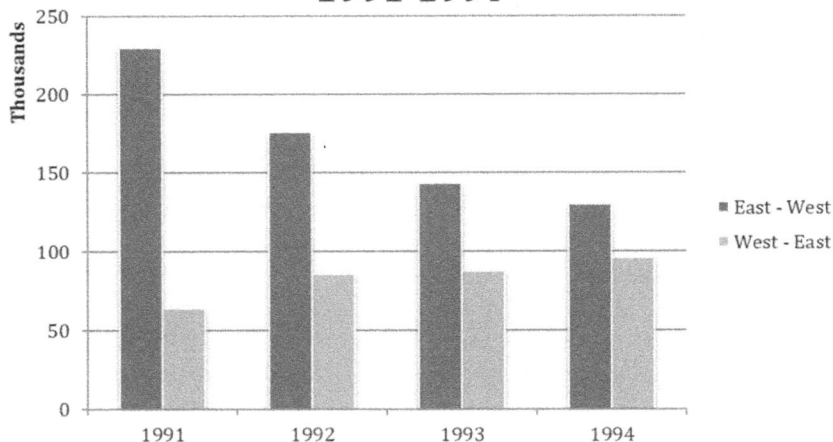

Graph 3: Internal Migration in United Germany, 1991–1994. *Statistisches Bundesamt.* "Genesis Data Set – Binnenwanderung" (1989–1994).

---

53 For more on trends in wage convergence, see Deressin, "Internal Migration in West Germany and Implications for East-West Salary Convergence," and Jennifer Hunt, "The Transition in East Germany: When Is a Ten-Point Fall in the Gender Wage Gap Bad News?" *Journal of Labor Economics* 20, no. 1 (2002), 148–169.

The persistence of this wage imbalance coupled with the reduction in the East German labor force capacity as a whole resulted in unemployment rates that were both higher and more enduring than previously expected. In addition, wage and employment differences continued to support the maintenance of a high east to west migration rate even as privatization wound down.

The effects of emigration were most immediately felt in the larger urban areas in the East such as in Leipzig and Dresden, where a combination of factors led to the emigration of younger professionals and their families. Leipzig, which had been a central location of protest and dissent in the 1980s, had already been losing population before the fall of the Wall due to the deportation of dissidents to the West, as well as a reduction in the general population who were redistributed to other areas of the GDR in response to a chronic housing shortage within the city.[54] This trend continued through the revolution of 1989/1990. Out of a population of 535,000 in 1989, 15,800 people left Leipzig for the West; in 1990, the number was over 17,000.[55]

From 1990 to 1994, Leipzig continued to lose young professionals to the West. The housing shortage that had been endemic in Leipzig since the early 1980s was a key factor in the loss of population from the city center.[56] Although Leipzig continued to lose population, many apartment buildings were so dilapidated that they were not fit to serve as dwellings once they were vacated. In 1991, 10,000 households were waiting to be reassigned to new housing, but only 4000 new apartments could be found. In 1992, only a quarter of the 10,000 housing applications could be filled.[57] In the GDR, when options for migration were more limited, young couples or single mothers often lived in together with parents or other family members. In the more open atmosphere of unified Germany, they simply moved out of the city to East Berlin or even farther afield to the West.

As migration from Leipzig persisted, the proportion of young people in the total population declined, with the largest decrease seen in those aged 20 to 30.[58] The loss of this young cohort can be attributed both to the chronic housing shortage as well as to the lack of educational and training opportunities in the East,

---

54 Eva Kolinsky, "Introduction," in *Between Hope and Fear: Everyday Life in Post-Unification East Germany*, ed. Eva Kolinsky (Keele: Keele University Press, 1995), 17.

55 "Bevölkerung/Wanderung, 1989–1990." *Stadt Leipzig Amt für Statistik und Wahlen* (August 12, 2006).

56 Kai-Uwe Arnold, *Leipzig, 1954–1979: Trümmer, Abriss, Neuaufbau* (Leipzig: Strom & Strom, 2004), 54–62.

57 Mathias Orbeck, "Einwohnerzahlen in Leipzig sind wieder gesunken," *Leipziger Volkszeitung*, February 16, 1994.

58 Stadt Leipzig, *Statistisches Jahrbuch – 1993* (Leipzig: Stadt Leipzig, 1994), 145–149.

after unification. In June 1991, there were only 1400 positions for 2700 young people seeking apprenticeships in Leipzig.[59] Although there seemed to be a surplus of positions by 1994, this can be attributed not to the creation of new employment and training opportunities but rather to the effects of emigration: there were simply not as many young people applying for positions in Leipzig.

As housing stock, employment, educational, and training opportunities were received in the eastern cities, young East Germans from rural areas migrated to urban areas. The emigration of the young to urban areas further exacerbated the low birth rates and the "aging" and deskilling of the eastern rural hinterlands. This demographic phenomenon reflects and supports the further economic stagnation and high unemployment figures that have persisted in the eastern states well into the twenty-first century.

Although all areas of western Germany experienced some degree of immigration from the East in the immediate period after unification, the states of Bavaria and Baden-Wurttemberg attracted the largest number of migrants from the former GDR.[60] This was due to the relatively close proximity of the border (for the Bavarian case, in particular), as well as to the increased demand put on the West German manufacturing and automobile industries under the influence of the temporary "unification boom" caused by the demand for western products in the East.[61] Unlike major West German cities such as Hamburg, Bremen and Cologne, all of which had established communities of foreign-born migrants, the migration of East Germans to smaller urban areas with little to no social network entailed a major adjustment for both the migrant and the receiving community alike.

---

59 Ute Starke, *Jugend in Leipzig vor und nach der Wende* (Leipzig: Universität Leipzig Gesellschaft für Jugend- und Sozialforschung, 1992), 156.

60 Steffen Maretzke and Ferdinand-Otto Möller, "Wanderungsverflechtungen zwischen den neuen und alten Bundesländern im Jahre 1991," *Geographische Rundschau* 45, no. 3 (1993), 192.

61 West German GDP grew at a rate of 4.6% in 1990 while employment rose from 28 million to 28.7 million, as the unemployment rate sank to 7.2%. Notably, the number of registered unemployed in western Germany only declined by about 300,000, indicating that at least half of the new jobs in western Germany were taken by persons who had moved or were commuting from eastern Germany. The dramatic improvement in the western German figures resulted from the opening in eastern Germany of a new market of 16 million and the simultaneous availability of many new workers. Many east Germans did not want the shoddy good produced at home, preferring western consumer products and food. Moreover, many easterners were coming West to find work. By the end of 1990 as many as 250,000 were commuting to work in the West, and that number is estimated to have grown to 350,000 or even 400,000 by the middle of 1991. For more see Frank Heiland, "Trends in East-West German migration from 1989 to 2002," *Demographic Research* 11 (2004), 173–194.

The border town of Hof in northern Bavaria, which had spent 40 years on the economic margins of the FRG, quickly became uneasy with its position at the center of the new Germany, created after unification. From January to November 1990, over 15,000 East Germans from Saxony and Thuringia registered at the Hof labor office.[62] The realization that unification had not solved the problem of East–West migration was met with alarm. A November 1990 article in *Der Spiegel* characterized the potential pool of migrants from the East as merely the tip of the iceberg: "Many in the area [surrounding Hof] fear that [the amount of migration so far] is merely the vanguard of an incoming invasion. A gigantic reserve army of job-seekers stands ready in eastern Germany."[63] However, in contrast to the foreign labor migration of the postwar economic miracle, the post-unification migration of East Germans to the West was unsolicited and not legally subject to regulation. As German citizens, East Germans who moved West to search for work could not simply be sent back home.

This invasion of West German space elicited a visceral reaction, perceptible in descriptions of everyday interactions between East and West Germans. In border towns such as Hof, which experienced both permanent official migration into the city as well as commuter migration from nearby border towns, the friction between East and West quickly overrode the previous atmosphere of friendship and solidarity that accompanied the arrival of the first migrants in August of 1989. On the first anniversary of the fall of the Wall, Silvia Matthes, who migrated with her husband form the East via Prague in November 1989, gave a speech as a part of an official ceremony at the Hof City Hall in which she reminisced about the "warmth and affection" with which she and her husband were initially received. However, in a later interview with *Der Spiegel*, her public speech merely recollected the welcoming atmosphere that had since become mere memory:

> Later [after the ceremony], in a small circle of people, Matthes described the hatred that she has experienced for several weeks on the streets of Hof: "Now we barely dare to leave the house . . . The people who were so nice first are suddenly only revolted by our presence." The warmth of former days, the euphoria of the first weeks after the border opening is in Hof is now a long time past; now hatred and aggression rules. Matthes has worked as a cleaning woman since her arrival in Hof from Prague. However, even her clients have changed their attitudes toward her. "I am no longer happy to live here," she says bitterly. "I think that now the people in the West are showing their true face."[64]

---

62 "Es rumpelt in den Betrieben."
63 "Es rumpelt in den Betrieben."
64 Stephan Lebert, "Bleibt, wo ihr seid," *Der Spiegel*, December 12, 1990.

In Hof, aggression was not only directed toward permanent migrants, but also toward East German commuters and visitors alike. Just 13 months after the collapse of the border, the center-left daily paper *Süddeutsche Zeitung* reported that there was so much hostility and distance between the inhabitants of Hof and its former GDR "sister city" of Plauen (just 30 km away in the eastern state of Saxony) that it "seems as if there has been another wire fence erected" between them.[65] As friction between East and West grew in Hof, inhabitants of Plauen were often targeted as the source of overcrowded stores, excessive traffic, and black marketeering. One (anonymous) group went so far as to blanket the streets of Plauen with flyers that simply read, "*Scheiß Sachsen, bleibt wo ihr seid! Alle Hofer.*" ("Shitty Saxons, stay where you are." Signed, "All citizens of Hof.")[66]

> The mood In Hof, complains [SPD Bundestag representative] Döhla, "is quite explosive." The citizens have had simply enough of the "mad traffic," enough of the eternally congested shops. "We must now be careful to avoid pouring even more oil onto the fire." Regularly, visitors from the new neighbor state complain about the willful damage to their cars. One resident of Plauen, who had a kilo of sugar poured in the gas tank of his car asked whether it would be possible to get a license plate from Hof, "so that nobody can recognize me."[67]

A main point of contention of the citizens of Hof toward East German commuters was that they were taking advantage of West German hospitality to gain an unfair and unearned advantage. One common complaint was that unemployed (and benefit collecting) workers were taking advantage of their free time to drive into Hof in order to work illegally, undercutting pay rates, undermining native industry, and keeping native unemployment high. Hof's representative to the German Trade Federation (DGB), Sapp Schummi, warned of the phenomenon of East Germans collecting unemployment benefits, yet using their free time during the week to commute to Plauen to earn black market DM. The situation created so much tension, Schummi warned, that it had the potential to even spark a "sort of a civil war."[68] City official Peter Tschoepe was reluctant to even announce when the concert hall (which just 1 year prior had held "thousands of refugees") had a sold out performance because it would "only create [more] bad blood." – "If I make an announcement], the people of Hof will only say, 'Yes, it is only [sold out] because [the tickets] were bought by those people from other there [Plauen] – they have enough money.'" This is not an exaggeration, stresses Tschoepe. "You

---

65 "Wieder vereint," *Süddeutsche Zeitung*, November 21, 1990.
66 Döhla über Ossi-Haß," *Frankenpost*, October 26, 1990.
67 Döhla über Ossi-Haß."
68 Lebert, "Bleibt, wo ihr seid."

should hear the tirades that are unleashed every time someone sees a Mercedes from 'over there' driving down one of our streets."[69]

While campaigning against the CDU (which had pushed for early and quick unification), SPD candidates in Hof did not hold back from utilizing the increase in conflict involving East Germans in the city. As reported in *Der Spiegel*,

> Even Hans Büchler, the SPD top candidate from Hof to the Bundestag, goes there [utilizes the conflict between East and West]. In an election speech to an audience of 20 in a somber restaurant, he speaks freely about "how badly those from the GDR handle money." The SPD man is also not embarrassed to remark that every Hofer with a relative over there is poor, because "the East Germans are so greedy, that after the third visit one is broke."[70]

While the atmosphere of conflict between East and West was certainly more intense in the border regions such as Hof/Plauen, the same general themes can be traced in rhetoric concerning East–West migration and difference throughout Germany in the period immediately following unification. The change in life in the West brought on by the migration of East Germans was frequently explained in terms of deficit – or how East Germans as a people did not live up to the West German ideal. Central to these characterizations was the idea that East Germans were expecting more than they deserved; in terms of relationships with relatives, the use of West German space, unfair access to employment via a willingness to work for less than the West German wage, and access to benefits from the state. These characterizations frequently relied upon gender for definition. Gendered characterizations of migrants and migration helped views of both East and West German identities in the period after unification.

4.2 Migration and Gendered Identities in United Germany, 1989–1994

Historically, human migration is often treated as if its significance can only be found in its net effect on population patterns. In other words, the aggregate effect of migration is recorded without concern for the characteristics of its individual migration streams. While it is true that an examination of net internal migration between East and West Germany reveals much about the nature of the relationship between the eastern and western regions after unification (namely, a net population loss in the East caused by a long period of economic stagnation), a view of net migration statistics does not reveal the full impact of German mobil-

---

69 Lebert, "Bleibt, wo ihr seid."
70 Lebert, "Bleibt, wo ihr seid."

ity. When examining the East to West and West to East movements independently, a much more nuanced picture of mobility in the years after unification begins to emerge. Above all, it is the shift in the gender balance of migration streams that quickly comes to attention. When these streams are further analyzed according to age group, these gender distinctions become even better defined.

The following sections investigate the gendered nature of internal migration in the first 5 years after German unification. While migration has been acknowledged as important in its reflection of economic imbalance between the eastern and western regions of united Germany, the social and cultural consequences of the gendered nature of German mobility require more exploration. When examining gendered trends in migration in juxtaposition with the evolution of conceptions of East/West difference, it becomes evident that contact through migration was a vital factor in the formulation and proliferation of these gendered debates in the aftermath of German unification.

East-West Migration by Gender, 1989-1994

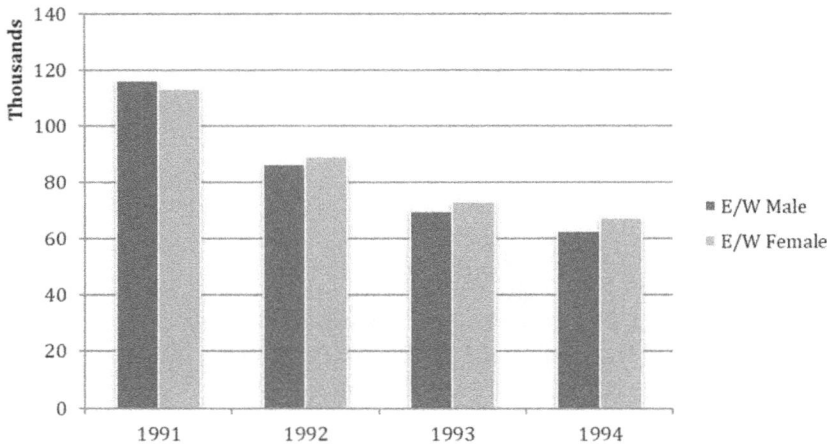

Graph 4: "East-West Migration by Gender, 1989–1994." *Statistisches Bundesamt.* "Genesis Data Set – Binnenwanderung" (1989–1994).

As shown in Graph 4, there was a dramatic shift in the gender balance of East–West migration from 1989 to 1994. While migrants from 1989 and 1990 were predominately male, by 1994 there had been a significant shift that put female migrants in the majority. When data are further separated by age, it becomes evident that the biggest shift toward the feminization of East–West migration took place among women aged 18 to 25. While males made up the majority of migrants in the two older productive cohorts (25–30 and 30–50), the proportion of female migrants in the university- and apprenticeship-age cohort (19–25) steadily increased as privatization took hold (graph 5).

East to West Migration (18-25) by Gender, 1991 - 1994

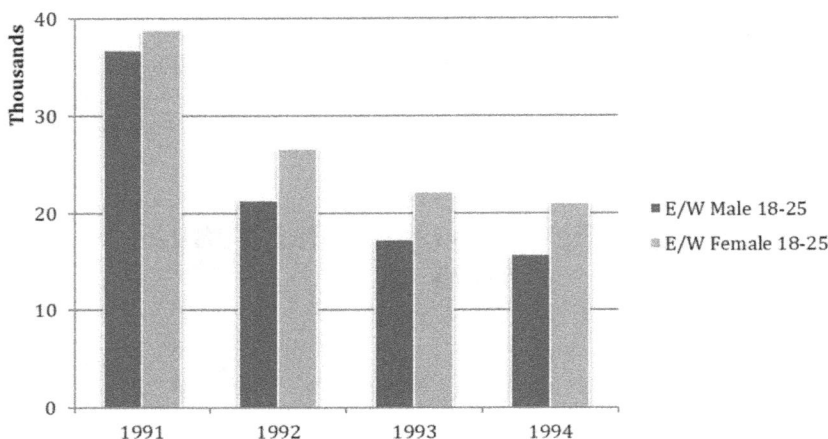

Graph 5: "East-West Migration (18–25) by Gender, 1991–1994." *Statistisches Bundesamt.* "Binnenwanderung," *VII B. Wanderungstatistik* (Wiesbaden: Statistisches Bundesamt, 2005).

The significant presence of women going westward is indicative of the multi-faceted transformation from the socialist "employment" society of the GDR to the "capitalist risk" model of the Federal Republic. Women who had been educated in the GDR or had recently entered the workforce tended to be more willing to take risks (here, to migrate), in order to stay relevant through western education or by establishing a presence in the western work force. As will be explored below, not only did the transfer of West German models entail the shake-up of political, economic, social, and cultural structures in the eastern states, but it also involved a rethinking of the significance of gender, particularly the role of women as workers, in unified Germany.

East to West Migration (25-30) by Gender, 1991-1994

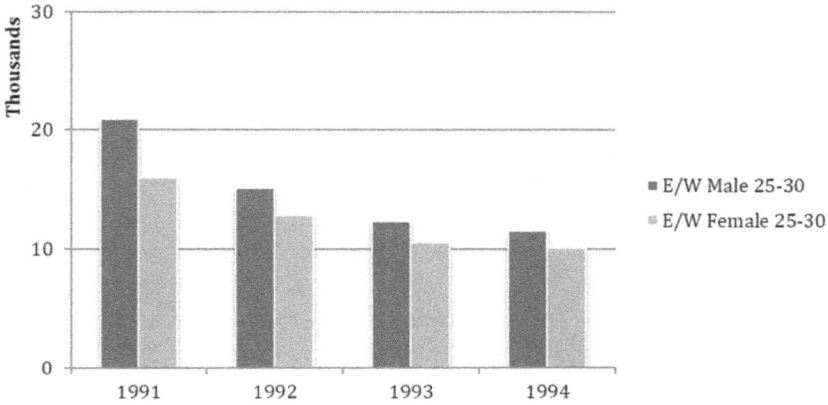

Graph 6: "East-West Migration (25–30) by Gender, 1991–1994." *Statistisches Bundesamt.* "Binnenwanderung," *VII B. Wanderungstatistik* (Wiesbaden: Statistisches Bundesamt, 2005).

East-West Migration (30-50) by Gender, 1991-1994

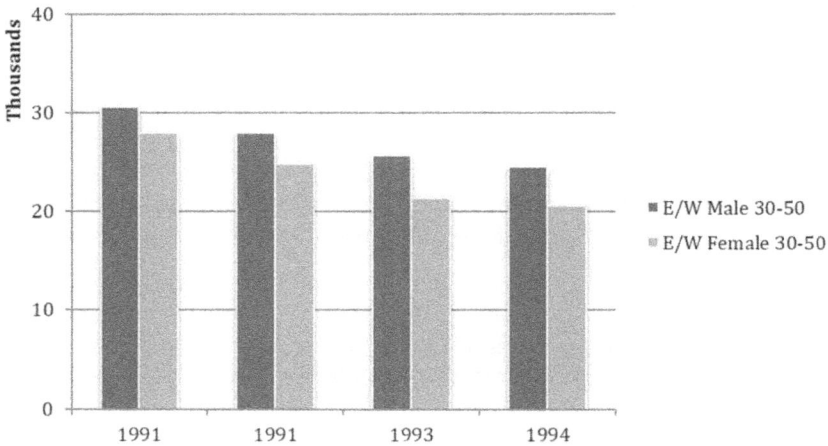

Graph 7: "East-West Migration (30–50) by Gender, 1991–1994." *Statistisches Bundesamt.* "Binnenwanderung," *VII B. Wanderungstatistik* (Wiesbaden: Statistisches Bundesamt, 2005).

4.2.1 The Right to Work in the GDR: Women in a Full Employment Society

The SED leadership realized early after the establishment of the GDR in 1949 that it was necessary to utilize women as full-time workers in order to establish a strong industrial economic workforce. In the first constitution of the GDR, drafted in 1949, a number of measures were enacted with the goal of fully integrating women into the workforce.[71] These measures included the policy of equal pay for equal work (a provision most struggled for in the postwar years in the West), protection against unfair dismissal based on sex, up to 40 days paid leave for children's sickness, and paid leave for additional training and education.

The first phase of the *Frauenförderpläne* (Women's Development Program), was established in the early 1950s and set forth provisions for employers to develop programs specifically to give access to further training and education to women. The fruits of these policies were seen rather quickly and by the early 1960s, the large educational and qualification gap that had existed between men and women in the immediate postwar era had begun to close.[72]

As had been widely the case in the Cold War socialist societies, although the official doctrine of the GDR was that of equality between men and women, this equality was not considered in terms of gender hierarchy and division of household work. Although the doctrine of "equal pay for equal work" was established with the first GDR constitution in 1949, in 1989, women still made proportionally less than men in similar positions. Although there was a much less gap than between West German men and women, women were still heavily overrepresented in traditionally "female" occupations in the GDR. In addition, few females held positions of power and authority either in the workplace or in government.[73]

The implementation of *Frauenpolitik* in the 1960s and 1970s introduced several measures that sought to further encourage women to become working mothers and led to a large proportion of females in active employment. However, policies that gave all responsibilities to the female partner, such as a year of maternity leave (*Mutter/Babyjahr*), the establishment of a shorter workweek for

---

71 Volkskammer der Deutsche Demokratische Republik, *Die Verfassung des Deutsche Demokratische Republik* (1949). For more on women's rights in postwar West Germany see Robert G. Moeller, "Protecting Mother's Work: From Production to Reproduction in Postwar West Germany," *Journal of Social History* 22, no. 3 (1989), 413–437.

72 Sabine Schenk, "Employment Opportunities and Labor Market Exclusion: Towards a New Pattern of Gender Stratification?" In *Reinventing Gender: Women in Eastern Germany since Unification*, ed. Eva Kolinsky and Hildegard Maria Nickel (London: Frank Cass, 2003), 56–60.

73 Myra Marx Ferree, "The Rise and Fall of 'Mommy Politics,' Feminism and Unification in (East) Germany," *Feminist Studies* 19, no. 1 (1993), 92.

working mothers, and one household day each month, created a seeming mandate from the state, which removed the male/partner/father from any responsibility for the home or the children.[74] Because the social support surrounding the care of dependent children was considered to be largely a marriage between women and the state's social policy, in many cases, the state effectively filed the role of the father, allowing single mothers to work full time and care for children without the necessity of paternal support.

To summarize, the SED saw the compatibility of full-time female employment and motherhood as vital to the success of the socialist project. Although formal legislation provided a right to equal status and equal pay under the law to both women and men, labor market segregation still existed in the East, although to a lesser extent than in West Germany. Furthermore, although the state provided additional support for working mothers, these measures often served to increase the so-called double burden felt by single and married mothers alike, since fathers could take less responsibility for childcare and housework.[75]

In spite of the inequalities faced by women within the economic and social structures in the GDR, the right to work became a central part of many East German women's identities. As unification resulted in the transformation of the East German employment society, the rate at which risk was assumed was markedly as seen in Graphs 6 and 7 in the high numbers of participation in the between 1991 and 1994 for both the 18–25 and 25–30 female cohorts. As the West German attitudes toward working motherhood were transferred to the East, women were also at greater risk of unemployment as eastern industry was privatized. This increased risk, however, did not decrease the desire of many East German women to remain in full-time employment. As a result, many East German women were willing to alter their personal plans for having a family after unification and were increasingly willing to move West in order to remain active in the labor force.

4.2.2 East German Men and Women After Unification

In the first decade after the *Wende*, East German women were often referred to as the "losers" of unification. They lost not only because the state institutions sup-

---

74 Marina A. Adler and April Brayfield, "East-West Differences in Attitudes about Employment and Family in Germany," *The Sociological Quarterly* 37, no. 2 (1996), 253–257.

75 For more on the double burden of career and home see Ferree, "The Rise and Fall of 'Mommy Politics,'" as well as Annette Sørensen and Heike Trappe, "The Persistence of Gender Inequality in Earnings in the German Democratic Republic," *American Sociological Review* 60, no. 3 (1995), 398–406.

porting working motherhood were dismantled in the processes of unification, but also because, as a group, they were seen as unemployable due to the limits motherhood put on their availability. To reconfigure East German social structures to match West German norms, East German women were typically quite literally the first to get fired and the last to get hired. Constructed in opposition to West German women, who typically chose early between family and professional life, the East German woman and her (now historic) structurally facilitated ability to balance both career and children with or without a male partner, was now perceived as being unable to exist alongside West German gender norms.

The period between the opening of the borders and the signing of the unification treaty was a period of profound hope for many sectors of German society. Many women's right groups in both East and West Germany hoped to not only preserve, but to even advance women's rights. However, West German and East German feminists did not necessarily subscribe to the same brand of feminism. The inability of these two groups to work together as a lobby led to some minimal gains in terms of the western agenda (such as the limited legalization of abortion), but on the whole, the concerns raised by East German women regarding working motherhood were largely ignored. Social services supporting working motherhood were shut down, severely limiting the ability of many East German women to remain in full-time employment.

Unsurprisingly, reproduction has been at the center of debates concerning East German women, and their ability to sustain careers within the western system. The perception of the inherent neediness of East German working *Muttis* (Mommies) has caused some East German women to put off childbearing indefinitely in order to establish a career. In the early 1990s, there were even reports of East German women who underwent voluntary sterilization in order to become employable in the West.[76]

The image of the mobile East German women helped to construct East German men as immobile. Although some West German women did move east as professionals or as a part of family migration, the predominance of West German men in eastward professional migration reinforced the image of East German men as non-agents. Most of the West–East migration in the post-unification era was driven by the need for western expertise. As a result, West German professionals, mostly male from 30 to 50 years of age, migrated east in order to fill management and bureaucratic positions as GDR structures were reshaped according to West German specifications.

---

76 See Irene Dölling, Daphne Hahn and Sylka Scholtz, "Birth Strike in the New Federal States: Is Sterilization an Act of Resistance?" in *Reproducing Gender: Politics, Publics and Everyday Life after Socialism*, ed. S. Gal and G. Klingman (Princeton: Princeton University Press, 2000), 135.

West-East Migration by Gender, 1989-1994

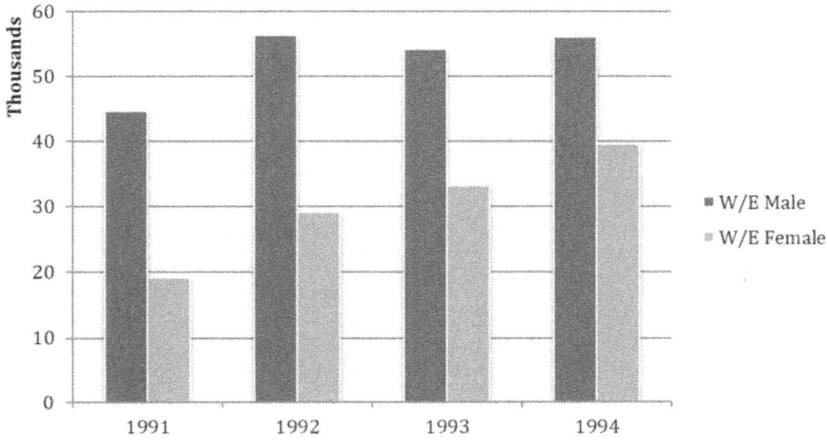

Graph 8: "West-East Migration by Gender, 1989–1994," *Statistisches Bundesamt.* "Genesis Data Set – Binnenwanderung," (1989–1994).

West-East Migration (18-25) by Gender, 1991-1994

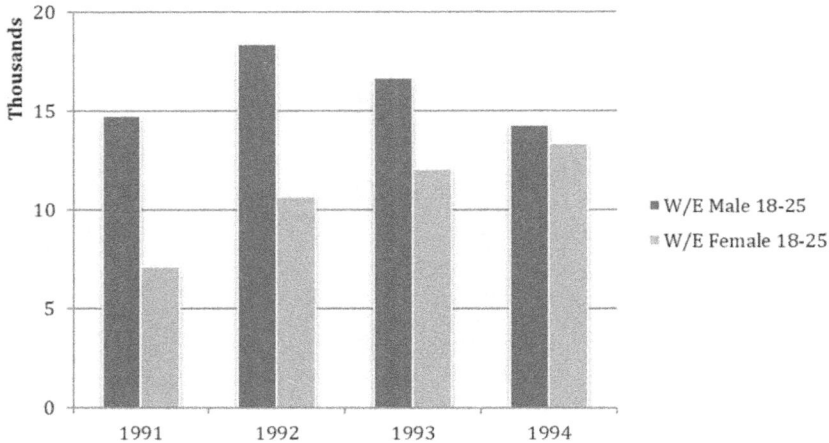

Graph 9: "West-East Migration (18–25) by Gender, 1991–1994." *Statistisches Bundesamt.* "Binnenwanderung," *VII B. Wanderungstatistik* (Wiesbaden: Statistisches Bundesamt, 2005).

West-East Migration (25-30) by Gender, 1991-1994

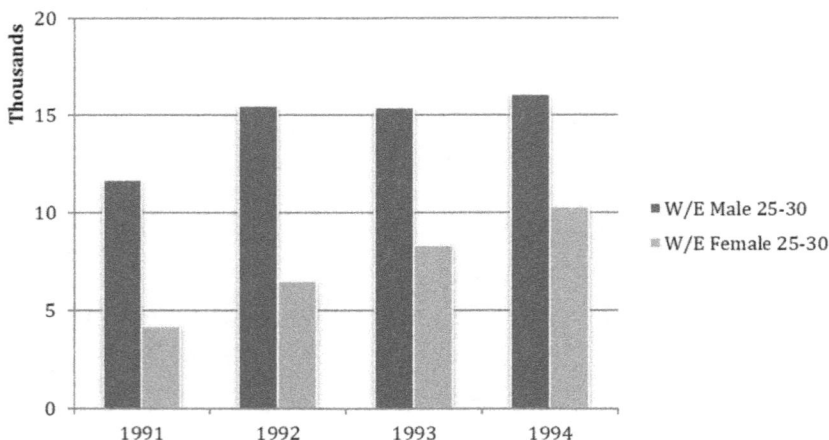

Graph 10: "West-East Migration (25–30) by Gender, 1991–1994." *Statistisches Bundesamt.* "Binnenwanderung," *VII B. Wanderungstatistik* (Wiesbaden: Statistisches Bundesamt, 2005).

West-East Migration (30-50) by Gender, 1991-1994

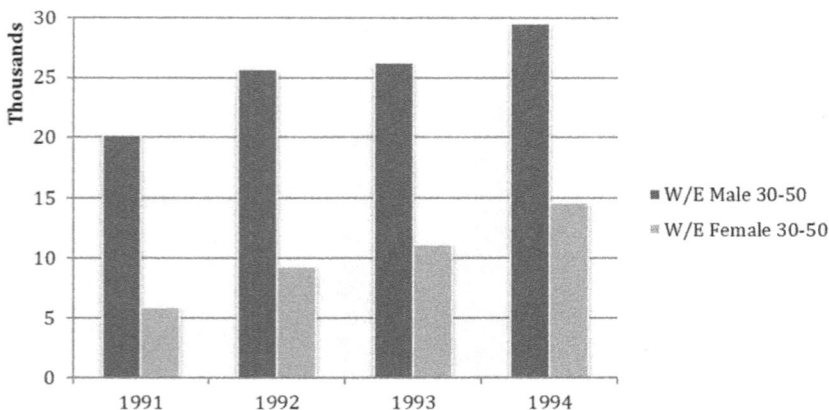

Graph 11: "West-East Migration (30–50) by Gender, 1991–1994." *Statistisches Bundesamt.* "Binnenwanderung," *VII B. Wanderungstatistik* (Wiesbaden: Statistisches Bundesamt, 2005).

As can be seen in Graphs 7-11, demographically, West–East migration had less impact than East–West migration. Seeing East Germany as a sort of hinterland, many West German males chose to establish a second residence as a commuter, while maintaining a main residence (and keeping their spouses and children) in the West. This trend would worsen the demographic decline in the eastern states in the late 1990s. As the German economy entered a period of stagnation, investment tapered off and companies began to fold; many of these West German managers simply returned home to their families in the West.

Although East German women were popularly characterized as the "losers of unification," East German men were targets of gendered characterizations as well. The East German man was physically weak, overweight, and hopelessly out of style when compared to the image of the chic and headstrong western man. Socially, he was constructed as shy and unable to form or voice an opinion in a work environment. The inability to physically and socially measure up to the West German standard, constructed *Ostmänner* (eastern men) as generally lacking what was required to compete and be successful in the new capitalist risk society of the united Germany.

The physical characterizations of *Ostmänner* often took the form of caricature, after unification. The stereotypical *Ostmann* was often pictured as balding, badly dressed, and overweight, with a big beer belly; in short, the antithesis of the *Schickimicki* image of a young, fit, and stylish West German professional. The pervasiveness of these stereotypes is highlighted in a short story by the West German author Stefan Berkholz. Two West German friends catch up over a drink at a bar, one having just returned from a vacation at the Baltic Sea, a popular East German holiday destination. The vacationer proceeds to describe the typical *Ossi* to his friend as such: "The *Ossi* is always pale in the face, as if he had just spent ten years locked in a cellar. [You could always tell an East German] by the shabby jogging suit they wore each morning to the breakfast buffet!"[77] In the same volume, Karl Scheithauer, a West German journalist, describes the typical *Ostmann* aesthetic: "The eastern man is typically dressed in dove gray, pale beige or ocher green, with a white shirt and horrible glasses."[78] From these and other physical characterizations of *Ossis*, it is apparent that outward appearance and style were important guideposts, segregating western style from eastern sloppiness. The stark distinction between eastern and western masculinity also appears in Peter

---

77 Stefan Berkholz, "So Isser, Der Ostler," in *Stiefbrüder: Was Ostmänner und Westmänner voneinander denken*, ed. Katrin Rohnstock (Berlin, Elefanten Press, 1995), 64.
78 Karl Scheithauer, "Männerpositionen," in *Stiefbrüder: Was Ostmänner und Westmänner voneinander denken*, ed. Katrin Rohnstock (Berlin, Elefanten Press, 1995), 37.

Hoffman's 1995 examination of the importance of the appearance of youth in the western job market: "Youth is important, and if the western man is no longer young, then he at least wants to appear so."[79] *Ossi* men are portrayed at the opposite end of the spectrum from the western ideal image of youth.

The incompatible physicality of the eastern man – unhealthily pale and overweight, aids in his exclusion from the competitive western labor market. This not only had consequences for the economic health of the eastern states, but also fundamentally changed the social lives of many ex-GDR citizens by eliminating the workplace as a center of social identity. *Wessi* managers were imported to take over newly privatized companies and other high-ranking positions. *Ossi* managers were either displaced or demoted to work under the *Wessi*. This trend resulted not only in the demoralization of the *Ossi*, who had previously held a position of authority, but it also reinforced the construction of *Ossi* men as uncreative, unmotivated, and timid. In his study examining the proliferation of "East–West alterities" among journalists, Dominic Boyer lists how *Wessis* and *Ossis* were constructed in opposition to each other in the mainstream western press (East vs. West): "formulaic vs. creative, consensus minded vs. conflict minded, pessimistic vs. optimistic, backward vs. cosmopolitan, deductive vs. inductive, erotic vs. unerotic, warmth vs. austerity, natural vs. paternal, idealist vs. pragmatist."[80] In popular discourse, the qualities that were valued most positively in the capitalist-risk society were all attributed to the West.

Popularly constructed, therefore, the *Ostmann*, who was socialized in a now defunct (and therefore, inherently flawed) full-employment society, was incompatible with a capitalist-risk society that required a creative, individualistic, and pragmatic approach. Thus, *Wessi* managers were put up as the ideal type for success in the capitalist society while the stereotyped *Ossi* man simply did not fit into and could not succeed within the western system. This is reflected in the subordination and exclusion of the *Ossi* from a mixed –work environment, as described by Peter Hoffmann, "With the free journalists from the West, the boss went with them to eat, developed relationships and chatted with them. Toward the easterners, he maintained an air of disgust."[81]

East German journalist, Frank Rothe, experienced the label of *Ossi* as an assault on his identity. At parties, he was forced to hide his so-called *Ossi*-ness, lest

---

79 Peter Hoffmann, "Die Sieger im Osten haben etwas verloren," in *Stiefbrüder: Was Ostmänner und Westmänner voneinander denken*, ed. Katrin Rohnstock (Berlin, Elefanten Press, 1995), 21.
80 Dominic Boyer, "On the Sedimentation and Accreditation of Social Knowledges of Difference: Mass Media, Journalism and the Reproduction of East/West Alterities in Unified Germany," *Cultural Anthropology* 15, no. 4 (2000), 483–484.
81 Hoffmann, "Die Sieger im Osten haben etwas verloren," 29.

he be ostracized. According to Rothe, "The minute someone finds out I am from the East, the tone of the conversation changes. They only want to know how it is 'over there.'" However, it was during a job interview for a position at a western media outlet that his eastern identity became most obviously detrimental to his future as a journalist in united Germany. During the interview, he was questioned solely upon his political affiliations and activities in the GDR. He did not get the job. Later, he learned that he probably did not even have a chance. "Later someone from NDR (*Norddeutsche Rundfunk*) told me that the station had previously had bad experience with *Ossis* and they wouldn't hire any others. If this is true, I don't know. It only made it clear to me that it was not so easy to lose one's past."[82]

Even the language used to describe unemployment set *Ossis* and *Wessis* apart. Although unemployment was highest in the new eastern states, after unification, unemployment increased in all regions in Germany as a result of an economic down cycle influenced by the enlargement of the EU and the costs of unification. Even more than a decade after unification, however, the unemployment rate in the East remained consistently more than twice that in the West. Dialogues concerning how German masculinity has been affected by periods of unemployment also show the presence of a clear East–West divide.

In her essay, "What makes a man into a man?" Janine Berg-Peer, a West German manager, discusses how unemployment differently affects West and East German managers. Using her experience as a "re-employment" agent, Berg argues that unemployment is less of a threat to the masculinity of *Ossi* managers because their role within the husband-wife relationship does not depend upon being the breadwinner. Berg-Peer: "The East German manager remains a man to his wife when his function as the breadwinner of the family is no longer guaranteed." For the West German manager, however, the circumstances are quite different: "A western manager, who no longer can maintain the status of his family, is no longer a man."[83]

The construction of an *Ossi* masculinity in the rhetoric surrounding the transformation of East German work identities reflects the increase and persistence in the manufacture of difference between East and West, since unification. Negative physical and social stereotyping of *Ostmänner* in western discourse had resulted in the production of the East German man as incompatible, with and incapable

---

82 Frank Rothe, "Die Dinosaurier im Bernstein: Ich, Das Überbleibsel aus einer implodieren Galaxis," in *Das Buch der Unterschiede: Warum die Einheit eine ist*, ed. Jana Simon, Frank Rothe and Weite Anderasch (Berlin: Aufbau Verlag, 2000), 58.
83 Janine Berg-Peer, "Was macht den Mann zum Mann?" in *Stiefbrüder: Was Ostmänner und Westmänner voneinander denken*, ed. Katrin Rohnstock (Berlin, Elefanten Press, 1995), 78.

of, participating in the new social market economy in united Germany. Reinforced by demographic patterns that had led to the continued westward migration of the young and talented (and female), these gendered stereotypes that have their roots in the period immediately following unification have endured.

As the examples in this chapter have illustrated, gendered stereotypes of both East German men and women often were articulated through a comparison to a West German ideal. While East German women were primarily defined through their reproductive capacity and their willingness to migrate to remain in full employment, East German men were characterized through their lack of action and their physical incompatibility with the West German model.

Chapter 5 will explore the lasting power of these gendered characterizations, tracing the mutual influence of mobility and discourse surrounding the East/West conflict and identity in the decade following the end of privatization. As economic instability continued to plague the eastern states in the late 1990s, western and foreign investment stagnated as well. As West–East migration greatly declined, there was a resurgence in East–West mobility. As in earlier periods, the most likely to depart were young, professional, and female. What was different in this period however was that the migrants moving to the West after 1997 increasingly belonged to a generation that had spent the majority of their formative years in united Germany. While economic stagnation in the eastern states can be seen as a root cause for the increase in emigration in the later half of the 1990s, it is clear that the East/West stereotypes still hold power, well into the twenty-first century.

5 German Mobility and a New Generation, 1994–2004

If the development of the East has a name and a permanent address, it is "Neue Messe, Messe Allee 1, 04356 Leipzig."[1]

On April 1, 1996, *Bundespräsident* Roman Herzog cut the ribbon to open the *Neue Messe* (New Trade Fair) complex outside of Leipzig to great pomp and circumstance. Located just outside of city limits to the north, this ultramodern achievement of five exhibition halls, crowned by an impressive steel-buttressed glass entrance hall, offered over 100,000 square meters of exhibition space. This modern glass and settle complex however, sat in stark contrast to the backdrop of outdated GDR-era shopping centers and warehouses. The symbolism of the modern commercial phoenix rising from the ashes of the dustbin of history was more than visual. The opening of the new trade fair complex was heralded by the German press as nothing less than the ushering in of a new era – a sign of the official arrival of the *Aufschwung Ost* (Upswing East). In sum, it signaled that the painful process of unification had finally given way to a period of stabilization, growth, and parity for the East. After the complete reconfiguration of the structure and society of the GDR, unification, in all its capitalist glory, had finally arrived.

In addition to the rhetoric surrounding its significance for German unity – a unity founded in the hope of economic parity between East and West – the opening of the new trade fair grounds also represented a hopeful move toward the restoration of Leipzig as a center of European economic life after the destruction and division wrought by the twentieth century. Historically, Leipzig had held a monopoly on trade fairs in central Europe from 1507, when Emperor Maximilian I declared the city's traditional trade fairs, which had been growing steadily since the twelfth century, to be "imperial" trade fairs. This status, in effect, banned other trade fairs from operating within a 15-mile radius of the city and made other cities dependent upon Leipzig as an imperial marketplace.[2]

For the next three centuries, Leipzig continued to grow in economic importance, as it became the central trade point for English and Polish goods, heralded as the so-called marketplace of Europe. Upon the foundation of the German Reich in 1871, Leipzig was made the seat of the German Supreme Court as well as the home of the national library. With the establishment of additional trade fair

---

1 Dirk Meyhöfer, "Palast des Aufschwungs," *Kulturspiegel*, February 26, 1996.
2 Ernst Hasse, *Geschichte der Leipziger Messen* (Leipzig: Zentral-Antiquariat der Deutschen Demokratische Republik, 1963), 7–32.

https://doi.org/10.1515/9783110716221-006

grounds and the opening of the (at the time) largest long distance train station in Europe, the population continued to grow throughout the early twentieth century, reaching its peak at just over 713,000 in 1939.[3]

The decline in both the size and influence of Leipzig as the commercial enter of European trade began with the Second World War. Allied bombings destroyed 25% of all buildings within the city. The focus of the Soviet Union on reparations rather than reconstruction made many areas inside the city uninhabitable. By 1950, the population had declined to 613,000.[4] The division of Germany by the Allied occupation forces and the permanent establishment of the two Cold War states in 1950 officially removed Leipzig from its previous position of central importance in the European market. Although COMECON continued to hold economic fairs and demonstration trade shows twice a year in Leipzig that attracted several western visitors, the market was limited to Eastern Europe. Suburbanization of new housing stock combined with the focus of the GDR on heavy industry and strip mining in the lands surrounding the city meant that throughout the GDR era, Leipzig continued to lose population rather than stabilize or grow.[5] When the Wall fell in 1989, the population of Leipzig stood at just 530,000 – a loss of 88,000 in 40 years.[6]

Along with the German unification came the hope that Leipzig would regain its former status as a center for industry and trade. The opening of the *Neue Messe* in 1996 was a signal that Leipzig was ready to retake (or at least share in) the place as center for trade and innovation. As an article in the nationally weekly newspaper *Die Zeit* proclaimed, "It is a great day for the city, for the country, for the economy and for the whole commercial world. And of course, 'for the people.'"[7] While the tone was noticeably more subdued in the (east) Berlin paper *Berliner Zeitung*, the construction of the *Neue Messe* was definitely seen as a move in the right direction:

> About all, the new exhibition supplies the region with a feeling of hope that the promise of "Upswing East" has yet to fulfill. Unemployment is 16 percent. In the city, there is virtually no longer any large-scale industry. Leipzig leads Germany in vacant office space. The decision to build the new exhibition grounds and not to let the fair go under was the right one. The city thrives on the show – and is growing with it. The hotel industry is already booming, and transportation links have been strengthened.[8]

---

3 Frank-Dieter Grimm, "Return to Normal – Leipzig in Search of its Future Position in Central Europe," *GeoJournal* 36 (1995): 321–324.

4 Frank-Dieter Grimm, "Return to Normal – Leipzig in Search of its Future Position in Central Europe.

5 For more on the history of the *Leipziger Messe* in the GDR see Kai-Uwe Arnold, *Leipzig, 1954–1969: Trümmer, Abriss, Neuaufbau* (Leipzig: Strom & Strom, 2004).

6 Grimm, "Return to Normal – Leipzig in Search of Its Future Position in Central Europe," 324.

7 Manfred Sack, "Der Leipziger Kristallpalast," *Die Zeit,* April 12, 1996.

8 Peter Kirnisch, "Alte Messe an neuem Ort," *Berliner Zeitung,* April 13, 1996.

Despite high hopes that Leipzig would recover economically, and furthermore that it might even regain its position as marketplace to the world as it had when it lay at the crossroads of the *via regia* and *via imperiali* in the eleventh century, announcements that Leipzig was "back" and "in luck," were short lived.[9]

As the global economic importance of the European Union grew in the late 1990s, the hopes that Leipzig would establish itself again by bridging the Cold War eastern and western markets diminished. Despite attempts to revitalize infrastructure and garner new industrial investment from foreign or West German companies, Leipzig continued to shrink as it struggled to gain a foothold in the now post-Cold War "European" economy. While the opening of modern facilities did attract some attention, the decision to focus on specialty fairs rather than to adopt the previous *Muster Messe* model meant that the potential for Leipzig to grow to international prominence was no longer there.[10] Western cities such as Hannover and Frankfurt (Main), which had established parallel fairs during the Cold War, continued to maintain and strengthen their hold on the European market after unification.[11]

After the privatization phase ended in the mid-1990s, the initial enthusiasm of foreign and West German investors for the potential of the eastern market dropped off sharply. As businesses closed and projects ended, many of the West German managers and professionals who had come East during the unification boom returned to the West. This movement consisted not only of professionals returning to their western homelands but also for young East German graduates seeking training, employment, and university educations in the West and abroad. For Leipzig, this developed very quickly into a surplus of apprenticeships, as opposed to the shortage that had occurred in the immediate aftermath of unification. As the infrastructure in the city itself was revitalized, and industry began to pick up after 2000, a new wave of migration began to pull young rural migrants into Leipzig, while a great number of native-born *Leipziger* began to look West for their own futures.

This chapter traces the intersection of three forces – migration, identity politics, and nostalgia – in united Germany after the end of formal privatization in

---

9 "Leipzig im Glück," *Die Zeit*, January 23, 1996.
10 The *Muster Messe* model was used in Leipzig from 1895 and involved major manufacturers across many industries displaying and demonstrating their wares. During the Cold War, the same model was maintained, only limited to industries in the Eastern Bloc. After unification, the motto was transformed from "*Muster Messe*" to "*Messe und Mehr*" (trade fair and more). Instead of a vast sampling of goods across several industries, fairs were much more specialized. As a result, Leipzig became one of several *Messe-Städte* (trade fair cities) across Germany, as opposed to the dominant fair destination it had been in the past.
11 Marco Brontje, "Facing the Challenge of Shrinking Cities in East Germany: The Case of Leipzig," *GeoJournal* 61 (2004), 17–19.

1994. In many ways, the preceding intersection of economic stagnation, migration, and demographic consequences seen through the lens of Leipzig brings out more general trends in regard to the interaction between East and West in the period following the conclusion of privatization. While many leading political and economic experts lauded the coming of the *Aufschwung Ost* with the decline of East–West migration from 1994 to 1997, this stabilization was short lived. In the long term, these were consequences of general change and the peak of western investment in the East immediately following privatization. For a brief time window, migration slowed because all who had found a job either in the East or West had already found one, and those still unemployed tended to stay unemployed.

An examination of internal migration patterns from 1998 to 2004 indicates that emigration again increased as the first generation to be schooled in united Germany came of age, while there was a concurrent decline in eastward migration as investment started to taper off. Westward movement in this period was disproportionately of the young and often female. Seeing little future in the East, the brightest career-minded East Germans continued to look West and even further abroad for education, training, and employment.

As in the period immediately following unification, gender and generation continued to be important factors in determining who would migrate, where, and for what reason. In addition to a continuing movement to the West of young skilled people, there was also a sharp rise in the urban migration of young rural women. These women migrated not only to larger cities in the West, but also to urban areas in the East.[12] A decade after unification however, the demographic consequences of this skewed migration began to appear. The increased emigration of young women has intensified the decline in the birthrate in the eastern states. Reaching a low of 0.77% in 1994, the birth rate in East Germany remained well below the West German average since unification.[13] This trend has exaggerated the aging of the population as the young continue to make their exodus. These departures have eroded the already low potential for international investment in the eastern states (outside of major cities such as Berlin and Leipzig), and threatened to turn the eastern states into the *mezzogiorno* (comparative to the chronically economically depressed region of southern ideally) of Germany.[14]

---

12 Ralf Mai, Abwanderung aus Ostdeutschland: Strukturen und Milieus der Altersselektivität und ihre regionspolitische Bedeutung (Berlin: Peter Lang, 2004), 107–138.
13 Statistisches Bundesamt, Germany's Population by 2060: Results of the 12th Coordinated Population Projection (Wiesbaden: Statistisches Bundesamt, 2009), 12.
14 Nicholas Werz, "Abwanderung aus den neuen Bundesländern von 1989 bis 2000," Aus Politik und Zeitgeschichte 39 (2001), 27.

An examination of internal migration between East and West Germany in the decades after unification uncovers patterns of movement that reveal much about the consequences of economic and demographic development in the eastern states. Distinct phases of internal migration intersect with economic cycles of boom and bust, periods of recovery, and stagnation. As previous chapters have established, the massive westward movement that had brought down the Berlin Wall figured prominently in calls from both East and West for rapid unification. While a total of more than one-third of the workforce was eliminated in the eastern states, emigration continued in full force. Westward migration affected all of eastern Germany in this initial period, while all major urban areas in West Germany, in particular those along the border, served as reception areas.[15]

Meanwhile, the eastern migration of West German professionals steadily increased, as the machinery of system transfer and privatization was set into motion. However, many of these western managers and professionals hired to oversee the transformation of East German companies and institutions often commuted from their homes in the West rather than establish residency. While they were counted statistically as having migrated (changed residence), these commuters often maintained homes and families in the West, which limited the civil, social, political, and economic impact of these immigrants in the eastern states.

When formal privatization ended in 1994, rates of eastward and westward migration began to converge. From 1994 to 1996, the rate of East–West migration remained relatively stable at around 160,000 a year. Concurrently, West–East movement increased from only around 11,000 in 1989 to a high of over 150,000 in 1997. The result was a near zero net migration in 1997, with the eastern population losing just 1,000 inhabitants to the West.

The convergence of eastward and westward migration coincided with a cyclical upswing in employment as the German economy rebounded for the first time since unification. After experiencing an initial economic boost after the fall of the Berlin Wall, the German economy followed the rest of western Europe into a recession lasting 1992–1994. While unemployment rates in the western states experienced an initial drop in 1989/1990, they rose again with the onset of the recession, which in turn reduced the opportunities for East Germans in the western states.[16]

As seen in Graph 12, this momentary balance between eastward and westward migration was not so much a sign of stabilization as it was a sign of the changing of the guard – a mere gap between the period of volatile growth in the post-unification

---

15 Franz-Josef Kemper, "Internal Migration in Eastern and Western Germany: Convergence or Divergence of Spatial Trends after Unification?" Regional Studies 38, no. 6 (2004), 665.
16 Frank Heiland, "Trends in East-West German Migration from 1989 to 2002," *Demographic Research* 11 (2004), 185–187.

Migration between Eastern and Western Germany, 1989-2004

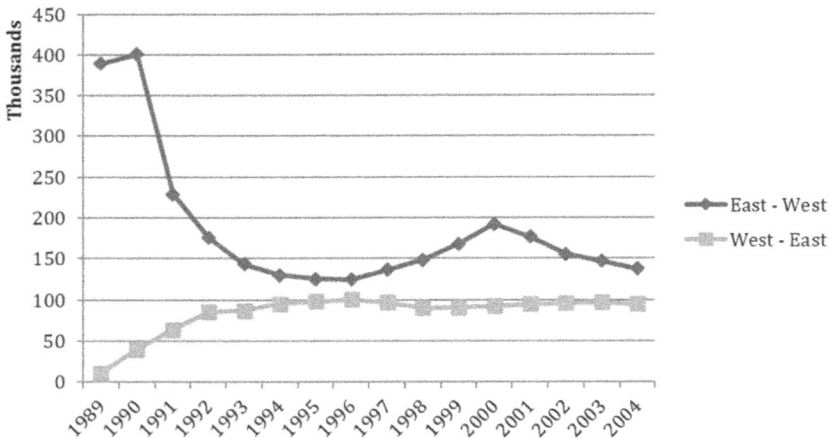

Graph 12: "Migration between Eastern and Western Germany, 1989–2004." Data source: *Statistisches Bundesamt.* "Binnenwanderung," *VII B. Wanderungstatistik* (Wiesbaden: Statistisches Bundesamt, 2005).

period and the stagnation that set in after 1998. At the time, however, experts and the media alike were cautiously optimistic that the eastern states would not only be able to maintain their population level, but possibly even experience growth. There are several explanations for this optimism. By 1996, some of the chronic problems, such as dilapidated housing, failing infrastructure, and pollution, that were primary obstacles to foreign and West German investment were beginning to be cleaned up. Major investments in infrastructure and successes such as the opening of the *Neue Messe* and the new Reichstag building in Berlin were presented as the physical embodiment of the promise of West German modernization for East German recovery.

Wage convergence, which had played such a major role in the call for rapid unification after the fall of the Berlin Wall, was seen as the primary factor in achieving demographic stabilization. At the time, economic experts argued that convergence was the key because an immediate increase in wages would in turn increase the standard of living in the eastern states. Once standards of living in East and West were on par with each other, the impetus for migration would be removed. However, the initial boost toward total wage convergence had been misleading. The most influential factor in the rise of wage in the early 1990s was not the establishment of new full-time jobs in the East, but rather a narrowing of the gap between eastern and western wage rates amongst wage labor in the industrial and service sectors.[17] As a result, while unskilled workers became less likely to move, skilled labor continued to do so at about the same rate. The concurrent growth in management opportunities for West Germans in the East balanced out net migration rates. In short, the evening out of migration between East and West combined with the upswing in the economic cycle resulted in undue economic optimism despite the lack of any real quantifiable growth.[18]

In addition, there was also a sharp rise in the emigration of young women from rural areas in the East to urban areas in the East as well as the West. This long-term migration trend had resulted in a higher decline in the eastern birthrate and a drastic aging of the population and had called into serious question the prospect for an economic turnaround and revival of investment in the East. The loss of a high proportion of the most productive portion of the population resulted in a skill gap that further discouraged investment possibilities in the East long after the initial period of high emigration. In addition, a considerable percentage of westward migrants were young and female, which would contribute to the stark decline in birthrate in the East. Thus, the prolonged emigration of productive females that has lasted decades has contributed to a cycle of emigration and structural weakness in the eastern states that in turn, prevented growth and investment in the area.

The phenomenon of *Ostalgie* coincided with the resurgence in the urgency of the westward movement of young East Germans. As the region struggled to establish itself economically, the revival of Eastern products and the production of films, television programs, and literature about everyday life in the GDR, sought to prove that one could and did live a *"ganz normales Leben"* (completely normal life) in the GDR, but that some aspects of life were preferable to that in the West. The sudden commercialization of the GDR, although often criticized as glossing over the dark side of German communism, provided the generation coming of age in the late 1990s and early 2000s with a foothold to identify with the GDR on their own terms. In short, the commercialization of the GDR made it accessible to those who had very little or no experience living in it. The combination of the westward emigration of a younger generation, the persistence of stereotypes of difference between East and West, and the *Ostalgie* for everyday life in the GDR has extended the longevity of the regional divide between East and West.

---

17 Jennifer Hunt, "The Transition in East Germany: When is a Ten-Point Fall in the Gender Wage Gap Bad News?" *Journal of Labor Economics* 20, no. 1 (2002), 153.

18 Although there was a shift toward a "spirit" of optimism in the media, most economic experts were halting in their prognoses for an economic boom in the East. Hunt, for example, warned against the consequences of a possible brain drain in the East in her analysis of the migratory flows of the mid-1990s.

In order to understand the full impact of mobility in the post-privatization period, it is useful to go beyond net migration, analyzing each stream independently. While mapping out net migration rates is indeed useful in gaining a big picture view of the overall shape of mobility, net figures alone obscure certain characteristics of migration. Gender, age, economic status, and educational level prove to be vital components in understanding the intricacies at work in both the causes and consequences of large-scale internal migrations. While determining the rate of net migration may yield a rough idea of how much movement occurred, it cannot say much about exactly who migrated, or why.

In the case of internal migration in Germany after unification, disaggregating the two different migration streams to the East and West in germs of gender and age proves to be the most helpful in explaining the intersection between the determinants of migration as well as its consequences. While an assessment of net migration goes to a certain point in explaining the long-term perpetuation of western and eastern flows founded upon economic inequality, establishing trends in the gender and age of migrants helps determine how this migration has shaped not only the economic aspects of German society after unification, but also the social and cultural attitudes concerning ideas of "east" and "west" as well.

5.1 Internal Migration and *Aufschwung Ost*

In 1998, the national news magazine *Focus* reported the shocking news that West Germans were migrating to the East in significant numbers. Based upon preliminary national migrations statistics from 1997 to early 1998, and peppered with interviews from well-known social scientists including economist Gert Wagner from the German Institute for Economic Research, the article claimed that this shift in the balance of internal migration signified nothing less than a "new feeling of unity" among East and West Germans.

> In 1993 population researchers warned that the former GDR was literally "bleeding away" its human capital. A dramatic decline in the birth rate and massive emigration to the West depopulated the land between the Elbe and the Oder. Sociologists emphasized a "demographic shock." Five years later there is no more talk of that. The great train from the West to the East is growing apace: the migration balance in favor of the West is becoming smaller. Experts soon expect a full reversal of the trend. Already this first year, [1998] could see more westerners migrating to the East than the other way around.[19]

---

19 Wanderung: Es Bewegt sich was. Das Neue Einheitsgefühl der Deutschen," *Focus*, September 21, 1998.

Despite this optimistic tone, 1998 did not live up to its promise. As the German economy dipped into a mini-recession, unemployment in the East began to rise. Along with the economic downturn came a resurgence in the emigration of East Germans to the West. At the same time, West–East migration slowed considerably. The *Aufschwung Ost* was an illusion that remained entirely unrealized.

The convergence of net migration rates was portrayed in the press as a sign of economic stabilization, when in reality a number of factors not directly related to the labor market also influenced the development of migration in the two decades after unification. The demographic problems that began with the so-called birth strike in the eastern states immediately following unification were compounded by the preponderance of young women choosing to go West. The elimination of skilled positions and limited growth of service sector jobs and other wage work made the western states even more attractive to the most potentially productive sector of East German society.

As the mechanisms for investment in the eastern states ramped up after privatization, the increase of West Germans migrating to the East balanced the westward movement. However, as the German economy entered an economic down cycle in 1998, this eastward movement dropped off while there was a significant increase in the westward movement of young women. This renewed state of decline, both promoting and aided by the rise in *Ostalgie* (eastern nostalgia), has nurtured the discussions surrounding East/West difference that are still going strong more than 20 years after unification.

The following section will explore the gender and age composition of both westward and eastward migration in the decade from the end of privatization in 1994 to the apparent stabilization of migration rates in 2004. Presently, most historical and contemporary study of internal migration has focused upon the net gains and losses in order to indicate the relative prospects for productivity and growth. Analyzing each migration stream by gender and age group reveals forces that are impossible to factor into an argument that relies upon net migration alone.

5.1.1 East–West Migration and Gender, 1991–1997

East to West movement was highly gendered in the initial phase of migration from the fall of the Berlin Wall in November 1989 to formal unification in 1990. As discussed in Chapter 2, most westward migrants during this initial phase were young and male, most looking to take advantage of what might have been a temporary window to escape the GDR before it became evident that the border would remain open. Many were unskilled hourly blue-collar workers that took advantage of the wage imbalance between the East and West to fill open gaps in the West German labor market.

The gendered story of unification, with East German women set in the losing role, has been well established.[20] Shortly after unification and the implementation of system transfer, East German women began to utilize emigration as a coping strategy for sudden unemployment. As discussed in Chapter 3, a combination of the restructuring of the East German economy and a loss of social provisions that supported working motherhood resulted in many women looking to the western states in order to remain a part of the labor force.

Migration from Eastern to Western Germany by Gender, 1991-2004

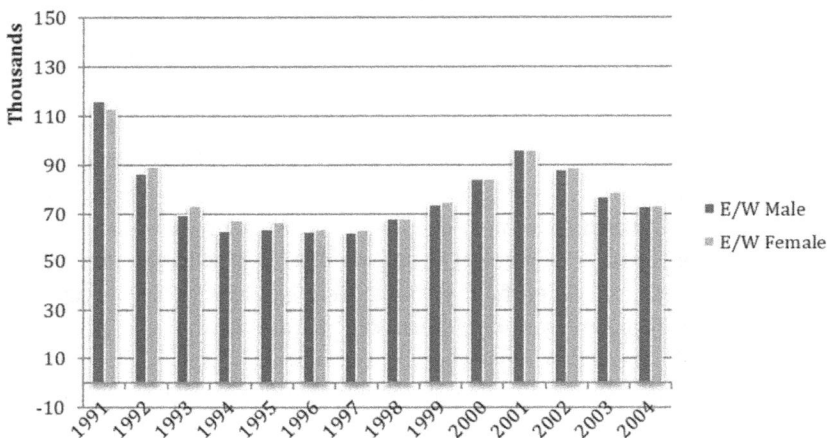

Graph 13: "Migration from Eastern to Western Germany by Gender, 1991–2004." Data source: *Statistisches Bundesamt.* "Binnenwanderung," *VII B. Wanderungstatistik* (Wiesbaden: Statistisches Bundesamt, 2005).

In sum, the sudden gender shift in migratory flows can be seen as reflective not only of the construction of a post-GDR East German society in the image of the West, but also the reconfiguration of gender regimes. As can be inferred by graph 13, the young, male-driven migration that accompanied the fall of the Berlin Wall and

---

20 See Ferree, "The Rise and Fall of 'Mommy Politics,'" as well as the edited collection of interdisciplinary essays edited by Eva Kolinsky and Hildegard Maria Nickel, *Reinventing Gender: Women in Eastern Germany since Unification* (London: Routledge, 2003). Also see the collection of interviews with East German women in the aftermath of unification compiled by Dinah Dodds and Pam Allen-Thompson, *The Wall in My Backyard: East German Women in Transition* (Amherst: University of Massachusetts Press, 1994).

lasted until unification gave way to a significant female emigration as the labor market was restructured according to West German standards. Not only were many jobs lost as formerly state owned conglomerations were dismantled and sold off, but also as many full-time positions held by women were eliminated as the economy was reshaped to reflect a new gender regime – where men were lifelong participants in the labor market and women were expected to participate in career work only when young and childless.[21]

The economic and social pressures caused by the transformation also had an almost immediate impact on birth rates in the new eastern states. The combination of high unemployment and a loss of state support for working motherhood drove women to drastically alter their plans, limiting childbearing or postponing motherhood altogether. As a 1993 report in *Der Spiegel* decried, many young East German women would "rather get a dog" than have a child in unified Germany. Karin Werner, an unemployed engineer, who at the time worked as a consultant for the unemployment office in Dresden, explained that many East German women felt that the new Germany is a hostile environment in which to raise children: "If I were to have a child now, I would not even be able to begin to estimate what I would be able to offer him. In my work [at the unemployment office in Dresden], I hear many women utter the phrase, 'This state will get no child of mine!'"[22] In 1994, the birthrate in the eastern states had fallen to 0.7% – half of the rate in the western states, and at the time, by far the lowest in the world.[23]

Meanwhile, rapid wage convergence commenced, bringing wages in the eastern states for wage laborers to 75% of western levels by 1994, while also driving unemployment to nearly double that of the West. At the time, it was reported that wage convergence had been particularly positive for women whose wages had increased vis-à-vis men in the period from 1991 to 1996.[24] However, this rise in wages only measured women who had chosen to stay in eastern Germany. In addition, this group consisted primarily of unskilled wage laborers, not skilled workers. By 1996, the majority of skilled workers between the ages of 30 and 50 had either left the job market with early retirement, had already moved West, or had accepted a lesser position outside of their original field in order to stay in the

---

21 For more on West German gender regimes, see Robert G. Moeller, "Protecting Mother's Work: From Production to Reproduction in Postwar West Germany," *Journal of Social History* 22, no. 3 (1989), 413–437.

22 "Lieber ein Hund," *Der Spiegel*, September 20, 1993.

23 Michael Sontheimer, "Land ohne Kinder," *Die Zeit*, October 7, 1994.

24 Jennifer Hunt, "The Transition in East Germany: When is a Ten-point Fall in the Gender Wage Gap Bad News?", 154.

labor market when all other options (unemployment benefits, retraining programs, ABM jobs) had been exhausted.[25]

An analysis of westward movement in terms of age and gender reveals some interesting aspects of the nature of migration after privatization. As illustrated in Graph 14, examining the westward flow in 1991–1997, one can come to some rudimentary conclusions. While the rate of migration for those near or above retirement age remains pretty constant, there is a distinct decline in the number of migrants under the age of 18. This indicates a decline in the rate of family migration (migration with at least one parent and minor children) from its peak around unification. This is consistent with larger total migration in 1989–1990, when more families migrated as a unit.

Migration from Eastern to Western Germany by Age Cohort, 1991-2004

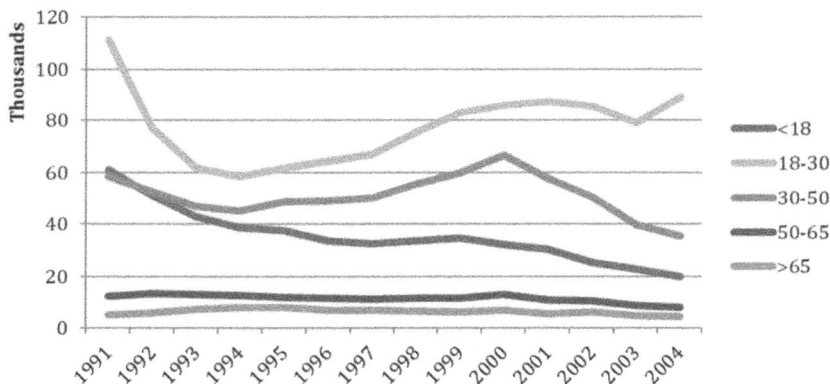

Graph 14: "Migration from Eastern to Western Germany by Age Cohort, 1991–2004." Data source: *Statistisches Bundesamt.* "Binnenwanderung," *VII B. Wanderungstatistik* (Wiesbaden: Statistisches Bundesamt, 2005).

After steadily declining from 1991 to 1994, migration of those aged 30–50 (typically an age group consisting of individuals who have already established a career), rose slightly from 1995 to 1997. This is generally consistent with the end of stopgap measures such as ABM schemes and federally sponsored retraining programs.[26]

---

25 *Arbeitsbeschaffungsmaßnahmen* (ABM) refers to temporary (612 months) federally funded minimum wage assignments administered by local governments during periods of high unemployment.
26 Vanessa Beck, Debbie Wagener, and Jonathan Grix, "Resilience and Unemployment: A Case Study of East German Women," *German Politics* 14, no. 1 (2005), 11.

The largest and most volatile of migration streams – consisting of migrants aged 18- to 30-year-old – represents the most mobile portion of the population. In many ways, 18- to 30-year-old students, trainees, and professionals were the freest to migrate westward to work, because in most cases they had only recently began their career and could be safely inserted into a new workplace at a junior level. After unification, this stream somewhat mirrored the curve of the cohort aged 30–50 in 1991–1996, dipping to a low of 54,000 migrants in 1997. While this was still a much higher rate of migration than that of the other age groups, this decline is consistent with the perception of economic stabilization at the time.

Analyzing this migration stream by age and gender leads to some helpful insights concerning the general flow of migration from East to West. However, it also obscures some important clues as to the complex relationship between the decision to migrate and prospects for economic revival. At first glance, the convergence of eastward and westward flows from 1991 to 1997 indicates a move toward economic stabilization in the eastern states. However, an analysis of the East–West migration flow by gender indicates a different story.

As demonstrated in Graphs 15–21, once the migration stream is subjected to a year-by-year analysis by age and gender, a strikingly different picture of mobility emerges that is sensitive to the economic situation in the eastern states after privatization. While the actual volume steadily decreased from its peak in 1989 until it converged with the column of eastward migration in 1997, the shift in migrant sex ratio by age group suggests that this perceived recovery, no matter how enthusiastically lauded by politicians, was merely the calm before the storm. As a new generation of works and students came of age in the late 1990s, emigration to the West among younger East Germans rose, in response to the lack of opportunities and economic stagnation in the eastern states.

For those aged 30–50, while the overall volume of migration fell, the proportion of female versus male migrants steadily increased in 1991–1997. At the same time, the volume of migrants under the age of 18 was cut in half. Traditionally, migrants under the age of 18 usually move as part of a family unit. In this case, the increase of male migration in proportion to female migration with the concurrent decline in the migration of children suggests that more males were migrating on their own to the West rather than coming as part of a family unit.[27] This trend corresponded with the end to many retraining programs in the East and also signifies that continued economic stagnation and unemployment had encouraged men to become more flexible in their willingness to relocate – with or without

---

27 Ralf Mai, Abwanderung aus Ostdeutschland: Strukturen und Milieus der Altersselektivität und Ihre Regionalpolitische Bedeutung, 156–162.

family – after privatization. In sum, while it may have appeared that some stabilization was occurring because the actual volume of migration was decreasing while net migration rates converged, in reality, the indication of an increase in male migration while the number of migrants under 18 decreased indicates that more migration was occurring with employment as the primary determinant.

1991

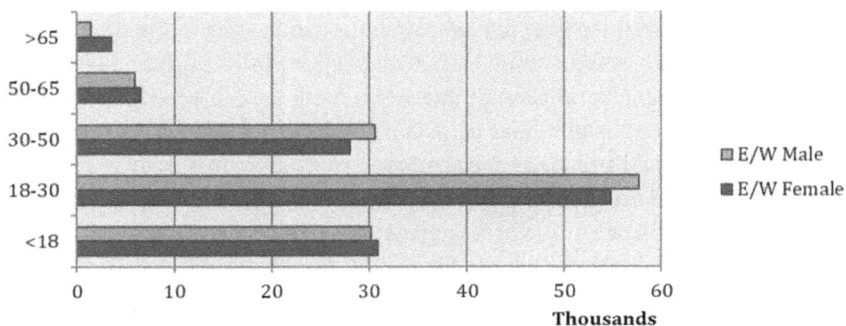

Graph 15: "Migration from Eastern to Western Germany by Age and Gender, 1991." Data source: *Statistisches Bundesamt.* "Binnenwanderung," *VII B. Wanderungstatistik* (Wiesbaden: Statistisches Bundesamt, 2005).

1992

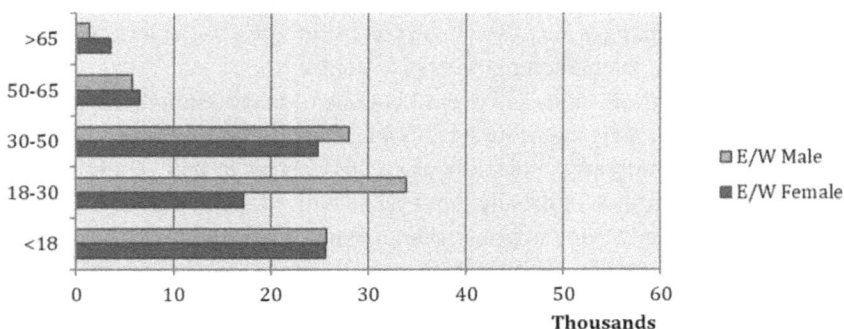

Graph 16: "Migration from Eastern to Western Germany by Age and Gender, 1992." Data source: *Statistisches Bundesamt.* "Binnenwanderung," *VII B. Wanderungstatistik* (Wiesbaden: Statistisches Bundesamt, 2005).

1993

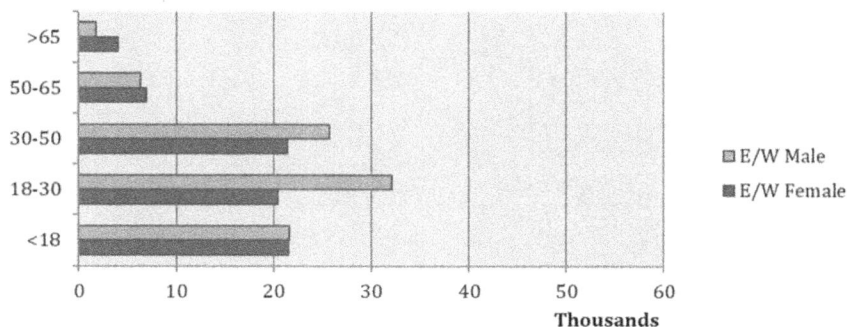

Graph 17: "Migration from Eastern to Western Germany by Age and Gender, 1993." Data source: *Statistisches Bundesamt.* "Binnenwanderung," *VII B. Wanderungstatistik* (Wiesbaden: Statistisches Bundesamt, 2005).

1994

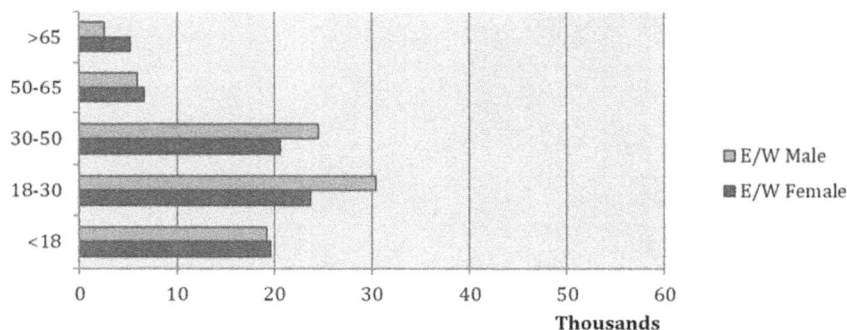

Graph 18: "Migration from Eastern to Western Germany by Age and Gender, 1994." Data source: *Statistisches Bundesamt.* "Binnenwanderung," *VII B. Wanderungstatistik* (Wiesbaden: Statistisches Bundesamt, 2005).

The second major point that can be culled from the disaggregation of each year by age and gender comes with an examination of migration among those aged 18–30. Again, while the total volume of migration decreased, the proportion of migrants between the ages of 18 and 30 started to increase after the end of privatization. Furthermore, in 1992–1997, there were more female than male migrants in this cohort who emigrated to the West. In the hardest hit regions, the gender disparity

1995

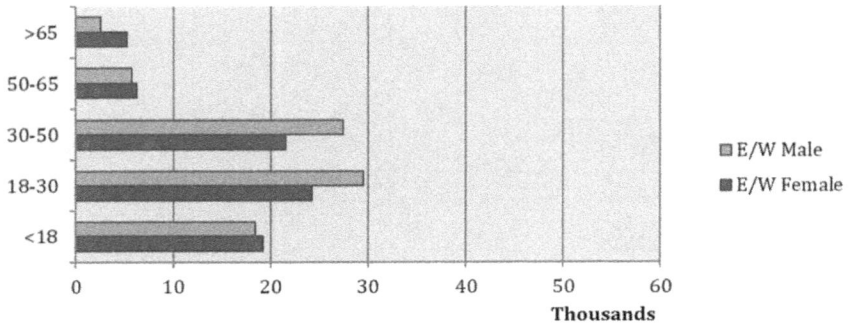

Graph 19: "Migration from Eastern to Western Germany by Age and Gender, 1995." Data source: *Statistisches Bundesamt.* "Binnenwanderung," *VII B. Wanderungstatistik* (Wiesbaden: Statistisches Bundesamt, 2005).

1996

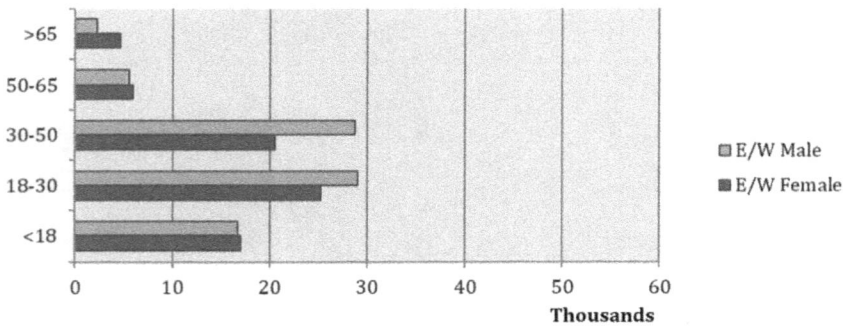

Graph 20: "Migration from Eastern to Western Germany by Age and Gender, 1996." Data source: *Statistisches Bundesamt.* "Binnenwanderung," *VII B. Wanderungstatistik* (Wiesbaden: Statistisches Bundesamt, 2005).

was even more pronounced. In the eastern state of Saxony-Anhalt, for example, the number of female migrants outnumbered male migrants, two to one.[28]

This example reflects two interrelated trends: the restructuring of the East German economy in the image of the West and the continuing expectation of East Ger-

---

[28] Vanessa Beck, Debbie Wagener and Jonathan Grix, "Resilience and Unemployment: A Case Study of East German Women," 8.

1997

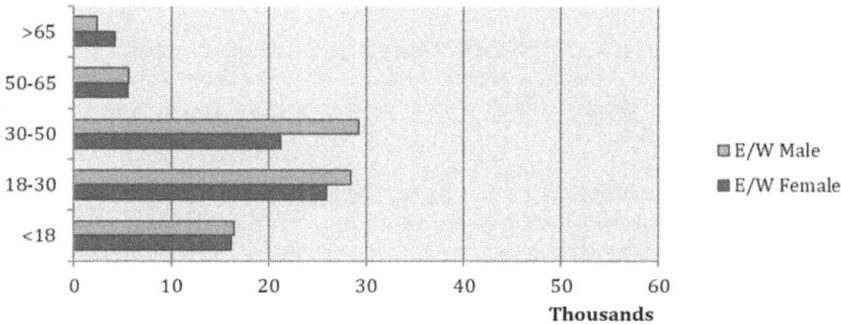

Graph 21: "Migration from Eastern to Western Germany by Age and Gender, 1997." Data source: *Statistisches Bundesamt.* "Binnenwanderung," *VII B. Wanderungstatistik* (Wiesbaden: Statistisches Bundesamt, 2005).

man women to remain in full employment. Contrary to the popular West German belief that the adaptation of West German gender roles would offer the "worn out *Ossi-Mutti*" (eastern mommy) a welcome break, in the phase following the end of privatization, East German women continued to look for work despite having weathered long-term unemployment. In addition to the view that work was an integral part to one's identity, the combination of high male unemployment as well as the prevalence of single parenthood in the eastern states, made full-time employment necessary for survival for many East German women. For many, a career could not simply be cast aside as the consequences of unification for full-time working motherhood became clear. In the period before the economic collapse in 1998, the continuing expectation of many East German women to maintain full employment was targeted by many West Germans as contributing to the "inflation" of employment figures in the eastern states. Labeled *"Arbeitsarme Ostfrauen"* (underemployed Eastern women), according to researcher Debbie Wagener, they "refused to bow to the common social expectation that they would return to the home and stop exacerbating unemployment figures."[29]

A 1998 debate between the conservative sociologist, Ulrich Beck and then SPD shadow minister, Christiane Bergmann echoed the prevalence of the attitude that the high rate of unemployment of East German women did not require a solution,

---

29 Debbie Wagener, "Women, Identity and Employment in East Germany," in East German Distinctiveness in a United Germany, ed. Jonathan Grix and Paul Cooke (Birmingham: University of Birmingham Press, 2002), 126.

rather that the problem was the expectation of the existence of a significant female labor force:

> Bergmann: What upsets me the most is that there is clearly a democracy deficit in the East. The slogans we heard on the street in 1989, "Democracy – now or never" are gone now. It is more important that people find their place in society, which [for East German women] is through gainful employment.

> Beck: What you see as the solution is the problem. There is no return to full employment. It is dead. Businesses need only a fraction of the jobs to produce more than before . . . at the same time we have more job seekers willing to work. [German] female employment is on its way out in the European Union, getting further and further away like the taillights on a car. If West German women were to think the same [about employment] as East German women, unemployment would rise dramatically.

> Bergmann: The findings of the Commission are, however, that the employment expectations of women in the East have no realistic relationship to the actual employment opportunities available. In plain language [they are saying]: "Eastern women, get back to the stove."[30]

In conclusion, a disaggregation of migration statistics by age and gender reveals that 1991–1997, although the volume of migration from East to West Germany decreased overall, the bulk of these losses came in non-productive categories of retirement age (50–65, 65+) and children under the age of 18. The gender-specific emigration of males between the ages of 30 and 50 and females aged 18–30 reflects not only contemporary concerns of momentary unemployment and economic stagnation in the East in the mid-1990s, but also a distrust that, despite the rhetoric of politicians lauding the imminent arrival of the *Aufschwung Ost*, there was any hope for an eastern recovery. The refusal of East German women to "get back to the stove," reflected the persistence in belief in the right to work, despite being offered the so-called comforts of western womanhood. As will be examined later in this chapter, these attitudes toward work would filter down to the next generation of East German women, fueling further emigration as this new generation sought to make a place for themselves in united Germany.

5.2 Migration from Western to Eastern Germany, 1991–1997

The movement of thousands of West German managers and professionals into the eastern states commenced in July 1990. Although numerically, the volume of

---

30 Sylvia Schreiber and Hajo Schumacher, "Ein Leben jenseits der Arbeit," *Der Spiegel,* August 24, 1998.

eastward migration does not compare to the rate of migration into the western states, this cadre of entrepreneurs, managers, bureaucrats, and professionals has had a significant impact on the form that unification took on the ground. The nature of the power relationship inherent in this migration, which some have described as that of a colonizing force, has also helped redefine the complicated and contentious relationship between *Besserwessis* and *Jammerossis* in the two decades after the fall of the wall.[31]

Unlike East to West migration, which has been the subject of several studies, there has been very little research done examining the determinants of eastward migration. However, by aggregating the migration data, some preliminary inferences can be made as to the makeup of these migration streams. Migration from

Migration from Western to Eastern Germany by Gender, 1991-2004

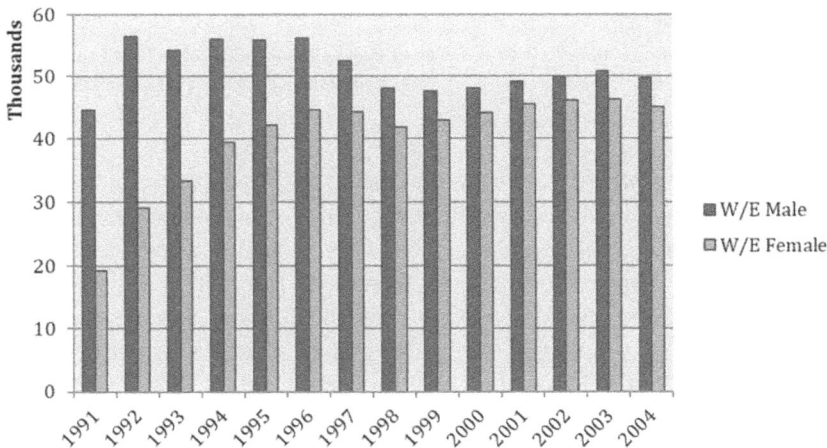

Graph 22: "Migration from Western to Eastern Germany by Gender, 1991–2004." Data source: *Statistisches Bundesamt.* "Binnenwanderung," *VII B. Wanderungstatistik* (Wiesbaden: Statistisches Bundesamt, 2005).

---

31 For a discussion on the applicability of postcolonial theory to the East German context, see Chapter 1 in Paul Cooke, *Representing East Germany since Unification: From Colonization to Nostalgia* (New York: Berg, 205), 1–26. See also Marc M. Howard, "An East German Ethnicity? Understanding the New Division of United Germany," *German Politics and Society* 13, no. 4 (1995), 49–70. as well as Thomas Baylis, "Transforming the East German Economy: Shock without Therapy," in *From Bundesrepublik to Deutschland* ed. Michael Huelshoff, Andrei Markovits and Simon Reich (Ann Arbor: University of Michigan Press, 1993), 77–92.

Migration from Western to Eastern Germany by Age Cohort, 1991-2004

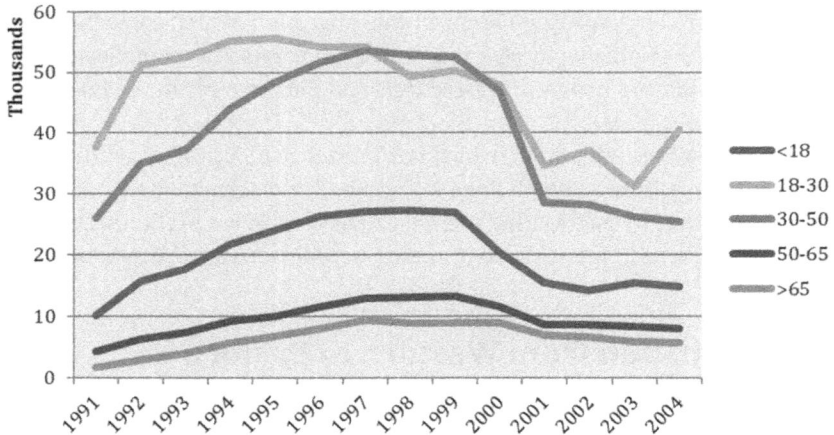

Graph 23: "Migration from Western to Eastern Germany by Age Cohort, 1991–2004." Data source: *Statistisches Bundesamt.* "Binnenwanderung," *VII B. Wanderungstatistik* (Wiesbaden: Statistisches Bundesamt, 2005).

West to East was overwhelmingly male, leading up to the end of privatization in 1994, and predominantly male thereafter. Examining the overall data on age distribution, it becomes evident that the eastward migration of 18- to 30-year-olds clearly outpaced that of 30- to 50-year-olds from 1991 through 1997.

When viewed in the context of anecdotal information on the processes of system transfer involved in unification, it can be inferred from the age distribution that most of these West to East migrants in the first seven years were young professionals. As discussed in Chapter 4, these migrants migrated to the east primarily to advance in their professional lives, not to establish or maintain families or set down roots in the community.

While the migration streams remained predominantly male, the proportion of female-to-male migrants increased significantly from just under 25,000 in 1991 to a high of just over 70,000 in 1997. One must consider that some of the increase in female migration is the result of return migration to the East. Although there has been no official study of return migration using state-level statistics, there has been research published that made use of sample data from the GSEOP (German Socioeconomic Panel).[32] A recent study using this data estimates that in 1990–2006, approximately 18% of East Germans who migrated to the West ended up returning to the East within 3 years.[33]

1991

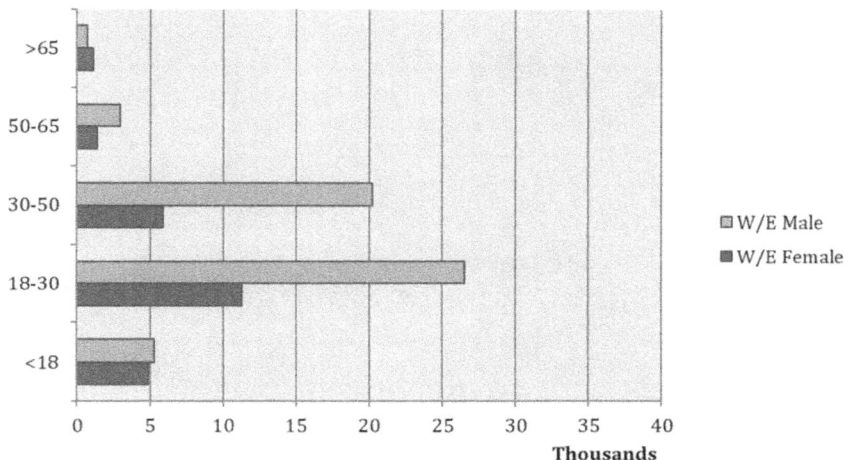

Graph 24: "Migration from Western to Eastern Germany by Age and Gender, 1991." Data source: *Statistisches Bundesamt.* "Binnenwanderung," *VII B. Wanderungstatistik* (Wiesbaden: Statistisches Bundesamt, 2005).

An examination of Graphs 24–30 shows very clearly that the largest increase in West–East migration occurred among females between the ages of 18 and 30. Taking into account that the largest increase in East to West migration in the same period also occurred amongst females between the ages of 18 and 30, in can be inferred that at least some of this eastward movement of young women at this time could be attributed to return migration.

---

32 The German Socioeconomic Panel (*Sozialökonomisches Panel*) is a household-based longitudinal study that began in 1984 with data taken for adult members of households under study, annually. Since 1990, East German households have been included in the dataset.
33 Nicola Fuchs-Schündeln and Mattias Schündeln, "Who Stays, Who Goes, Who Returns?" *Economics of Transition* 17, no. 4 (2009), 713–716.

1992

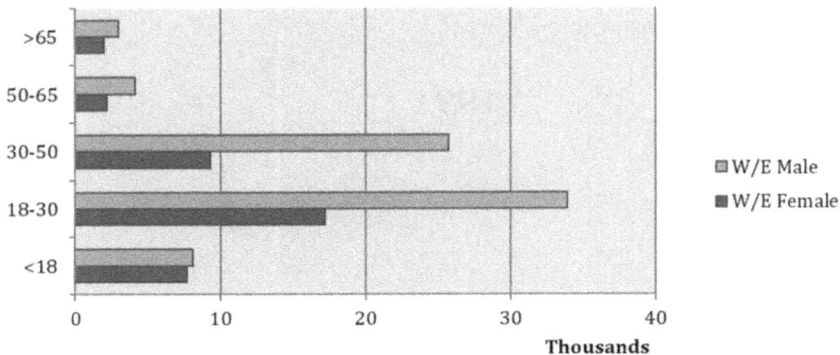

Graph 25: "Migration from Western to Eastern Germany by Age and Gender, 1992." Data source: *Statistisches Bundesamt.* "Binnenwanderung," *VII B. Wanderungstatistik* (Wiesbaden: Statistisches Bundesamt, 2005).

1993

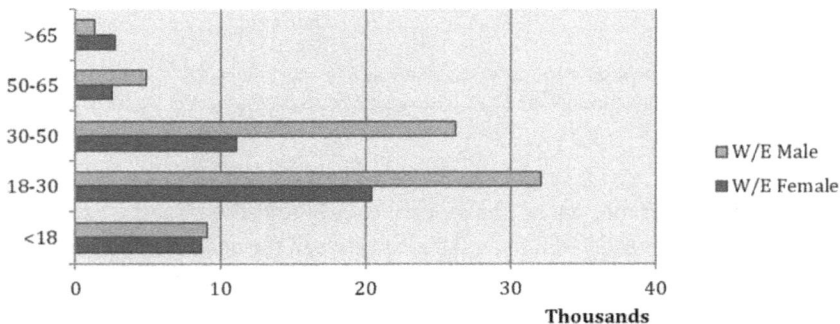

Graph 26: "Migration from Western to Eastern Germany by Age and Gender, 1993." Data source: *Statistisches Bundesamt.* "Binnenwanderung," *VII B. Wanderungstatistik* (Wiesbaden: Statistisches Bundesamt, 2005).

Return migration alone cannot account for the drastic jump in the volume of female migration between the ages of 18 and 30 in 1991–1997. Whereas in 1991, the proportion of female migration to the East had only been 42% of the male rate, by 1997, it had increased to 91%. There are a number of possible explanations for this drastic rise, including an increase in opportunities for female managers and professionals to work in the East and/or an increase in the attractiveness of East German universities to West German female students. One explanation that seems less

1994

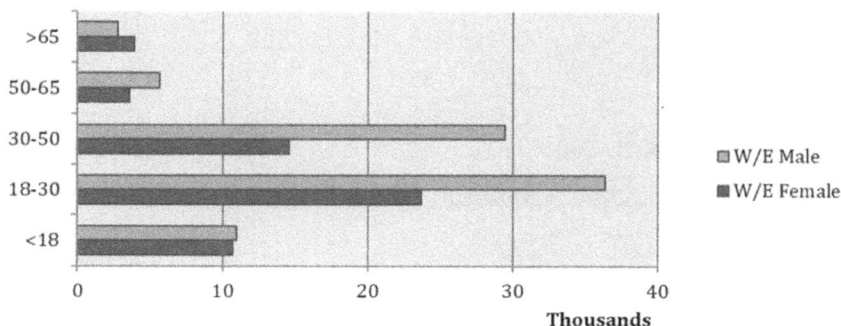

Graph 27: "Migration from Western to Eastern Germany by Age and Gender, 1994." Data source: *Statistisches Bundesamt.* "Binnenwanderung," *VII B. Wanderungstatistik* (Wiesbaden: Statistisches Bundesamt, 2005).

1995

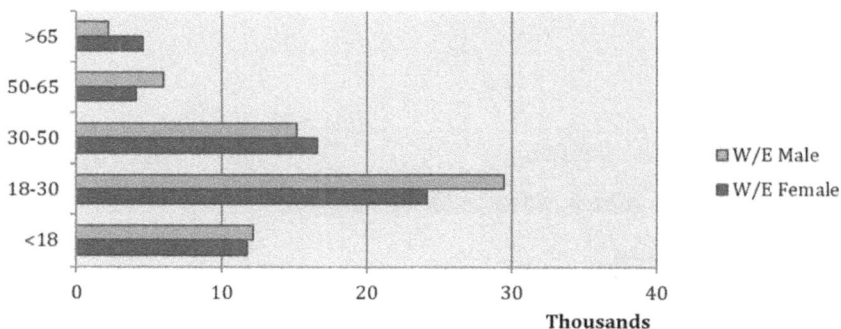

Graph 28: "Migration from Western to Eastern Germany by Age and Gender, 1995." Data source: *Statistisches Bundesamt.* "Binnenwanderung," *VII B. Wanderungstatistik* (Wiesbaden: Statistisches Bundesamt, 2005).

likely would be an increase in the volume of family migration, because there is no concurrent increase in the number of migrants under the age of 18. However, there is not enough evidence to make more than a preliminary hypothesis about the determinants of this rise.

Although net migration figures move toward convergence, an examination of East to West migration and West to East migration, 1991–1997 by establishing the gender and age composition of each stream by year reveals that the upswing that

1996

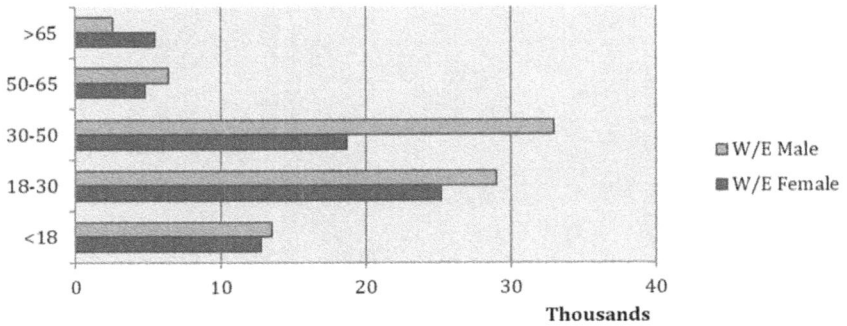

Graph 29: "Migration from Western to Eastern Germany by Age and Gender, 1996." Data source: *Statistisches Bundesamt.* "Binnenwanderung," *VII B. Wanderungstatistik* (Wiesbaden: Statistisches Bundesamt, 2005).

1997

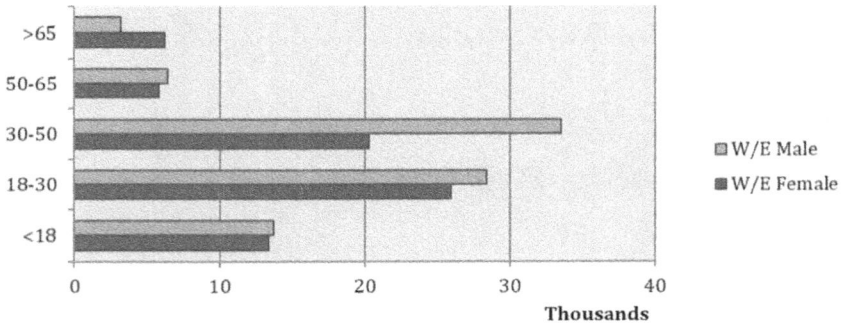

Graph 30: "Migration from Western to Eastern Germany by Age and Gender, 1997." Data source: *Statistisches Bundesamt.* "Binnenwanderung," *VII B. Wanderungstatistik* (Wiesbaden: Statistisches Bundesamt, 2005).

had been predicted for the better part of a decade in the eastern states was still quite a long way off.

1998

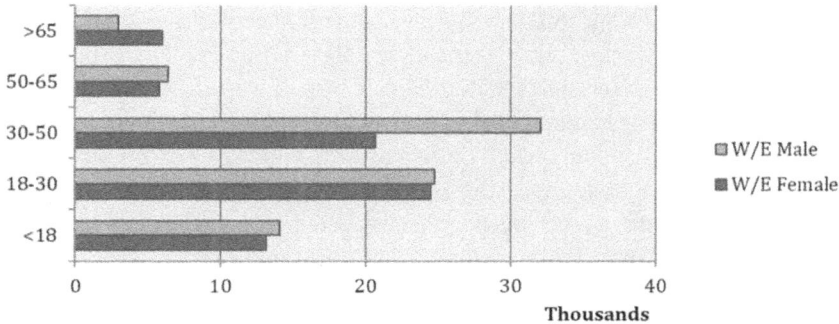

Graph 31: "Migration from Western to Eastern Germany by Age and Gender, 1998." Data source: *Statistisches Bundesamt.* "Binnenwanderung," *VII B. Wanderungstatistik* (Wiesbaden: Statistisches Bundesamt, 2005).

1999

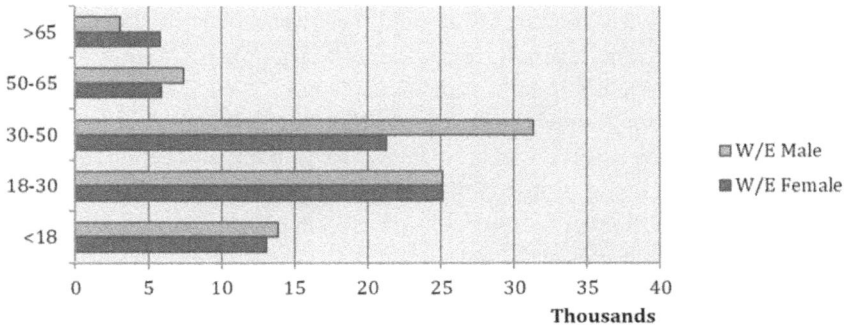

Graph 32: "Migration from Western to Eastern Germany by Age and Gender, 1999." Data source: *Statistisches Bundesamt.* "Binnenwanderung," *VII B. Wanderungstatistik* (Wiesbaden: Statistisches Bundesamt, 2005).

5.2.1 East–West Discourse After Privatization

From unification to the end of privatization, portrayals of East and West in the national press and popular culture had focused on a general state of hopelessness within the eastern states, as well as establishing a gendered discourse in which East Germans were cast as incapable of functioning after the transformation from the "socialist employment" society of the GDR to the "capitalist risk" society of the West.[34] As explored in Chapters 3 and 4, these differences were often portrayed as insurmountable; as traits bred into East Germans as a result of their socialization in the GDR. At this time however, it was expected that these incompatibilities would be washed away by the inevitable "blossoming landscapes" that would overtake the eastern states under the guidance of western expertise, much as the economic miracle had overtaken the West in the 1950s.

In the post-privatization period, there was a shift toward a more differentiated view of East-West issues, focusing more on dialogue than dissonance. A 1996 article in *Die Tagezeitung* (*taz*) for example, reported on a conference panel including two Green party activists – one West German, one East German. The key to being able to work together, these two claimed, is to be able to "forget history" in order to focus on the present. The *taz* reporter characterized the spirit of the summit as such:

> They chose not to address how *Ossis* and *Wessis* have dealt with each other since 1989, or if after seven years of German unity whether they react to each other at all. Instead of wallowing in the past, when we did not know each other, they focus on the present. "Must we be the same?" asks the moderator Marianne Birthler at the end of the East-West dialogue. "Can we not accept with wisdom that we are different? Can we not see this as an opportunity?"[35]

The call to "accept the wisdom that we are different" was a far cry from the rhetoric of incompatibility that characterized commentaries on East–West difference in the immediate aftermath of unification. In September 1998, a book review was published in the national newspaper *Die Zeit* claiming that right-wing violence was a part of everyday life in the eastern states. According to the author, this was nothing less than a lack of proper civil society in the eastern states alongside a lack of willingness of the East German politicians to speak out against xenophobic and nationalistic behavior:

> This is reflected in everyday things that shape the climate. The teacher does not condemn the swastikas on the jackets of his students, because he does not want to argue. There is right-wing violence here in the West, but in contrast to the new federal states, it is not embedded in a right-wing culture of everyday life. To be right wing, nationalist and xenophobic is normal for many East German youths today . . . when East German politicians do not openly react to right wing extremism and xenophobia, they need a strong kick and plenty of

---

34 The British German studies scholar, Eva Kolinsky, was the first to contrast the "socialist employment society" of the GDR with the "capitalist risk society" of the West, where a different socialization of competition was needed in order to secure and maintain employment throughout one's lifetime. Eva Kolinsky, *Women in Contemporary Germany: Life, Works and Politics* (Providence, R.I.: Berg, 1993), 16–18.
35 Jens Rubsam, "Vorwärts und nichts vergessen!" *taz*, October 22, 1996.

support from their western counterparts. If there it has ever been worth it to be insulted as a *"Besserwessi"* it is now.[36]

This article is not only notable for the patronizing tone of the (West) German report, which had been quite common since the xenophobic attacks on asylum seekers in the eastern city of Hoyerswerda in 1991, but also for the backlash against the use of stereotypes to advance East–West clichés. Three weeks later, the paper published a series of letters to the editor from both East and West Germans, criticizing not just the author of the article, but also the paper itself for publishing such inflammatory generalizations about East Germans. Silke E. of Treptow (East) gave a stern warning:

> In recent months, time and again, your newspaper has portrayed the image of the 'ordinary East German': It is something simple, easy to manipulate. His life revolves around orderliness, cleanliness, and diligence. Through the experience of forty years in the GDR, he has been damaged, thrown back into a pre-modern stage. The traits of tolerance and democracy have been completely bred out . . . What you may lose by such posturing is not just the support of the major democratic parties in the East, but also the great liberal daily and weekly press.[37]

Meanwhile, Axel H. of Erfurt (West) also chastised the author for spreading "prejudices and generalizations" with the purpose of blaming the East for what was, in his eyes, a "German" problem:

> How often are the *Ossis* (who themselves use that name now without negative connotation) called upon to tear down the wall in their heads? Such [news] items spread prejudices and generalizations have very little to do with reality. Needless to say, the right-wing movement is not to be underestimated, but the actions of a few should not be applied to (East) German society as a whole![38]

John N. (West), posed the following question:

> I have been living for two years as a "westerner" in Leipzig. I do not experience the atmosphere of right-wing violence the author describes . . . many East Germans cannot identify with the Federal Republic. Does the present-day Federal Republic identify with the East German?[39]

In these responses, eastern and western voices unite against the use of blanket stereotypes to characterize eastern Germans. This was a signal of sorts that the public as a whole was beginning to tire of the nature of the East–West debate as

---

36 Andrea Böhm, "Haß, nur Haß: Im Osten gehört die Gewalt von rechts zum Alltag. Die Politiker schauen Weg," *Die Zeit*, October 1, 1998.
37 "Solche Klischees Schmerzen," *Die Zeit*, October 1, 1998.
38 "Solche Klischees Schmerzen."
39 "Solche Klischees Schmerzen."

it had developed over the decade since the fall of the wall. Soon, however, the tone again would shift significantly as the economy again faltered, raising tensions in the West as well as in the East as unemployment rose again. The exodus of young people alongside the rise of the phenomenon of *Ostalgie* changed the nature of the East/West debate itself from one of direct confrontation of problems in communication, such as these letters to the editor discussed above, to that of general disengagement from personal responsibility.

5.3 Internal Migration from 1998 to 2004: The Exodus of a Generation

After achieving a near-zero net migration balance in 1997, a combination of the weakening of the German economy and the coming of age in the East of the first generation to be schooled in unified Germany triggered a second wave of emigration from the eastern states into the West. While net migration rates converged through 1997, the roots of the resurgence in westward migration can be seen as far back as 1995, when wage convergence stalled for skilled workers in the East.[40] Unemployment figures in the East also continued to rise after a period of false stabilization in 1994 and 1995. As seen in Table 1, from 1995 to 2004, the unemployment rate in the eastern states began to increase, averaging around 18%, which was more than twice the rate in the western states.

The German economy entered a state of near-recession in 1997 that substantially weakened the West German labor market, temporarily driving down westward movement due to a lack of available positions. As the German economy recovered, the labor market in the West rebounded while the eastern market remained weak. While the demand for skilled labor in the West increased, the only measurable growth in the East occurred in the unskilled service sector. The increase in available positions in the West combined with an atmosphere of stagnation and lack of opportunity in the East encouraged a new type of migrant to emigrate. These migrants, members of the first generation to come of age in a united Germany, were increasingly more likely to move West in order to attend university, undertake apprenticeships, or to begin a career.

Although less dramatic than the increase in westward migration, there was also a considerable shift in West to East movement that coincided with the dip in the German economy and the rebound of the West German labor market. Many

---

40 Hans-Werner Sinn, "Germany's Economic Unification: An Assessment after Ten Years," *Review of International Economics* 10, no. 1 (2002), 116.

West German migrants of the early 1990s who had come either as entrepreneurs or in a professional management positions left as their contracts ended or their business collapsed. In many cases, they were not replaced. As unemployment in the West decreased, motivation to take a position in the eastern states also declined.[41]

Table 1: Unemployment in Western and Eastern Germany, 1994–2004 (percentages).

	Total	West	East
1994	9.6	8.1	14.8
1995	9.4	8.1	13.9
1996	10.6	8.9	15.5
1997	11.4	9.6	17.7
1998	11.1	8.6	17.8
1999	10.5	7.6	17.3
2000	9.6	7.2	17.1
2001	9.4	7.6	17.3
2002	9.8	7.2	17.7
2003	10.4	8.2	18.5
2004	10.4	8.5	18.7

Source: *Bundesagentur für Arbeit*. http://www.destatis.de. Accessed 10.5.2010.

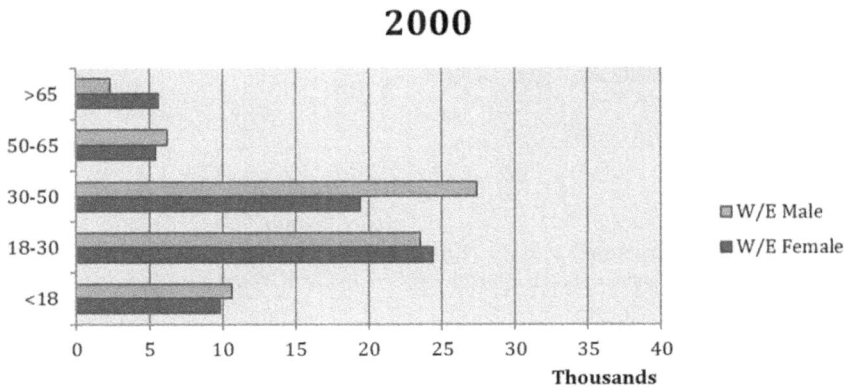

Graph 33: "Migration from Western to Eastern Germany by Age and Gender, 2000." Data source: *Statistisches Bundesamt.* "Binnenwanderung," *VII B. Wanderungstatistik* (Wiesbaden: Statistisches Bundesamt, 2005).

---

41 Nicholas Werz, "Abwanderung aus den neuen Bundesländern von 1989 bis 2000," *Aus Politik und Zeitgeschichte* 39 (2001), 28–29.

2001

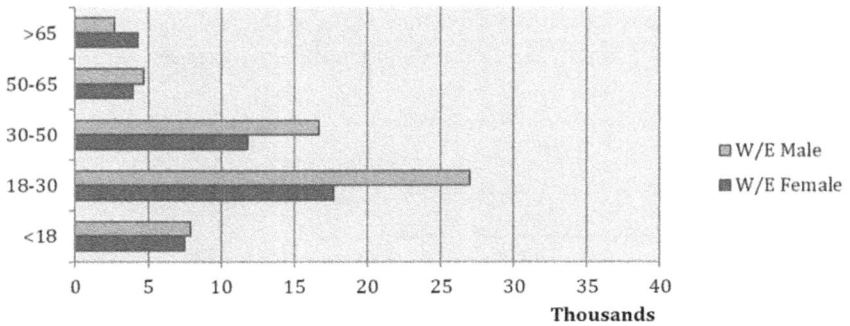

Graph 34: "Migration from Western to Eastern Germany by Age and Gender, 2001." Data source: *Statistisches Bundesamt.* "Binnenwanderung," *VII B. Wanderungstatistik* (Wiesbaden: Statistisches Bundesamt, 2005).

2002

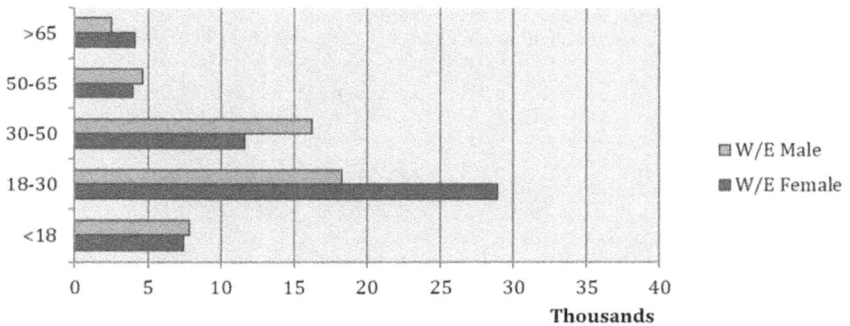

Graph 35: "Migration from Western to Eastern Germany by Age and Gender, 2002." Data source: *Statistisches Bundesamt.* "Binnenwanderung," *VII B. Wanderungstatistik* (Wiesbaden: Statistisches Bundesamt, 2005).

The age and gender composition of West to East migration shifted in the period 1999–2004. As indicated in an examination of the Graphs 31–37, there has been a distinct decrease in the number of male migrants between 30 and 50 years old, which is indicative of the withdrawal of investment from the East. Meanwhile, the volume of female migrants aged 18–30 has increased substantially. While no formal studies have specifically examined the increase in young female migration into the eastern states, anecdotal evidence points to one possible explanation. The lower cost of living in the eastern states could prove attractive to students. How-

2003

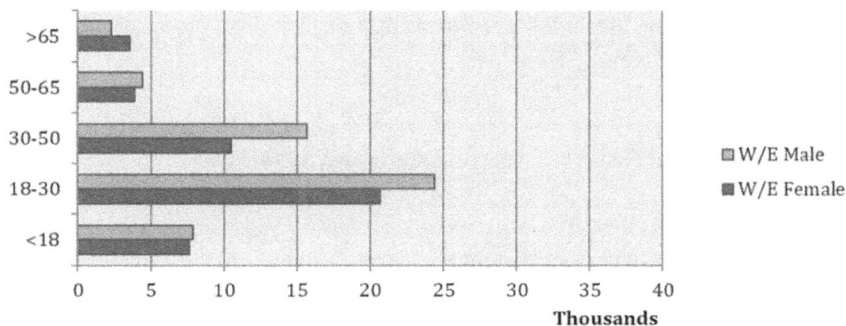

Graph 36: "Migration from Western to Eastern Germany by Age and Gender, 2003." Data source: *Statistisches Bundesamt.* "Binnenwanderung," *VII B. Wanderungstatistik* (Wiesbaden: Statistisches Bundesamt, 2005).

2004

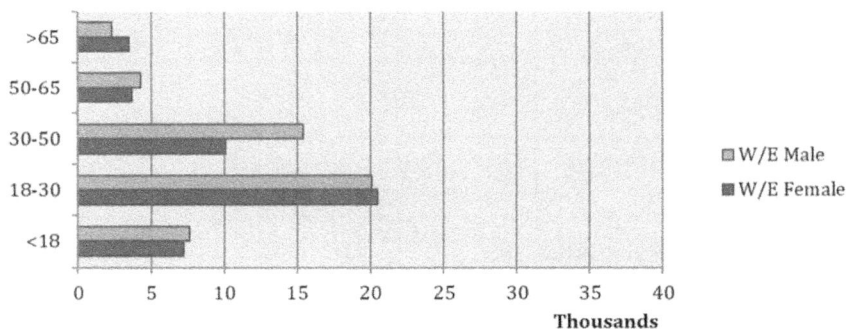

Graph 37: "Migration from Western to Eastern Germany by Age and Gender, 2004." Data source: *Statistisches Bundesamt.* "Binnenwanderung," *VII B. Wanderungstatistik* (Wiesbaden: Statistisches Bundesamt, 2005).

ever, once their studies are completed, most return to the West to work. As a 2006 report issued by the Institute for the German Economy warned, the "East German states are training Bavarian elites."[42]

---

42 Barbara Dribbusch, "Im Westen Ackern, im Osten Altern; Ost-West Wanderung: Ältere oder Studenten kommen in den neuen Bundesländern, Jüngere auf Jobsuche verlassen sie," *taz*, September 30, 2006.

In addition, a major portion of this increased migration consists of migrants returning to the eastern states. While in 1994, only 30% of those migrating to the eastern states could be identified as return migrants, by 2004, those returning accounted for more than half (56%).[43]

5.3.1 Migration from Eastern to Western Germany, 1998–2004

As in the period 1991–1996, the composition of East to West migration has been highly gender and age-specific. Compared to the previous period however, there was an increase in the volume of 18- to 30-year-olds emigrating to the western states. Over time, this age group has become progressively larger, peaking in 2003 at just over 87,000 compared to 54,000 in 1996.

The increase in the number of migrants between the ages of 18 and 30 is the result of the coming of age of the first East German generation to have been educated in unified Germany. Knowing little of the GDR and having completed most (if not all) of their schooling in unified Germany, this generation responded to the prolonged economic drought in the East by seeking apprenticeships and univer-

1998

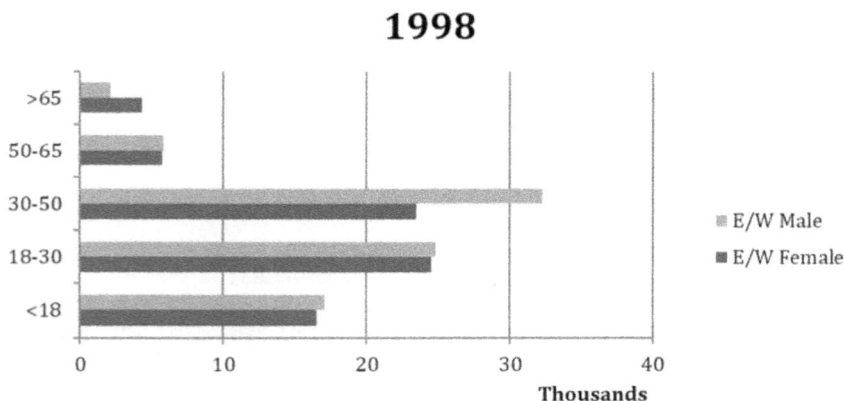

Graph 38: "Migration from Eastern to Western Germany by Age and Gender, 1998." Data source: *Statistisches Bundesamt.* "Binnenwanderung," *VII B. Wanderungstatistik* (Wiesbaden: Statistisches Bundesamt, 2005).

---

[43] Grit Beck, "Wandern gegen den Strom. West-Ost-Migration in Deutschland," in *Bevölkerungsgeographische Forschung zur Migration und Integration,* ed. Frank Swiaczny and Sonja Haug (Wiesbaden: BiB, 2004), 103–105.

1999

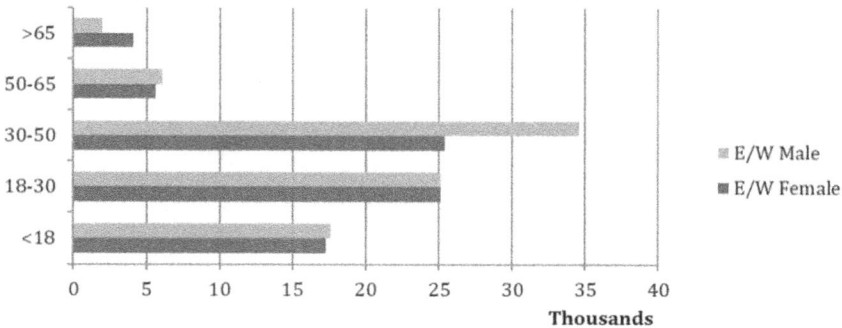

Graph 39: "Migration from Eastern to Western Germany by Age and Gender, 1999." Data source: *Statistisches Bundesamt.* "Binnenwanderung," *VII B. Wanderungstatistik* (Wiesbaden: Statistisches Bundesamt, 2005).

2000

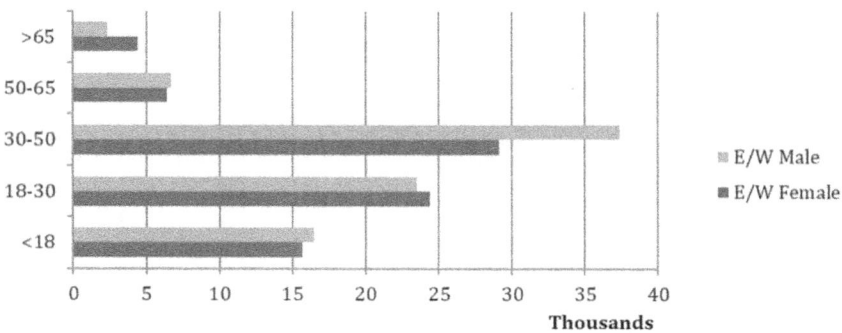

Graph 40: "Migration from Eastern to Western Germany by Age and Gender, 2000." Data source: *Statistisches Bundesamt.* "Binnenwanderung," *VII B. Wanderungstatistik* (Wiesbaden: Statistisches Bundesamt, 2005).

sity spots in the West.[44] "There was no question that I would go to the West for university," explains Nicole Dreyer, who left a farming village in the rural eastern state of Mecklenburg West-Pomerania for the West German university city of Bremen in order to study marine biology:

---

[44] Ralf Mai, Abwanderung aus Ostdeutschland: Strukturen und Milieus der Alterselektivität und Ihre Regionalpolitische Bedeutung (Berlin: Lang, 2004), 207–219.

2001

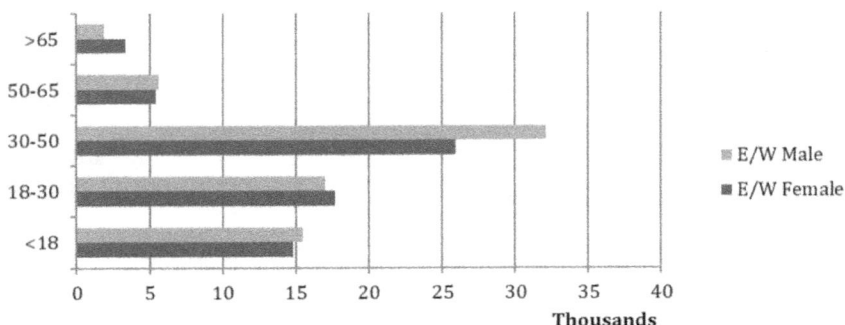

Graph 41: "Migration from Eastern to Western Germany by Age and Gender, 2001." Data source: *Statistisches Bundesamt.* "Binnenwanderung," *VII B. Wanderungstatistik* (Wiesbaden: Statistisches Bundesamt, 2005).

2002

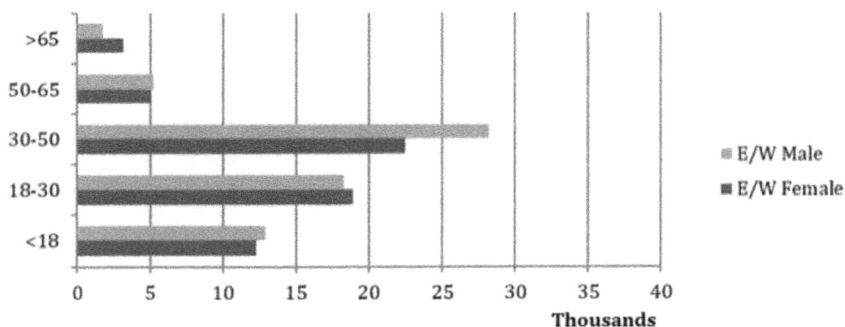

Graph 42: "Migration from Eastern to Western Germany by Age and Gender, 2002." Data source: *Statistisches Bundesamt.* "Binnenwanderung," *VII B. Wanderungstatistik* (Wiesbaden: Statistisches Bundesamt, 2005).

> In fact, the decision was quite easy. I did not feel secure in maintaining a place at an East German university . . . the university places were not guaranteed to last through the program. Even if I could finish my degree, I probably would have had to move to the West anyway because of the better job opportunities there.[45]

---

45 Eckhard Stengel, "Go West: Nicole Dreyer tauschte Meck-Pomm gegen Bremen und träumt von einem Job als Meeresforscherin," Frankfurter Rundschau, August 22, 2006.

2003

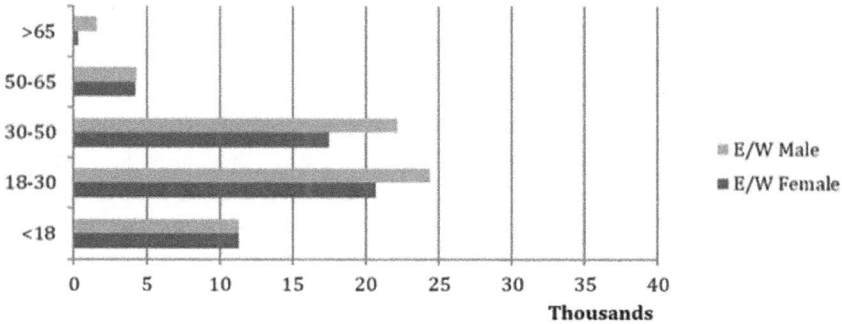

Graph 43: "Migration from Eastern to Western Germany by Age and Gender, 2003." Data source: *Statistisches Bundesamt*. "Binnenwanderung," *VII B. Wanderungstatistik* (Wiesbaden: Statistisches Bundesamt, 2005).

2004

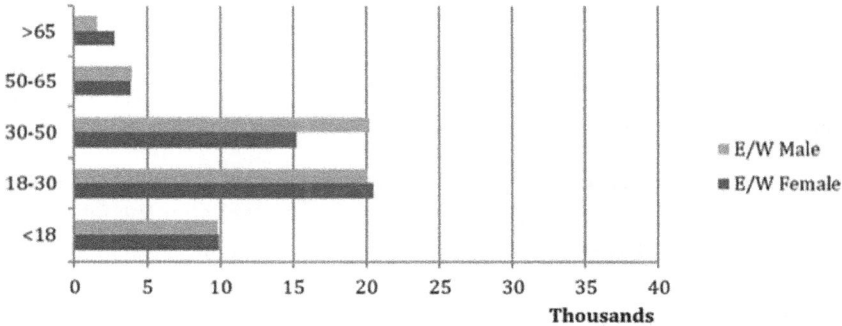

Graph 44: "Migration from Eastern to Western Germany by Age and Gender, 2004." Data source: *Statistisches Bundesamt*. "Binnenwanderung," *VII B. Wanderungstatistik* (Wiesbaden: Statistisches Bundesamt, 2005).

Dreyer in many ways embodies the typical East-West migrant of the new generation; she is young (20 years old), female, and from a rural background. Population researcher, Stefan Kröhnert, sums up the rural exodus simply as a phenomenon of "the smart women from the farmlands leaving the poor worker boys behind."[46] From 1998 to 2004, the volume of female migrants in the ages of 18–30 remained

---

[46] Simone Schmollack, "Bloß Weg hier," taz, June 25, 2007.

high. Women were leaving rural areas for eastern cities as well. In the same period, for every four women who went West, five women moved from a rural village or town of 1,000 or fewer inhabitants to a city of 10,000 or more.[47] This decimated places like Eggesin, for example, a rural town in Mecklenburg-West Pomerania, that have previously been the headquarters for the National People's Army during the GDR, but had shrunk from a population of 9500 in 1990 to just 5000 in 2007. Young people also departed nearby Ahlbeck, a small village close to the Polish border. The already tiny population decreased from 900 inhabitants in 1990 to just 775 in 2007. Furthermore, the absence of young people (and their future children) has elevated the average age in the village to 52.[48]

There are several theories as to why more young women than men chose to leave the East for prospects in the West. First and foremost, it is argued that women simply perform better in school than eastern men. As reported in the German English language online newsmagazine *Deutsche Welle*,

> Women in eastern Germany have tended to get better education. Germany's school system places students around the age of 10 on one of three educational tracks. In the east, 31 percent of women get in the highest, university bound track. Among men, the number was only 21 percent. Twice as many boys as girls drop out of school. Gottfried Richter, a regional administrator from the former industrial town of Elster Elbe in southern Brandenburg describes the situation thusly: "Girls have done better in school and had more choices. So over the past 10 years, they've taken their good report cards and left to find jobs." The boys, he added were more likely to stay where their friends were and where they had their roots even though the unemployment rate there is 19 percent.[49]

The continued prevalence of young female migration worsened the decline in the birth rate that began shortly after unification. Twenty years after the fall of the Berlin Wall, the demographic consequences of the shortage of young females is reflected in a drastic aging of the population as well as a significant decline in the number of young children. It has even been argued that a shortage of women has contributed to the increase in right-wing extremism and xenophobia in rural eastern Germany, because the unemployed young men who are left behind when the young women depart are unable to find partners.[50]

Once young women left for education or training, they were highly unlikely to return to the East. A primary factor in their proclivity to stay was their choice

---

47 Mai, Abwanderung aus Ostdeutschland, 156–157.
48 Schmollack, "Bloß Weg hier."
49 "Women Fleeing Eastern Germany, Leaving Men Behind," Deutsche Welle. http://www.dwworld.de/dw/article/0,,22578834,00.html. June 6, 2007. Accessed May 5, 2010.
50 Steffen Kröhnert and Reiner Klingholz, *Not am Mann: Von Helden der Arbeit zur neuen Unterschicht?* (Berlin: BIfBE, 2007), 142–151.

of partners. Anecdotal evidence indicates that those who found West German partners most often stayed in the West. According to an article in *Der Spiegel* covering a study by the Berlin Institute for Population Research exploring the "Crisis of Men" in the eastern states, the reasons behind the demise of the East go beyond macroeconomic dysfunction, to reflect the gendered stereotypes prevalent in the aftermath of unification:

> The crisis is also a story about women and men: the women who break away because they want more from life, who stand on their own two feet and desire to find a man who has standards as high as themselves; it is the story of men who want to remain, as they are, what they are, where they are. Therefore, it is predictable that an eastern woman would go into the glittering West; to snap up Mr. Right, get 1.34 children, never to return. However, the eastern man is lonely and childless, and the result is his unending self-pity and an unemployment rate in the double digits.[51]

According to a report in *Die Welt*, West German women who migrate to the East do not provide a potential solution to the lack of mates for East German men. The primary turn off is the characterization of eastern German men as lacking drive and ambition:

> The chic [female] CEOs from the West are in fact not the only ones with whom a large part of the boys have no chance. Even the ambitious women of the East say with best regards: "Hartz-IV candidates whose idea of an exciting weekend is a TV dinner with canned beer? – No thanks!"[52]

These remarks strongly recall discussions of East/West difference in the early 1990s when East German men were stereotyped as out of step and too timid to be successful in the capitalist "risk" society offered by the West. Almost 20 years on, although the constant chatter of difference had become somewhat muted, this underlying tone of incompatibility persists. In the eyes of western researchers, the cycle of demographic decline and economic stagnation is perpetuated by the lack of initiative and attractiveness of East German men.

Demographic consequences of emigration have influenced and reinforced characterizations of the East and its people, bringing back the old Cold War joke that the DDR stood not for the *Deutsche Demokratische Republik*, but rather for *Der doofe Rest* (the dummies left behind). In 2002, demographer Wolfgang Weiß was quoted in *Der Spiegel* as saying that the exodus of intelligent and engaged people from the East had become a "flight for life." Weiß claimed that this demo-

---

51 Andrea Brandt et al., "Geld oder Liebe?" *Der Spiegel*, June 4, 2007.
52 Hartz-IV refers to the controversial reform program that took effect January 1, 2005, merging long-term unemployment benefits with social welfare benefits, thereby reducing the overall total amount and duration of payments to the chronically unemployed.

graphic implosion had led to the "thinning out of intelligence in some rural areas – which had produced a "socially conditioned imbecility" among the remaining population. The solution, suggests Weiß, is to acknowledge that the East is too far-gone to benefit from further investment. It would be better to "convert the fertile land into organic farms and to use what is left over as land for retirement homes."[53]

Meanwhile, the commercial success of the phenomenon of *Ostalgie* – the "nostalgia for the East" – has performed a dual role, allowing East Germans to get back in touch with the material remnants of their past (or to develop a relationship with them in the first place), while also making it available for purchase and consumption. While "hip" young West German students purchased salvaged GDR era furniture to house in their retro style flats in the trendy East Berlin neighborhoods of Prenzlauer Berg and Pankow, beloved GDR brands such as the *Sandmannchen* children's cartoon and *Spee* laundry soap were brought back to life by West German entities.[54] The commercial success of films such as *Goodbye Lenin!* and *The Lives of Others* bring back certain feelings and experiences for older East Germans, while simultaneously discrediting the complexity of the East German experience by making it accessible for consumption by non-East Germans.

It is this unique combination of these two phenomena: continued westward migration due to a lack of opportunity in the East combined with a nostalgia rooted in a constructed memory of the GDR that has kept the conversation concerning the "essentiality" of East–West difference alive, more than 20 years after the GDR ceased to exist. This is a conversation that continues to hold power through a paradox of constant dialogue reifying East/West difference combined with a lack of willingness to confront the issues at hand on the level of the individual.

---

53 Irina von Repke, Andreas Wasserman and Steffen Winter, "Wieder der Doofe Rest? *Der Spiegel*, January 14, 2002.

54 The availability of consumer goods is a major subject of many commentaries on *Ostalgie*. This, in turn, has its roots in the consumer envy developed ruing the Cold War by East Germans toward the West as a result of the close proximity to West German goods. Ironically, the rapid push toward unification and the demand for West German goods drove most GDR manufacturers out of business. It was only in the mid- to late 1990s that GDR goods became available once again, though in many cases they were manufactured in West Germany by West German companies.

6 Conclusion

In March 2009, in honor of the twentieth anniversary of the fall of the Berlin Wall, the German Fulbright Commission hosted its yearly seminar in Berlin under the label, "1989–2009: New Hopes – New Challenges." Although it was meant to be an open investigation of the two decades of German unity for over 200 German and American scholars participating in Fulbright programs across Europe and the United States, the seminar organizers unfortunately seemed to fall short of their goal. The inaugural panel, "German Unification: Chances and Challenges," consisted of four members: three West Germans and one American, plus the moderator Margaret Heckle and the (West German) political editor of *Die Welt*. Over the course of 2 hours, personal stories covering the fall of the Wall, the political challenges of unification, and above all, the economic condition of the eastern states were discussed in earnest. What was missing however is what is missing in much of the discussion of German unity in the last decade – the voice of the East German people. The story of German unity, 20 years on, is still very much a West German tale.

As the eastern German states sank into demographic decline and economic stagnation in recent years, all too often, East German voices have been obscured in favor of West German admonishments, predictions, research, and prescriptions. Although the commentaries on the differences between East and West remain at the forefront of political, economic, social, and cultural discourse, each year as the anniversary of the fall of the Wall approaches, magazines and newspaper headlines inquire if there really is still a divide of which to speak.

The answer is still a resounding "yes," but as the economic situation in the East has deteriorated, and above all, a new generation of East Germans has made its way to the West to seek their fortunes, the nature of the debate has changed. Instead of the shocked portraits of eastern whininess or western snobbery, the debate oscillates between detailing the struggles of the everyday on the statistical level through detailed demographic reports and prognoses, and identifying the decline of difference by identifying the "exception to the rule" (i.e., "My neighbor came in 1995 from *over there*, but you can't even tell."). In both cases however, there exists a subaltern East German – male, overweight, unemployed, and without drive toward anything, save right wing extremism.

The phenomenon of *Ostalgie* coincided with the resurgence in the urgency of the westward movement of young East Germans. As the region struggled to establish itself economically, the revival of eastern products and the production of films, television programs and literature about everyday life in the GDR sought to prove that one could and did live a *"ganz normales Leben"* (completely normal

https://doi.org/10.1515/9783110716221-007

life) in the GDR. Moreover, some aspects of life were even preferable to those in the West. The sudden commercialization of the GDR, although often criticized as glossing over the dark side of German communism, provided the generation coming of age in the late 1990s and early 2000s with a foothold to identify with the GDR, on their own terms. In short, the commercialization of the GDR made the GR accessible to those who had little or no experience actually living in it.

On the other hand, the commoditization of life in the GDR has also altered its relationship with the West. The spectacle of *Ostalgie* variety shows featuring Katerina Witt parading various household goods and scrapbook mementos from life under "real existing socialism" have allowed the West to detach from trying to figure out what the relationship between East and West really was, is, or should be. The production of objects (many made by West German companies) allows the West German to handle, consume, and digest the East, at will. In my estimation, this detachment has manifested itself in a lack of engagement with the East Germans as people – for their concerns, their experiences, their hopes, or their dreams. Meanwhile, if the "bleeding out" of the eastern states continues as it has over the past two decades, there soon may not be any East German to consider in any case.

This book has traced the intimate ties between mobility and constructions of German identity from the end of the Second World War through two decades of German unity. The categorization of German refugees, evacuees, and expellees in both the FRG and the GDR exposes how tentative and frail the conceptions of "German" identity remained in the shadow of the war. Both German states, formed out of the rubble of war and carefully composed in political, economic, social, and cultural opposition, struggled not only to rebuild, but to redefine what being "German" would mean in the postwar world. Utilizing a combination of demographic and discursive source bases, examining the establishment and continual reconfiguration of the migrants, and the categories they fit into – or did not fit into – this work has shown that the establishment of categories of difference was key in controlling migration and migrants to fit various state and local narrative functions. From the foundation of migration as a function of victimhood in the days after the end of the Second World War to the continual discussion of what constituted "legitimate" migration – both in the East and in the West – German identities became bound up in definitions of belonging – and belonging became a very narrow category.

The threshold of the construction of the Berlin Wall intensified issues of legitimacy as the number of migrants fell in the 1960s and 1970s and then rose again in the 1980s. As the numbers increased, West Germans began to discuss again the issue of what constituted political (or legitimate) migration and what constituted economic (illegitimate) migration. This would serve as the foundation for the discourse surrounding migration after the fall of the wall, and a key issue in the quick decision toward unification.

On the eve of the fall of the Berlin Wall, the politicization of the escape from the GDR meant that those who arrived in the West were welcomed with open arms. However, as more migrants began to arrive and less space became available, GDR refugees were increasingly portrayed in terms of difference. As the story went, the socialization of East Germans in the totalitarian atmosphere of the GDR had made the vast majority unable to function within a western society of free market choice. Despite the euphoric images of East and West Germans joyfully celebrating that are firmly established as the historical memory of the day the Berlin Wall fell, the opening of the German–German border resulted in an escalation of negativity toward the East Germans who came to the West to stay.

The evolution of coverage of GDR refugees in the national, regional, and local press that followed indicates that as the West German space and resources became increasingly strained, East German "brothers and sisters" were portrayed as socially damaged, criminally corrupt, or as parasitical to the West German social system. The debates surrounding GDR refugees in 1989/1990 also destabilized a core element of the postwar West German identity by putting the security of the welfare state in direct conflict with aid for refugees of German blood. As emigration from the GDR continued with fervor, it became clear that the only solution to the conflict between the right to return and the problem of GDR refugees was rapid unification. However, the cessation of aid did not put a stop to the negative perception of GDR refugees.

The rapid change in the perception of GDR refugees that occurred between the fall of the Berlin Wall and unification was founded upon contact and perceptions of migration. These laid a foundation for a continuing and evolving discourse of difference between East and West Germans for decades after unification. While the initial economic shock caused by the wholesale restructuring of the GDR in the image of the West resulted in widespread unemployment in each of the five new eastern states, it was portrayed as a temporary situation that would be remedied once the economy in the East had stabilized. However, the "blossoming landscapes" promised by Helmut Kohl never materialized and the market did not grow as predicted. As it became clear that there would be no economic miracle in the East, the combination of this initial displacement of workers and a continued lack of new opportunities fueled a continuing emigration of skilled workers well into the twenty-first century.

The loss of a high proportion of the most productive portion of the East German population resulted in a skill gap that further discouraged investment in the East, long after privatization ended. In addition, a considerable percentage of westward migrants were both young and female, which according to demographic researchers, had contributed to the further decline of the birthrate in the eastern states, especially in rural areas. The prolonged emigration of productive females over the last two decades had aided in the perpetuation of a cycle of emigration and structural weakness that has in turn prevented growth, and made the region unattractive to investment, both domestic and foreign.

While many experts lauded the coming of the *Aufschwung Ost*, the labor market in the East seemed to be stabilized with the decline of East-West migration from 1994 to 1997. This was only a temporary consequence of the generational change. An examination of the internal migration patterns from 1998 to 2004 reveals that emigration once again increased as the first generation to be schooled in united Germany came of age, while there was a concurrent decline in eastward migration as investment tapered off. Seeing little future in the East, a disproportionate number of westward migrants in this period were members of the most productive (and reproductive) age group. In addition, there was also a sharp rise in the emigration of young women from rural areas to urban areas, both in the eastern and western states. This long-term migration trend has resulted in an even steeper decline in the eastern birthrate and a drastic aging of the population that has called into serious question the prospects for an economic turnaround and revival of investment in the East.

The future lies in the debates surrounding the prospects for economic revival in the eastern states. As this book has argued, there exists a real and tangible divide between East and West Germans, more than two decades after the fall of the wall. However, the voices debating the existence of unity come most often from the West. As long as East Germans are not included in this debate as equal partners, as opposed to deficient younger brothers, the gulf between the overarching, yet one-sided discourse on German unity and the demographic and economic stabilization of the eastern states will continue to persist.

In addition to pointing to the persistence of regional differences, understanding the complexity of the relationship between migration and mobility, gender, ethnicity, and identity throughout the volatility of the Second World War, Cold War, the collapse of the Soviet Bloc, German unification, the formation and partial dismantling of the European Union (economically (and often politically) driven by German polities and preferences), also aids in the understanding of the persistence of the fear of the other, and a rise in anti-migration rhetoric in the shrunken, yet still global world of the twenty-first century. Examining how the legitimate and illegitimate migration is continually redefined through political unrest, war, economic dislocation, and a global pandemic raises awareness of how powerful and present are the nineteenth and early twentieth century conceptions of ethnicity, belonging, nationality, and entitlement.

Examining German history through the lens of migration and mobility – and sensing the continuity between the need to extend shelter, aid, and legitimacy only to "deserving" individuals – fundamentally upends traditional historiography by placing issues of identity – not only defined through policy but also reflected in public narratives – at the forefront. Developing an integrated yet interdisciplinary historiography of German identity will begin to shift both academic and public discourse surrounding the rigidity of what is considered legitimate mobility, and who is considered to be German. Seeing migration and mobility, not as an aberration but as a common feature of life, will hopefully break down some of the barriers that reinforce destructive narratives of illegitimacy and otherness. Detailing patterns and the development of these narratives through periods of crises, as I have done within this book, is the first step toward understanding the connection between migration and identity, and can hopefully lead toward further examination of how "otherness" is defined, redefined, and used to reinforce regimes of exclusion.

Bibliography

Statistical Sources

Bundesrepublik Deutschland (West) – Statistisches Bundesamt Wiesbaden. *Statistisches* Jahrbuch für die Bundesrepublik Deutschland. Wiesbaden: Statistisches Bundesamt, 1952–1990.

Bundesrepublik Deutschland – Statistisches Bundesamt Wiesbaden. *Statistisches Jahrbuch für die Bundesrepublik Deutschland*. Wiesbaden: Statistisches Bundesamt, 1991–2006.

Deutsche Demokratische Republik – Staatliche Zentralverwaltung für Statistik. *Statistisches Jahrbuch der Deutsche Demokratischen Republik*. Berlin [-Ost]: Deutscher Zentralverlag, 1955–1990.

Stadt Leipzig – Statistisches Amt. *Bevölkerungsentwicklung, 1991–2003*. Leipzig: Amt für Statistik und Wählen Stadt Leipzig.

Statistisches Bundesamt Deutschland. "Genesis-Online Database." Online Resources. https://www-genesis.destatis.de

Newspapers and Magazines

Berliner Zeitung

Bild

Focus

Frankfurter Allgemeine Zeitung

Frankfurter Rundschau

Frankenpost

Hamburger Abendblatt

Kulturspiegel

Leipziger Volkszeitung

Neues Deutschland

Der Spiegel

Spiegel Extra

Süddeutsche Zeitung

Die Tageszeitung (taz)

Die Welt

Die Zeit

Other Primary Sources

Amnesty International. *The GDR Annual Report*. London Amnesty International, 1989.

Brandt, Willy. "Die Bedeutung der Massenflucht aus der Sowjetzone." *Gewerkschaftliche Monatshefte* 4, no. 4 (1953): 224–228.

Jürgs, Michael and Angela Elis. Typisch Ossi, Typisch Wessi: eine längst fällige Abrechnung unter Brüdern und Schwestern. München: C. Bertelsmann, 2005.

https://doi.org/10.1515/9783110716221-008

Rohnstock, Katrin. Stiefbrüder: was Ostmänner und Westmänner voneinander denken. Berlin: Elefanten Press, 1995.

Rohnstock, Katrin. Stiefschwester: Was Ost-Frauen und West-Frauen voneinander *denken*. Frankfurt am Main: Fischer Taschenbuch Verlag, 1994.

Simon, Jana, Frank Rothe, and Wiete Andrasch. *Das Buch der Unterschiede: warum die Einheit keine ist*. Berlin: Aufbau-Verlag, 2000.

Statistical Office of Berlin. "Refugees Flooding the Island of Berlin: Senate of Berlin Report." Berlin: Senate of Berlin, 1953.

Secondary Sources

Ackermann, Volker. Der "echte" Flüchtling: Deutsche Vertriebene und Flüchtlinge aus *der DDR, 1945-1961*. Osnabrück: Universitätsverlag Rasch, 1995.

Assmann, Aleida. *Das neue Unbehagen an der Erinnerungskultur: Eine Intervention*. München: C.H. Beck, 2013.

Bade, Klaus J. Europa in Bewegung: Migration vom späten 18. Jahrhundert bis zur *Gegenwart*. München: C. H Beck, 2000.

Bade, Klaus J. "German Emigration to the United States and Continental Immigration to Germany in the Late Nineteenth and Early Twentieth Centuries." *Central European History* 13, no. 4 (1980): 348-377.

Bade, Klaus J., and Jochen Oltmer. "Einführung: Einwanderungsland Niedersachsen – Zuwanderung und Integration seit dem Zweiten Weltkrieg." In *Zuwanderung und Integration in Niedersachsen seit dem Zweiten Weltkrieg*, edited by Klaus J. Bade and Jochen Oltmer, 11–36. Osnabrück: Universitätsverlag Rasch, 2002.

Bade, Klaus J., and Jochen Oltmer. "Flucht und Vertreibung nach dem zweiten Weltkrieg." In *Enzyklopädie Migration in Europa: vom 17. Jahrhundert bis zur Gegenwart*, edited by Pieter C. Emmer, Leo Lucassen and Jochen Oltmer. Paderborn: Schöningh, 2007.

Bade, Klaus J., and Jochen Oltmer. "Mitteleuropa: Deutschland." In *Enzyklopädie Migration in Europa: vom 17. Jahrhundert bis zur Gegenwart*, edited by Pieter C. Emmer, Leo Lucassen and Jochen Oltmer, 141–170. Paderborn: Schöningh, 2007.

Bartov, Omer. "Germany as Victim." *New German Critique* 80 (2000): 29–40.

Berdahl, Daphne. "The Spirit of Capitalism and the Boundaries of Citizenship in Post-Wall Germany." *Comparative Studies in Society History* 47, no. 2 (2005): 235–251.

Berdahl, Daphne. Where the World Ended: Re-Unification and Identity in the German *Borderland*. Berkeley, Calif.: University of California Press, 1999.

Blaschke, Monika, and Christiane Harzig, eds. *Frauen wandern aus: Deutsche* Migrantinnen im 19. und 20. Jahrhundert. Bremen: Universitätsdruck, 1991.

Blessing, Benita. "Review of Betts, Paul; Pence, Katherine, Socialist Modern: East German Everyday Culture and Politics." *H-German* July (2008).

Boltho, Andrea, Wendy Carlin, and Pasquale Scaramozzio. "Will East Germany become another Mezzogiorno?" *Journal of Comparative Economics* 24, no. 3 (1997): 241–264.

Boyer, Dominic. "Conspiracy, History and Therapy at a Berlin Stammtisch." *American Ethnologist* 33, no. 3 (2006): 327–339.

Boyer, Dominic "Media Markets, Mediating Labors and the Branding of East German Culture at Super Illu." *Social Text* 19, no. 3 (2001): 9–34.

Boyer, Dominic "Postcommunist Nostalgia in Eastern Germany: An Alternative Analysis." *Public Culture* 18, no. 2 (2006): 2006.

Brubaker, Rogers, and Frederick Cooper. "Beyond "Identity"." *Theory and Society*, 29no. 1 (2000): 1–47.

Castles, Stephen, and Mark Miller. *The Age of Migration*. New York: Guilford Press, 2009.

Chin, Rita C. K. The Guest Worker Question in Postwar Germany. New York: Cambridge University Press, 2007.

Connor, Ian. "German Refugees and the Bonn Government's Resettlement Programme: The Role of the Trek Association in Schleswig-Holstein, 1951–3." *German History* 18, no. 3 (2000): 337–361.

Cordeil, Karl. "The Role of the Evangelical Church in the GDR." *Government and Opposition* 25, no. 1 (2007): 48–59.

Decressin, Jörg. "Internal Migration in West Germany and Implications for East-West Salary Convergence." *Review of World Economics* 130, no. 2 (1994): 231–257.

Denham, Scott D., Irene Kacandes, and Jonathan Petropoulos. *A User's Guide to German Cultural Studies*, Social History, Popular Culture, and Politics in Germany. Ann Arbor: University of Michigan Press, 1997.

Diefendorf, Jeffery. In the Wake of War: The Reconstruction of German Cities after *World War II* New York: Oxford University Press, 1993.

Elliot, Mark. "The United States and Forced Repatriation of Soviet Citizens." *Political Science Quarterly* 88, no. 2 (1973): 253–275.

Fertig, Georg. "Eighteenth-Century Transatlantic Migration and Early German Anti Migration Ideology " In *Migration, Migration History, History*, edited by Jan Lucassen and Leo Lucassen. New York: P. Lang, 1999.

Fulbrook, Mary. German National Identity after the Holocaust. Maiden, MA: Blackwell, 1999.

Fulbrook, Mary. Power and Society in the GDR, 1961–1979: The 'Normalisation of Rule'? New York: Berghahn, 2009.

Fulbrook, Mary. The People's State: East German Society from Hitler to Honecker. London: Yale University Press, 2005.

Geddes, Andrew. The Politics of Migration and Immigration in Europe. London: Sage, 2003.

Gladen, Albin. Hollandsgang im Spiegel der Reiseberichte evangelischer Geistlicher: Quellen zur saisonalen Arbeitswanderung in der zweiten Hälfte des 19. *Jahrhunderts*. Münster: Aschendorff, 2007.

Glaeser, Andreas. Divided in Unity: Identity, Germany, and the Berlin Police. Chicago: University of Chicago Press, 2000.

Goeken-Haidl, Ulrike. Der Weg zurück: Die Repatriierung Sowjetischer Zwangsarbeiter Wahrend und nach dem Zweiten Weltkrieg. Essen: Klartext Verlag, 2006.

Green, Nancy L. and Francois Weil, eds. *Citizenship and Those Who Leave: The* Politics of Emigration and Expatriation. Champaign-Urbana, IL: University of Illinois Press, 2007.

Grundmann, Siegfried, and Irene Schmidt. "Zur Binnenwanderung in der DDR." Zeitschrift für Erkundeunterricht 42, no. 7 (1990): 235–241.

Harsch, Donna. Revenge of the Domestic: Women, the Family and Communism in the *German Democratic Republic*. Princeton, N.J.: Princeton University Press, 2007.

Hasan, Cil. Anfänge einer Epoche: Ehemalige türkische Gastarbeiter erzählen – Bir Dönemin Baslangiclari: Bir Zamanlarin Konuk Iscileri Anlatiyor. Berlin: Verlag Hans Schiller, 2003.

Heinemann, Elizabeth. "The Hour of the Woman: Memories of Germany's "Crisis Years" and West German National Identity." *American Historical Review* 101, no. 2 (1996): 354–395.

Herbert, Ulrich. A History of Foreign Labor in Germany, 1880–1990: Seasonal Workers, Forced Laborers, Guest Workers. Ann Arbor: University of Michigan Press, 1990.

Herbert, Ulrich. Geschichte der Ausländerpolitik in Deutschland: Saisonarbeiter, Zwangsarbeiter, Gastarbeiter, Flüchtlinge München: C.H. Beck, 2001.

Herf, Jeffrey. Divided Memory: the Nazi past in the two Germanys. Cambridge: Harvard University Press, 1997.

Hochstadt, Steve. "Migration in Preindustrial Germany." *Central European History* 16, no. 3 (1983): 195–224.

Hochstadt, Steve. Mobility and Modernity: Migration in Germany, 1820–1989. Ann Arbor: University of Michigan Press, 1999.

Howard, Mark. "An East German Ethnicity? Understanding the New Division in Unified Germany." *German Politics and Society* 13, no. 4 (1995): 49–70.

Hunn, Karin. "Nächstes Jahr kehren wir zurück" Die Geschichte der türkischen Gasarbeiter in der Bundesrepublik. Göttingen: Wallstein Verlag, 2005.

Jackson Jr., James H. Migration and Urbanization in the Ruhr Valley, 1821–1914, Atlantic Highlands, N.J.: Humanities Press, 1997.

Jarausch, Konrad. After Hitler: Recivilizing Germans, 1945–1955. Oxford: Oxford University Press, 2006.

Jarausch, Konrad. ed. After Unity: Reconfiguring German Identities. Providence, R.I.: Berghahn Books, 1997.

Jarausch, Konrad, and Michael Geyer. Shattered Past: Reconstructing German *Histories*. Princeton, N.J.: Princeton University Press, 2003.

Keller, Wolfgang. "From Socialist Showcase to Mezzogiorno?" *Journal of Development Economics* 63, no. 2 (2000): 485–514.

Klee, Katja. "Luftschutzkeller des Reiches": Evakuierte in Bayern 1939–1953: Politik, *Soziale Lage, Erfahrungen*, Schriftenreihe der Vierteljahrshefte für Zeitgeschichte Nr. 78. München: R. Oldenbourg, 1999.

Kolinsky, Eva Between Hope and Fear: everyday life in post-unification Germany: *A case study of Leipzig*. Keele: Keele University Press, 1995.

Kolinsky, Eva and Hildegard Maria Nickel eds. *Reinventing Gender: Women in Eastern Germany Since Unification*. Portland: Frank Cass, 2003.

Kossert, Andreas. *Flucht: Eine Menschheitsgeschichte*. München: Siedler, 2020.

Kulischer, Eugene. "Displaced Persons in the Modern World." *Annals of the American* Academy of Political and Social Science 262 (1949): 166–177.

Levy, Daniel. "Integrating Ethnic Germans in West Germany: The Early Postwar Period." In Coming Home to Germany?: The Integration of Ethnic Germans from Central and Eastern Europe in the Federal Republic, edited by David Rock and Stefan Wolff, 19–37. Oxford: Berghahn Books, 2002.

Lucassen, Jan. Migrant Labour in Europe, 1600–1900: The Drift to the North Sea. Wolfeboro, N.H.: Croom Helm, 1987.

Lucassen, Jan. Migrant Labour in Europe, 1600–1900: The Drift to the North Sea. London; Wolfeboro, N.H.: Croom Helm, 1987.

Meier, Charles. The Unmasterable Past: History, Holocaust and German National *Identity*. 2nd ed. Cambridge, Mass: Harvard University Press, 1997.

Meinicke, Wilhelm, and Alexander von Plato. *Alte Heimat – Neue Zeit: Flüchtlinge*, Umgesiedelte, Vertriebene in der Sowjetischen Besatzungszone und in der DDR. Berlin: Verlag Anst.Union, 1991.

Meyen, Michael and Uwe Nawratil, "The Viewers: television and everyday life in East Germany," Historical Journal of Film, Radio and Television 24, no. 3 (2004): 355–364.

Moch, Leslie Page. Moving Europeans: Migration in Western Europe since 1650. Bloomington: Indiana University Press, 2003.

Moeller, Robert G. War Stories: The Search for a Usable Past in the Federal Republic *of Germany*. Berkeley: University of California Press, 2001.

Neblich, Esther. "Das Umsiedlerproblem der Jahre 1945–1955 in der SBZ/DDR am Beispiel des Oberen Vogtlandes." *In Agenda DDR-Forschung*, edited by Heiner Timmermann, 248–275. Berlin: LIT Verlag, 2005.

Oltmer, Jochen. *Migration im 19. und 20. Jahrhundert*. München: R. Oldenburg, 2010.

Palmowski, Jan. "Citizenship, Identity and Community in the German Democratic Republic." In Citizenship and National Identity in Twentieth Century Germany, edited by Geoff Eley and Jan Palmowski (Stanford: Stanford University Press, 2004), 73–94.

Palmowski, Jan. Inventing a Socialist Nation: Heimat and the Politics of Everyday Life *in the GDR, 1945-1990*. Cambridge: Cambridge University Press, 2009.

Parisius, Bernhard, "und ahnten, daß hier die Welt zu Ende ist." Aufnahme und Integration von Flüchtlingen und Vertriebenen in westen Niedersachsens." In *Zuwanderung und Integration in Niedersachsen*, edited by Klaus J. Bade and Jochen Oltmer, 37–68. Osnabrück: Universitätsverlag Rasch, 2002.

Peck, Jeffrey, Mitchell Ash, and Christiane Lemke. "Natives, Strangers and Foreigners: Constituting Germans by Constructing Others." In *After Unity: Reconfiguring German Identities*, edited by Konrad Jarausch, 61–102. Providence, R.I.: Berghahn Books, 1997.

Pence, Katherine. "Women on the Verge: Consumers between Private Desires and Public Crisis." In Socialist Modern: East German Everyday Culture and *Politics*, edited by Paul Betts and Katherine Pence, 287–322. Ann Arbor: University of Michigan Press, 2008.

Pence, Katherine. and Paul Betts, eds. Socialist Modern: East German Everyday *Culture and Politics*. Ann Arbor: University of Michigan Press, 2008.

Poutrus, Patrice. *Umkämpftes Asyl: Vom Nachkriegsdeutschland bis in die Gegenwart*. Berlin: C.H. Links, 2019.

Reichling, Gerhard. Die Deutschen Vertriebenen in Zahlen: Umsiedler, Verschleppte, *Vertriebene, Aussiedler 1940-1985*. Bonn: Kulturstiftung d. Dt. Vertriebenen, 1995.

Reichling, Gerhard. Die Heimatvertriebenen im Spiegel der Statistik, Schriften des Vereins für Sozialpolitik, N.F., Bd. 6,3. Berlin: Duncker & Humblot, 1958.

Rist, Ray C. Guestworkers in Germany: The Prospects for Pluralism. London: Praeger, 1978.

Rubin, Eli. "The Order of Substitutes: Plastic Consumer Goods in the Volkswirtschaft and Everyday Domestic Life in the GDR." In *Consuming Germany in the Cold War*, edited by David Crew, 87–121. Oxford, New York: Berg, 2003.

Schroeder, Gregory F. "Ties of Urban Heimat: West German Cities and Their Wartime Evacuees in the 1950s." *German Studies Review* 27, no. 2 (2004): 307–324.

Schwartz, Michael. Vertriebene und "Umsiedlerpolitik": Integrationskonflikte in dem Deutschen Nachkriegs-Gesellschaften und die Assimilationsstrategien in der *SBZ/DDR 1945 bis 1961*. Oldenbourg: Oldenbourg Wissenschaftsverlag, 2004.

Stitziel, Judd. Fashioning Socialism: Clothing, Politics, and Consumer Culture in East *Germany*. Oxford: Berg, 2005.

Ther, Philipp. "The Integration of Expellees in Germany and Poland after World War II: A Historical Reassessment." *Slavic Review* 55, no. 4 (1996): 779–805.

Vedder, R.K., L.E. Gallaway, and G.L. Chapin. "The Determinants of Internal Migration in West Germany, 1967." *Weltwirtschaftliches Archiv* 106, no. 2 (1967): 309–320.

von Richthofen, Esther. Bringing Culture to the Masses: Control, Compromise and Participation in the GDR. Oxford: Berghahn, 2009.

Walker, Mack. Germany and the Emigration, 1815–1885, Cambridge: Harvard University Press, 1964.

Index

https://doi.org/10.1515/9783110716221-009

www.ingramcontent.com/pod-product-compliance
Lightning Source LLC
Chambersburg PA
CBHW030835090426
42737CB00009B/984